26 (11-93) 0

D - 8 - 06

BEYOND THE LIMITS

BEYOND THE LIMITS

A WOMAN'S TRIUMPH
ON EVEREST

by Stacy Allison
with Peter Carlin

LITTLE, BROWN AND COMPANY
Boston   New York   Toronto   London

Copyright © 1993 by Stacy Allison

First Edition

Library of Congress Cataloging-in-Publication Data

Allison, Stacy.
　Beyond the limits: a woman's triumph on Everest / Stacy Allison with Peter Carlin. — 1st ed.
　　p.　　cm.
　ISBN 0-316-03468-1
　1. Allison, Stacy.　2. Women mountaineers — United States — Biography.　　3. Mountaineering — Everest, Mount (China and Nepal)　I. Carlin, Peter.　II. Title.
GV199.92.A45A3　　1993
796.5'22'092 — dc20
[B]　　　　　　　　　　　　　　　　　　　　　93-18784

10　9　8　7　6　5　4　3　2　1
MV-NY
Published simultaneously in Canada by Little, Brown & Company (Canada) Limited

Printed in the United States of America

To my mother and my husband, David,
for your love and acceptance.

—SA

For Sarah Carlin Ames.

—PC

CONTENTS

ACKNOWLEDGMENTS

A special thanks to Wendy Allison-Petshow and John Petshow for your love, support, and airport service, Evelyn Lees for your adventurous spirit and friendship, Scott Fischer for believing in me, and Curt Haire for helping me see and feel the beauty of nature.

I would also like to thank Nancy Shute, Rick Wyatt, Peter Goldman, Liz Nichol, Bob McConnell, John Petroske, Steve Ruoss, Sue Giller, Barry Sochat, Brad Udall, Lynn Bornholdt, Catherine Crawford, my agents, Eric and Maureen Lasher, and my editor, Fredrica Friedman, for their help and encouragement.

Finally, thank you, Peter Carlin, for your patience and understanding.

—STACY ALLISON

Thanks to the following for the contents of their memories: Scott Fischer; Steve Ruoss; John Petroske; Brad Udall; Peter Goldman; Sherry Stripling (whose Everest '88 pieces for the *Seattle Times* were superb); Dave Hambly; Don Goodman; and particularly David Shute, for his always insightful analysis. Thanks also to Nancy Shute, for her zero-tolerance policy on sentence fragments. Much appreciation to the industrious team of Eric and Maureen Lasher, and to Fredrica Friedman, and also to Catherine Crawford. Thanks to Ted and Fran Ames, who lent their basement for several crucial weeks during the winter of 1992. Special thanks to Tony Green.

—PETER CARLIN

BEYOND THE LIMITS

1

BLOWN AWAY

WE were so close. From where we were sitting, curled in the dim light of a snow cave, the top of the world was only 3,000 feet away. Less than two days of climbing on the jagged North Face. But we weren't climbing.

We were hiding. Four American mountain climbers — Scott Fischer, Wes Krause, Samuel "Q" Belk, and me — tunneled into the side of Mount Everest, listening to the roar of the jet-stream wind. It was late in the climbing season and the winter winds had descended, tearing across the top of the mountain at 150 miles an hour. But for how long? Sitting up in my sleeping bag, balancing a cup of hot chocolate in my lap, I could imagine that the hurricane outside would vanish. In the dim light of the cave, I could overlook the life-squeezing pressure of life at 25,500 feet.

I could almost convince myself we wouldn't have to turn around when morning came. *Turn around?* Not after I had devoted years of my life to get here. Years spent dreaming of scaling this massive hill and then leaving my footprint on the crown of the earth. Now I was two-thirds of the way there — 25,500 feet up the North Face of Everest. Stranded in a snow cave . . . but so close.

I was determined to get to the top.

Hunched beneath the snow, I could imagine the grace of those final steps. Beyond the limits of gravity, human strength, and mental agility — out to where there are no limits. Nothing but the snow-covered mountain, the sky, and me, and right then it would be hard to tell where one ended and another began. I could have it all, but only if the jet stream rose off the mountain for one more day. Everything depends on the weather: even the best climber in the world won't get very high on a mountain shrouded in a storm or belted by gale-force winds. We'd worked so hard for so long, but on that cold night in the fall of 1987, I knew our entire expedition was on the brink.

The fifteen climbers on the 1987 American Everest North Face Expedition each had more than a decade of climbing experience. For two years most of us had committed our lives to climbing this one mountain. We spent two years maneuvering the bureaucracies of two governments, scraping for the money to cover airplane tickets, freight, climbing permits, and fees, convincing manufacturers to give us equipment and food. Two years planning and preparing and then three months on the expedition itself — the flight into Nepal, the trek from Kathmandu into Tibet and the yak-powered climb to Advance Base Camp, then the weeks of mountainside preparation. We built Advance Base Camp at the foot of the North Face, and then set up four intermediate camps on the mountain. We fixed our route up the mountain using ice screws, aluminum stakes, and rope to anchor a safety line up the steep sections, then dug snow caves in the steep mountainside and hauled up loads of food and gear to stock them. Only then could we set our sights on the summit. Set our sights, and hope the mountain would be kind to us as we tried to creep up her icy shoulders.

Kindness was a lot to hope for this high in the world. More, in fact, than what we'd been able to secure for ourselves. By the time the second summit team — our charismatic, blond team leader Scott Fischer, our more reserved deputy leader Wes Krause, the hyperkinetic young bond trader Samuel "Q" Belk, and me — set out for the mountaintop, an ugly wind was blowing through the expedition tents at base camp. So we moved with a redoubled sense of purpose. *I just want to climb,* Scott said when we left our Advance Base Camp. *Forget the bullshit and climb the mountain.*

The mountain cooperated for thirty-six hours. On the first day we climbed under calm, clear skies, moving from Camp 1 at 19,500 feet to Camp 2 at 23,500 feet by midday. We spent the night in the snow cave, then headed up again the next morning, climbing halfway up the White Limbo snowfield before a gathering snowstorm sent us scurrying back to Camp 2. The blizzard ravaged the mountain for four long days and nights, and when the sky finally cleared we scaled the 2,000 feet to Camp 3. But then the stubborn blasting wind descended and we were pinned down again.

We were running out of time. Climbers call the upper reaches of the world the Death Zone — above 19,000 feet the earth's atmosphere is too thin to support life. No matter how much you eat, your digestive system can't assimilate enough nourishment to keep you alive. After a few days your muscles start to atrophy. You grow weaker. Most climbers start to fade after a week, although some can hold on for two or even three weeks. Soon I'd discover how strong I was — this was our second night above 25,000 feet. It was our seventh night in the Death Zone.

A shower of loose snow tumbled in through the tunnel entry, settling onto my head, my shoulders, melting cold down my neck. As the empty hours passed I sat in silence, sharing the same thought as my three companions. *This can't be happening.* I needed success too much this year.

Yes, the summit was going to transform us all. For Scott and Wes — longtime climbing buddies as well as business partners — Mount Everest represented fifteen years of friendship. All the mountains they'd climbed together led to this one expedition, this one journey, to the peak of all climbing. And beyond it lay their business. It was so hard to keep an adventure guide service solvent. Having Everest on their résumés would add sizzle to Mountain Madness's reputation. Q's interest was less professional, but no less pressing. Born with money, Q insisted on proving his own worth. He traded bonds full-time during the week, then spent his weekends ripping through triathlons. As an experienced climber, Q was dead set on standing on the top of the world.

WHEN the storm first pinned us down at Camp 2, we tried not to seem concerned. Snowstorms never last forever, not even in the Himalayas. We had enough food in the cave to hold out for days, and then once the sky did clear nothing would hold us back. As it turned out, that storm was the worst autumn blizzard to hit Everest in more than forty years. But it did clear one night, and by the next afternoon we were in Camp 3. By then, the summit was only two days away . . . until we woke up the next morning and saw the gale-force winds ripping across the top of the mountain. So we went back to the cave, the four of us, back to talking and waiting. Two days passed and eventually we ran out of words. The wind kept blowing.

Then there was silence — the sound of breathing, the sputtering of the stove, the dry stuttering of the spindrift blowing in the tunnel. After seven days the altitude had weakened us, and it was too late in the season to retreat to base camp and wait for better weather. If we didn't get to the summit now, we couldn't try again. Unless the jet stream lifted by morning, we would have to go down. *Two years of work. A decade of training. A lifetime of hope.* Blown away.

Sleep wouldn't come. The cold air sank down through the tunnel, covering us like a dark, wet blanket. Lying closest to the entry, Q was curled into a ball, trembling under three layers of down. Scott flopped around in his bag, occasionally heaving up a great dispirited sigh. Wes lay still, his eyes burning. The minutes crept past. I swam in my sleeping bag, searching for the comfortable spot. But my body had been whittled away by the months of high-altitude effort, and comfort was beyond me. I was a stick figure of a woman, fragile bones jutting against pale flesh, muscles stretched taut like rubber bands: a body pulled to the breaking point.

Come on, morning. Our last chance would come with the daylight. I tried to push the hours along, pulling up the dawn by force of will-power. *Give me this one chance.* The dawn, and calm skies. Just two more days without the jet stream. *Please, please, I need this now.*

W H E N life gets tangled there's something so reassuring about climbing a mountain. The challenge is unambiguous. Ice and snow and rock. Self-discipline. Concentration. Focus. As you push higher you work yourself into a trance. Can I reach that ledge? Are my fingers strong enough to hold on to this crack? Will this ice screw hold? Eventually the weight of the world — the stalled career, the broken marriage, the shattered confidence — slides away. For those moments when it's just you and the rock and the ice and the snow, life always makes sense.

Climbing has always been more than a physical pursuit for me. Each mountain I face is another pinnacle in an internal adventure. An exploration of myself, an expression of my spirit. For ten years I had climbed, from desert cliffs in Utah to small mountains in the Cascade Range of the Pacific Northwest. Looking higher, I reached up into the clouds, then past the clouds. To larger mountains, and more complex climbs: Mount McKinley in Alaska, Ama Dablam in Nepal, Pik Kommunizma in the Soviet Union. I reached up, step by step, until I could see myself standing on the peak of the world's tallest mountain.

Mount Everest. Chomolungma to the Tibetans. Sagamartha to the Nepali. The Mother Goddess of the Earth to everyone living in its shadow. The top of Everest is the top of the world — 29,028 feet up into the empty Himalayan sky. The only spot on earth where you can't climb any higher.

I had to get up there. Usually I don't get obsessed about mountaintops — I had learned long ago that the time spent climbing in life means more than the time spent standing on a summit. But when my life turned sour, the tip of Everest gained significance. It was the top of the world! Reaching that windswept perch, I decided, would cleanse my spirit and heal my wounds. More than that, it would send me home with a title: The First American Woman to Climb Everest.

For so many years I wouldn't even allow myself to think I could get this far. Everest was for the big boys, and I was a very small woman. The climbing community has never had a lot of patience with women. It draws a distinct crowd — generally men equipped with a surplus of money, opinions, muscle, and testosterone. Imagine how welcome a petite blonde college dropout from Woodburn, Oregon, felt.

It came a step at a time, a decade of effort leading up to this one summit attempt, this journey to the top of the world. And now the world wasn't cooperating. Why did I think it would? I knew Everest wasn't like any other mountain. Only one of ten climbers who attempt the mountain stands on the summit. And for every three climbers who do scale the mountain, one dies trying. The facts aren't welcoming. But you don't plan a trip to Everest believing those facts will apply to you.

WHEN dawn finally came we got dressed for the summit — pulling our down climbing suits over the layers of polypropylene long underwear, polypro socks, plastic climbing boots, polypro and down gloves, a heavy pile hat, a neoprene face mask — then crawled out of the cave, pulled along by a fine thread of hope, and walked gingerly to the side of the ice tower that stood above our cave. Above us we'd see the summit, that great crooked pyramid on top of the world, the crown for the Mother Goddess. If she rose straight into a clean blue sky, we could try to push ourselves higher. But if she sent off a tail of white, if the winds were still ripping the snow from the hillside, we had to go down.

Wes turned the corner first. I didn't have to look up. I could read it in his shoulders. Wes slumped, then turned to see Scott, coming around the corner after us. I saw it in Scott's eyes, then heard his voice, shouting above the constant roar of the wind.

"Well, that's the ballgame."

Scott stomped back toward the snow cave, anguished, shaking his head. Wes stayed, staring into the sky. I turned my face upward and saw it, too. The thick plume of spindrift sailing from the mountain-top. The jet stream had not lifted. It was slamming against the mountain at 150 miles an hour for the third day in a row. And the thin thread of hope snapped.

BACK in the cave Scott's blond hair hung lank over dim eyes, his usually rosy cheeks looked pale and sunken. His chest caved in beneath his shoulders.

"If you guys want to wait another day," I said, "I can wait." Q looked up dimly and coughed. I was grasping at thin air. We had failed. It was over. Even so, Scott flashed a look at the rest of us, measuring reactions.

"One more day? Give it a shot?"

Q shook his head. The Death Zone was wreaking its havoc on him. He was losing wattage with every passing hour. "I can't stay up here another day," Q said. He'd been barely able to eat breakfast that morning. "If I don't go down today, I'm not going to get down."

Now just the sound of breathing, and outside the wind and then occasionally a light cloud of spindrift, floating through the tunnel and down into the cave. The cold drifted down my spine until I could feel it in my toes.

Scott picked up the walkie-talkie and called to our expedition mates waiting at base camp. *We're screwed. We're coming down.* The message was received, tenderly, and we started packing. Sleeping bags, Thinsulate pads, ice screws, rope, and cook gear over here, stoves, food, fuel over there. We'd carry the fragile gear, but the really soft and really hard gear could take the fast way down the Great Couloir, the chutelike valley just to the left of our route on the North Face. Camp 1 was just below the bottom of the chute; once the gear rocketed down, the other climbers would try to collect it.

We went back to the cave entry and slung on our packs. And we stood there for a moment, not looking at each other. Just stood there in the cold and the wind before taking the first step down. And then Wes moved, and Q followed, and then we were all moving. After two long years of planning and working and hoping, we were walking away from the summit. I could barely fathom the disappointment. I couldn't, not with the descent ahead of us. I still had to focus on getting down in one piece.

I turned to take a last look and my eyes fell on Scott's face. Tears were sliding down his cheeks. Did he see me watching him? It was only a moment, and he was wearing reflecting shades so it was impossible to tell. I turned around again and continued down dry-eyed. Whatever anguish I felt, I'd deal with it when we got down to safe terrain.

2

HEAVEN ON EARTH

I was seven years old when I first climbed. It was at a picnic on a blazing hot August afternoon in 1965, just a few weeks before the first day of second grade. Kids were everywhere, throwing baseballs and playing tag on the fields and hills. I was a blonde tornado then, a freckle-faced tomboy with skinned knees and dirty elbows, and after my parents spread our blanket on the grass, I ran off to look for some friends. A few hundred yards away, I noticed a group of boys swarming around a tall Douglas fir tree. Never a timid child, I strolled up to see what was going on. Peering over a few dirty shoulders, I saw the boys not only were playing around the fir, but also were inside, where lightning or blight had hollowed out the trunk. The cavern was large enough for five or six curious kids to squeeze into.

Squirming inside, I elbowed my way next to a small boy in a plain T-shirt. "We're climbin' it," he explained. Indeed, a boy was currently doing just that. Hoisting himself to where the walls of the trunk curved inward, he spread his legs wide and braced his feet against the rough wood. Grunting with the effort, he crept upward, moving one Keds-shod foot, then the other, in jerky two-inch increments. He gained about a foot before his left Ked started to slip. "Gangway!" he called, and jumped down.

Two other boys met similar degrees of success. A third got a little higher, but lost leg power after six feet, gasped deeply, and plummeted onto his hands and knees. As the other boys grew bored and wandered away, I hoisted myself up and braced my feet against the walls of the tree trunk. "Aw, man," cried the boy who'd just collapsed onto the soft floor of the cavern. "A *girl's* gonna try it!"

The remaining boys peered upward. Feeling their eyes on me, I pushed myself steadily up the walls, rocking my weight from one foot to the other. The trick, I learned, was to keep moving. Once you lost momentum, gravity would wrap its tentacles around your ankles. I rose higher. As the gap grew thinner, my legs were closer together, and it got easier. I was eight feet up, then ten, then twelve. At twelve feet, the gap closed, but I found a large knothole and crawled out onto a branch. I stood there for a moment, leaning against the tree trunk. The boys gathered outside the tree, gazing up at me. "I made it," I called down.

And then I heard his voice.

"Stacy!"

My father had come looking for me.

"*Stacy!*" he hollered. "Are you trying to kill yourself?" He peered around, looking over his shoulders. For what? He didn't seem to know. In any other situation he could pick me up and carry me back into the safe clutches of family discipline. But now his seven-year-old daughter had flown out of reach. Dad craned his neck and planted his hands on his hips. "Come on, Stacy. Get down from there."

But I'd been so pleased about getting up, I hadn't even considered getting down. Now my heart started pounding. Danger! I grasped the trunk and looked down at my father, still peering up at me, taking little steps back and forth on the grass. "I don't know how!" I wailed. I plastered myself against the trunk and held on tight.

Word of the crisis soon spread. Other fathers arrived and scratched their heads. "Now, that's a pickle," I heard one man say. More constructive comments were made and sorted through. Then my dad walked beneath the branch and shouted up to me. "Just sit down, honey. Grab on to the branch." I sat down unsteadily. "Wrap your arms around the branch," he instructed, "and lower yourself down as far as you can go. Now. Let go of the trunk. Reach down and wrap your arms around the branch." My legs swung in the air, and soon I felt him wrapping an arm around my knees. When he had both hands around my thighs, I made my body rigid and let go. In a flash, he hoisted me down and onto the ground.

Back on solid ground I grabbed my father's pant leg and sniffled, still shaken by fear and the thought that my wings were about to be clipped for the rest of the afternoon. He hugged me against his legs and patted my head. "Just stay on the ground from now on. Okay?"

A few minutes later, after everyone had returned to softballs and Frisbees, I went to get a drink of water. At the fountain, a man leaned down and smiled. "Were you the little girl up in that tree?" I nodded, wiping my mouth on my forearm. "Well, that's just great." He beamed down at me and gave my shoulder a squeeze. "All those boys couldn't climb it, but you could. And you got up there all by yourself."

I blushed and looked down. Yeah, it *was* pretty good, I thought. I was better than all those guys. I remembered standing on the branch before my father came, before his footsteps hardened the ground and softened my courage. Looking down at all the upturned faces had seemed like a dream, as if I'd suddenly taken flight and soared up into the air. It felt like a miracle, but it had really happened. I had done something wonderful, and now I knew I wasn't the only one who saw it. Bursting with new awareness, I ran off to find my family.

M Y family believed in movement. From the time we learned to walk, my parents kept us busy. With piano lessons. Tap-dancing lessons. Swimming lessons. Skiing lessons. There were five of us — my older sister, Wendy, then me, then our sister Sidney, our brother, Rodney, and our baby sister, Leslie. Mom and Dad both worked as educators, so they knew what happened to bored children. Busy hands, of course, stayed out of trouble.

But action never replaced order, and my parents took discipline seriously. Even with a litter of rowdy children in the house, we were expected to follow strict dinner table rules. We sat up straight, and passed food clockwise. Hands stayed folded until Dad picked up his fork. And to prevent us from gobbling our food, we knew we couldn't eat more than two bites without putting down our forks. Violators were reprimanded. Repeat offenders got a sharp rap on their knuckles.

My parents' high standards didn't end at the dinner table. Mom and Dad expected their four daughters and one son to keep backs straight no matter where we were. We would do well in school and be active outside the classroom. During the summers we'd take classes in summer school, or earn money picking berries. And the line we toed led past high school and into college. "It's the only thing you absolutely *have* to do," Mom would lecture, tilting her head back and crossing her arms to let us know she was serious. "You must go to college and get a degree."

Woodburn, Oregon, was the sort of small town where children paid attention to their parents. Just south of Portland in the Willamette Valley, the Woodburn of the late sixties was like a portrait of rural America. Berry fields ran to the edge of town, and the shopkeepers on the main street knew everyone's first name. Down at the high school, student demonstrations were limited to football games and dance squad concerts. It wouldn't last — if you listened carefully on the northern horizon you could hear the drumming feet of the super-highways and malls as the Portland suburbs marched in our direction. But for those last few years in the late sixties and early seventies, the northern Willamette Valley was sweet and green and wide open in every direction.

All that space gave us a lot of playing room, and with five kids in the family, competition was important to us. Winning a contest was a fast way to capture attention and prove one's individuality. For all of us the big sport was swimming. Swim lessons had been one of those healthy, structured activities that kept us away from trouble, so once we learned to keep ourselves afloat in a swimming pool, we started to compete.

And I could move in the water. For the first few years I raced, I never saw the back end of an opponent. I didn't even have to practice very hard. When I was nine or ten, still racing in the youth leagues, I could have the worst attitude of anyone on our team, then dive into the pool on Saturday morning and still jet past everyone. The glow of victory became second nature, I could track the meets with the line of blue ribbons marching across my bulletin board.

The problem was I never learned how to lose. Everyone *expected* me to win. As I edged into my teen years the thought of losing terrified me. Once I loved the sport for the friends I made at the pool, for the challenge, for the joy of moving through the water. Now none of that mattered to me anymore. Now it was all about winning. When swim meets approached at the end of the week, I would sink into waves of nausea. I couldn't stop trying to prove myself, week after week, and so the sport became little more than desperation and need.

No matter how fast I swam, I could always feel myself being pulled beneath the surface of the water.

When I realized how much I dreaded going to the pool day after day, I gathered up the courage to quit. My decision came a few days after I lost a race in a key meet, and when I told my coach he was beside himself. He glared down at me and wagged a long finger through the rank, chlorine-thick air in his office. "So does this mean you're going to quit every time your life gets tough?"

Well, no. Besides, a lot of things in life were already getting tough.

LOOKING back, childhood memories are always clouded over, images of reality collapsing into snapshots of emotion. In the jumble of my mind's eye our lives changed the day my father took a new job. When I was twelve he left his old school to work at the MacLaren School for Boys, an institution for Oregon's most troubled criminal youths. He accepted a raise and a promotion to work there, but also took on greater responsibility, trying to bring order to a world where none existed.

MacLaren stood in the north end of Woodburn, a desolate fortress surrounded by fences and trees. After a while my father took on the same characteristics. Never a big talker, Dad now brooded and sat impassively, gazing into space. When we did get his attention, his temper flared quickly. Work was difficult, and as the months passed, he grew closer to his coworkers. Their after-dinner telephone calls became a regular event. He'd talk briefly, then hang up and reach for his coat. "I'm going out" meant he was going to see his friends from work. They always had a lot of work to discuss, he explained.

At the time I didn't notice the pattern of change. I was fourteen years old, just floating into a new universe of friends and parties. And I wasn't the only junior member of the Allison clan itching to test her wings outside the family nest. We had three teenagers living in our house, and our time spent at home was generally limited to pit stops. A snack between school and the afternoon's projects. A quick dinner before the game. A few hours of sleep, then off to whatever the next morning held. . . .

At first I heard her screams in my sleep. They pierced the Saturday morning, echoing through the house, down the hall and into my adolescent dreams. I was out of my bed before I was awake, and halfway through the house before I realized I wasn't dreaming. You move fast when you hear your mother scream. Rod was two steps ahead of me and Wendy, Leslie, and Sidney were right on my heels. When we found them in the living room, my mother was lying on the floor, straining against my father's grasp. It hardly looked violent, because the scene was so familiar; they looked like children, horsing around on the living room floor. Only they weren't children. They were my parents, and Mom was still screaming — a wordless wail, like a siren — and struggling against Dad's grasp.

"Goddamn you." Words finally broke through her cries, but her voice was strange. They were words I'd never heard her use before.

"Calm down . . . Carole, please." He was pleading with her. Then I heard Wendy's voice.

"Mom? Dad?"

When they heard us, Mom quit flailing, and Dad relaxed his grip on her wrists and stood up, stepped back from us, and blinked unevenly.

"It's okay," he said softly. "Your mother's just upset." She sat up on the floor, holding her face in her hands. Soft, choked sobs escaped from between her fingers. She was still wearing her nightgown, but my father stood fully dressed. As we gathered around our mother he looked away from us, standing stiffly, his mouth open, but the words caught in his throat. Finally, he picked up his suitcase and headed for the door.

My father called us after that. I heard his voice and saw his handwriting on the checks that arrived each month. Beyond that he was a ghost in my life, a shaky voice on the phone, a tremulous figure floating in the background of graduations and school concerts.

Later I learned that the scene that morning began when my father announced he was leaving my mother to move in with a woman he'd met at work. My mother had never guessed her husband was even having an affair. It was her screams of surprise that woke us up.

After my father left I rarely saw him when he didn't appear to be drunk. He seemed to drink habitually, but he held on to his job, and the support checks arrived on schedule. But he was gone from our lives.

THE first year alone changed all of us. My mother managed to make it through the days, but nightfall sapped her strength. After dinner she retreated to her room, crying softly behind the closed door.

Torn from our strictly ordered lives, we each found our own way to rebel. Wendy, at fifteen the oldest in the family, strayed into the role of high school bohemian, dating the boys who rode motorcycles. Rod hung out with his own band of juvenile delinquents. My quest for attention and acceptance took a much more respectable form, at first. Ashamed of my father and what he'd done to our family, I looked for acceptance in the cliques that knotted the halls of Woodburn High School. I wore makeup and nail polish, and brushed my blonde hair until it performed just the right flip across my shoulders. I worked hard in class, went out for track, and even started swimming again. I pushed myself, but this time competing came easier. I no longer got sick before I raced.

As much as I sought out structure in life, I also valued freedom. I now cast a dubious eye at most of my mother's rules. She tried to be strict, but once our family foundation crumbled, family rules had little bearing on me. I could get away with it, too: as long as I got good grades I knew I had license to do whatever I wanted. When Mom forbade me to go away to central Oregon for the weekend with friends, I went anyway. Then I was no longer satisfied with mere overnighters. When I asked if I could go to Hawaii for a week when I was fifteen, she was apoplectic. "People like us don't just pick up and go to Hawaii," she sputtered. "We can't afford it." But she forgot that I had my own money, saved up from years of berry picking and unspent birthday checks. Once she left the house I called a travel agent and made my airplane reservation.

It felt good to defy my mother. When she set down a limitation for me, all I could think about was stepping across the line. I was still a good kid — still the good grades, the activities, the polite, well-spoken friends — but I was an adolescent, too. I thrived in high school or a few years, but once again I chafed against the limitations. By the end of junior year I spent most of my free time riding my bicycle on the country roads with Wendy or hanging around with her older crowd, getting stoned in the fields and pondering the world that waited outside Woodburn. When I started my senior year that fall, I felt as if I'd already left. I still did well in class, but high school had shrunk to a small part of my orbit. On nice winter days I wouldn't think twice to cut class and go skiing on Mount Hood. Still, an occasional midweek ski trip provided only temporary relief for the itchy soles of my feet. After seventeen years in Woodburn I had developed a painful case of wanderlust. I wanted to go everywhere, but anywhere was fine. Just away would do nicely, and the sooner the better.

CORVALLIS had to do. It was only an hour south of Woodburn, a quick hop from our doorstep down I-5 to the modern, highrise dormitories. But shifting my vistas to the campus of Oregon State University seemed a great leap into the future. So I set out eagerly that fall, packing my belongings into duffel bags and rushing headlong into the first horizons of adulthood. Deciding to study nutrition, I signed up for a slate of entry-level classes. But when I discovered that that particular major meant rounding out my studies with the Future Housewives of America in the home economics department, nutrition lost its appeal. When the next semester started, I switched to the biology department. Now I spent the mornings alongside 350 other freshmen, listening to intro lectures performed by assistant professors. I devoted the afternoons to peering into a microscope in hopes of identifying the intricate design of a pine tree's cell structure.

The more I learned about college, the more I realized I wanted to be someplace else. I'd just spent thirteen years in classes, and now something else was tugging at my sleeve. The world! I knew so much was going on out there, I wanted to be there when it happened, not read about it later. I got to know some of the other students in my dorm, but they seemed so disengaged. They put on makeup and whispered about their boyfriends and giggled just like the small-town high school kids I'd longed to escape when I left Woodburn. I'd left all right, but I certainly hadn't escaped. I was just as alienated as I'd felt in high school. The clouds in Corvallis hung just as low as they had in Woodburn. I wandered from class to class, from day to day. Sometimes it seemed the world was flat.

So I made for the hills, or I explored the town, walking or riding my bike on the neighborhood streets for an hour or two. I moved for the simple pleasure of going from one place to the next and back again. On my way out the door I occasionally bumped into a few like-minded people.

Evelyn Lees lived down the hall. She was a sophomore then, a nineteen-year-old geology major from Maryland. Evelyn walked with a kind of Gumby-esque gait, a long, loose-limbed shamble that was only accentuated by her standard uniform of baggy overalls. Despite the granny glasses, science-nerd interests, and up-the-country wardrobe, Evelyn was a strong athlete. Sure-footed and graceful, she thrived on physical movement, both as a personal challenge and as a way to bond with friends. Ev was lightning fast on her ten-speed, but when we went bicycling with my roommate, Lynn Bornholdt, she always hung back with us, even when her muscles were primed and the road clear. She preferred to ride along with us, never impatient, always encouraging.

W E became fast friends. Ev and I had the same appetite for the world, a restless yearning that usually kept us out-of-doors, sniffing after some new corner of the wilderness. When schoolwork clouded our minds at night we'd throw on shorts and T-shirts and go running in the darkness, dashing together down moonlit trails and roads that followed the river near campus.

Ev had taken a mountain-climbing class the spring before, and was filled with the glory of mountaineering. It was the perfect combination, she said, of beauty and strength, of abandon and discipline. Countercultural enough to be hip, but structured enough to be worthwhile. It wasn't exactly a women's sport, she conceded. All of the established climbers on campus were men, and few of them seemed to consider women as potential climbing partners. But that wouldn't stop her, or me.

That winter Evelyn introduced me to Lindsay Clunes, a graduate student she'd met the year before. At twenty-three, Lindsay was one of those charming golden boys mothers love to see escorting their daughters to the prom. He kept his button-down shirts pressed and his hair shiny and neat. Lindsay loved to have fun, and for him the best kind of fun came in intimidating packages. A hundred-mile bicycle ride, perhaps, or some extreme skiing off a secluded mountaintop.

If there was one thing Lindsay liked more than having an adventure, it was convincing other people to have an adventure with him. A few months after I'd met Lindsay, Evelyn and I bumped into him at a party one Saturday night. Bored with drinking beer and dancing, he convinced us to try something new.

Half an hour later we were back on campus. The night air was heavy with cold and as we walked across the grassy quad our breath draped silver plumes over our shoulders. Evelyn and I both carried climbing harnesses Lindsay had attached around our hips. Lindsay wore a rucksack, in which he carried his own harness, a long coil of blue Perlon climbing rope, and three quart bottles of Rainier beer. He led us to a fifty-foot Douglas fir, then stopped.

"Here she is."

After handing us each a beer, Lindsay took a long pull on his own bottle, then leaned down and propped it on a root. He stepped into his harness and tightened it around his waist, then hoisted himself up and started skyward, climbing the branches like a ladder. When he'd climbed about twenty-five feet, Lindsay reached into his rucksack for the bundle of rope. Looping it across a thick branch, he let both ends drop to the ground. Then he hooked the rope to the carabiners — metal loop snap-links — attached to his harness and swung into open air. Bouncing gently against the tree trunk, Lindsay started sliding down, falling as smoothly as a spider on a thread. He stopped about five feet off the ground and looked down at us.

"Lesson one," he said. "When you're in midair, don't ever let go of your brake hand." Lindsay released his right hand and the rope shot through the carabiners. He landed on his feet with a thump.

"Because you'll come down a little faster than you want to."

Evelyn had learned to rappel in her climbing class, so she was up and down in five minutes. When it was my turn, Lindsay climbed up with me. When we got to the branch where the rope hung, I sat down and he sat across from me. After making sure I had securely run the rope through the carabiners, Lindsay showed me how to place my hands. Then he sat back. "Okay," he said. "You're ready. Go."

"Go?"

"Getting off the branch is the best way," he said evenly. Then: "You've gotta trust the rope and carabiners."

I looked down.

"They'll hold you," Lindsay said.

I looked at him again.

"Honest."

My lips pursed, the cold night air whistled through my nose. But I gathered my courage, tightened my brake hand on the rope, and jumped into the empty air . . . slid a few inches and then jerked my hand up to stop the flowing rope.

Sure enough, holding my hand up created enough friction to lock the rope in the carabiners. I wasn't falling, but that didn't stop me from spinning crazily in midair.

"Lindsay!"

"You're okay!" he said. "Keep your brake hand tight, and hold your legs out!"

I extended my legs. One foot glanced off the tree trunk, but the other hit it square on. When I got both feet solidly on the bark, I regained control, bending my knees and bouncing slightly.

"Excellent!" Lindsay shouted, clapping his hands. "Now lighten up your brake hand, and let some rope go."

I slid a few inches, then stopped with a jerk. Trying again, I let another inch go by. Then another.

"That's it. Now walk down the tree," Lindsay called.

I slid downward, walking my feet down the bark. First I summoned the courage to trust the rope's grasp on me in midair, then learned how to loosen the grasp to lower myself. As I lost altitude I gained confidence, and then I was on the ground next to Evelyn, looking up toward Lindsay, still sitting on the branch and beaming down at me. Something surged in my chest. The night lit up around me. I had jumped out into the blackness and come down on the other side. What a revelation!

"Did you like it?" Evelyn asked.

"I *loved* it."

We spent an hour or two taking turns running up the branches and sliding down the rope, but time didn't exist for us then. The night was cold and quiet and still, and we were the only people awake in the dark, maybe the only ones alive. Just us and the tree, the branches creaking and bouncing under my weight, the fir needles clashing softly against themselves, and then the whirring of the carabiners as they slid down the Perlon rope. Scampering up a tree like kids, sliding down a rope like climbers. It was childlike and thrilling at the same time.

And from that night forward, thoughts of climbing filled my waking hours. The attraction was as magnetic as it was mysterious. Suddenly my soul was caught up in a world I'd barely known existed. Mountain climbing, and its even more inscrutable offshoot, rock climbing. People actually climbed up cliffs, pulling themselves up hair-thin cracks, tiptoeing across nubbin-sized rock pimples. Yes, *people really did this!* Just realizing this life existed, this intense collaboration of nature and physics and human strength, launched me forward, and now I needed to know: could I do it, too? Was I strong enough, brave enough, smart enough to dance on the edge of my limitations?

Plodding through the dreary Corvallis winter, I harbored dreamy images of snowy mountain peaks rising into clear, blue skies. Of a chain of climbers ascending the mountainside. Marching up the snowy glaciers, scaling the sharp cliffs, and then taking those last precious steps up onto the summit. I wasn't exactly sure how they did it. The climbers of my daydreams — rugged, smiling men and brave, powerful women — were extensions of the climbers I'd already met. People who blended structure and freedom so seamlessly, all learning the same fundamentals, but then having the freedom to channel what they knew into their own distinct movements. I still wasn't quite sure what they did. The climbers in my dreams seemed to be powered more by sheer will than specific abilities. But even if I could fill a large book with everything I didn't know about mountain climbing, that was a book I definitely wanted to read. More than that, I wanted to take a running start and dive into the pages.

When Curt Haire offered to take us with him to Zion, I knew this was my chance.

MANY climbers tend to a kind of backwoods machismo, a terse, squint-eyed braggadocio about storms braved and peaks conquered. But when Curt invited Evelyn and me to drive to Utah with him, he made the wilderness sound soft, even gentle. He was full of its beauty. "Zion's like a miracle," he promised. "It's heaven on earth."

That was high praise from someone who had almost decided to complete his education in a Catholic seminary. Curt was older than us, a graduate student in counseling who worked as a supervisor in our dormitory. He wore wire-rim glasses and a thin, ascetic beard, and though he'd opted against the priesthood, Curt's gentle, detached bearing still had the self-composed contemplation of a clergyman.

One late winter afternoon Evelyn and I had noticed Curt sorting his ropes and harnesses in the lounge of our dormitory. We walked over to say hello, and soon prompted Curt to launch an impromptu lecture. Climbing, he said, was more than a physical sport. It was an intellectual game, requiring as much strategy as strength and daring. Even in my most gilded fantasies I'd never guessed climbing could be so intellectual or so serious. Or so romantic. This last observation was Evelyn's and my favorite joke. I mean, we weren't idiots, we could count. There had to be ten guys for every woman who tried to climb. So we sat down and asked Curt to tell us more. He went to his room and came back with a book about the mountains in Oregon. The pages showing the ones he'd climbed were marked off, and his neat handwriting listed the date of the climb, the weather conditions, and the other members of the climbing party.

We all became friends, and a few weeks later Curt announced he was going to spend spring break in Utah. "I'd love to have some company," he said. "And there's no better place to learn the basics."

Of course we'd go. Never mind that neither Evelyn or I had any climbing gear. This was our big chance, and what's a few details when you're eighteen and starved for adventure? We made a quick trip to Corvallis's one climbing store to buy helmets, harnesses, and a rope, loaded up our warm clothes and sleeping bags, borrowed a tent, and figured we could probably get by without the rest.

Then we piled into Curt's muddy Subaru and pointed south on Interstate 5. We drove straight through to the high desert of southwestern Utah, trading off shifts behind the wheel. Seventeen hours after we left Corvallis we drove into the mouth of the Virgin River canyon, and then took our first walk beneath the park's curving, iron-stained cliffs. In the distance we watched two climbers rappel down an orange-bathed ridge. "That'll be you," Curt said, "at the end of the week."

The setting sun ignited the cliffs, and everywhere the glowing landscape filled me with a radiant sense of wonder and magic. Zion is like that, even before the dusk splashes it with color. It's in the colors from the sun and the natural oranges, reds, and yellows streaking the

smooth sandstone. The sagebrush and rabbitbrush that dot the rolling hills, the flowering cacti on the mesas, the lush cottonwoods
nestled close to the river. It's all that, and something less tangible,
too. I felt it at that moment, and later I watched it happen to other
people. The land has a distinct magnetism, a pull that steals your
breath and leaves you wandering beneath the cliffs, not quite sure if
you'll ever leave. The Indians felt it, too. They knew the spirits ran
wild in the canyon, and so they would hunt and walk through Zion,
but never let the sun set on them in there. The sweet air between the
cliffs was full of something they didn't understand, and they didn't
want to risk surrendering to its power.

In that moment I could feel it tugging me; the colors on the walls
and the valleys and in the purple, red, fuchsia, and yellow blooms on
the cactus, the spicy pull of sage and juniper on the warm breeze. All
that lying between the soft, undulating, distinctly feminine sandstone
cliffs. The feeling of enchantment was in the air, a feeling that I'd just
found a home. I was in the right place, and now I was open for
anything.

I T was just before midnight when Curt led me away from the
campsite and into the darkness. Under a bright full moon and a gal-
axy of stars, the world was reborn. We walked through the trees and
into the Virgin River canyon, where the sandstone cliffs cut shadows
in the moonlight. Desert creatures chirped in the night and the river
washed gently beneath the trail. Everything in the night was new and
mysterious. I wasn't sure where we were going, and when I thought
about it, I wasn't even sure Curt wasn't planning to put the moves on
me when we got there. But even the dangers of the unknown were
far more enticing than what lay behind, and with the perfume of the
juniper deep in my lungs I cast my fate to the stars and followed Curt
up the trail to Angels Landing.

It's an easy walk at first. The trail is paved, and the pitch of the
canyon is slight. But after two miles the trail veers into Refrigerator
Canyon, a deep, shadowed vein in the rock. Hidden from the light of
the moon, we descended into blackness. It was very still in the thin
canyon. A few pebbles rattled across the path ahead. I moved closer
and wrapped my forearm around the crook of Curt's elbow.

"Don't tell me you're scared," he said, softly.

"No way," I whispered. "I just don't want you to trip."

Half a mile later the canyon gave way to a series of switchbacks carved into the edge of the cliff. Then the trail gave way, and we scrambled up a quarter-mile of steep, crumbling sandstone. Finally, we stood atop Angels Landing, a stark, flat buttress almost 2,000 feet above the canyon floor.

While the sweat cooled on our backs, we sat on the dusty shelf, reclining above a surreal world. In the moonlight Zion looked like a landscape from outer space. But I could follow the path through the murky canyon and trace the switchbacks up the cliff to where we sat. My veins still singing, I looked down and flipped a pebble out into the empty air. It was late, already past two A.M. And poised on that cliff above the rocky Utah wilderness, I'd never felt more awake. As if I'd walked out past the fringe of reality, beyond anything I could recognize or grasp as part of my past. I wanted to absorb everything around me, to forget what I already knew for the sake of everything I needed to discover.

FROM the moment we drove beneath those spectacular sunset-blazed cliffs, everything about Zion seemed to glow. That week it seemed as if every sunrise unveiled new textures in the rock. Learning to climb introduced a whole new level of beauty and challenge in the world. New strategies to mount, puzzles to solve, climbing skills to master. I was quick to absorb the basic skills of rock climbing: how to belay another climber by running rope through the carabiners attached to my harness, letting it slide while they moved up, but always poised to lock it in my carabiners if they fell; how to stand on the rock, always keeping my center of gravity over my feet; how to place protection, wedging a hexagonal piece of aluminum securely into a crack, and then running the rope through an attaching carabiner.

It was all the most basic stuff, but everything I learned electrified me. And the more I learned, the more I realized mastering the sport involved more than ropes and carabiners or how to look at a rock wall and locate the best finger grips and toeholds. Climbing was a set of values: the freedom earned by confronting weakness and having the courage to accept limitations; being brave enough to challenge nature, but smart enough to respect it. Roping up, I grew to understand, meant more than participating in a sport. It was entering a culture; even joining a religion. Climbers shared an unspoken communication, a mutual trust built on mutual passions. All who climbed knew about the dangers that faced them. How easy it would be to grab the wrong handhold forty-five feet above hard ground and feel the lip of rock start to give. The same rule held for everyone: the higher you climb, the harder you fall.

That fact alone excludes a massive number of potential participants. It's just not a sport you can do casually. There's no such thing as sandlot rock climbing, or pickup mountain expeditions. The sport requires strength, commitment, and focus, plus a certain hunger for achievement. Knowing this, anyone serious about climbing can tell a few things about fellow climbers even before they say hello.

The campground at Zion is like any other National Park car camp. A few cinderblock toilets stand in subtle spots. A blacktop road, pocked with speed bumps, winds around between campsites. The sites themselves are mostly dirt, each with its own parking space, wooden picnic table, and flat area for tents. The park designers took pains to emphasize the camp's natural setting, but, inevitably, tire tracks and tennis-shoe waffles outnumber animal tracks.

During the summer families in station wagons take up most of the sites. But when we arrived, barely into spring, it was easy to find a spot to pitch our tents. Only a few sites were taken, mostly by small groups of climbers. Once we pulled the Subaru into the campground and started unloading our gear, it didn't take long for another climber to come striding over, booming his greetings. "Welcome aboard," he called. "Whatcha climbing?"

Curt stepped up and shook his hand, while Evelyn and I looked at each other, then looked back at our visitor. And blinked.

Scott Fischer's friends called him the Blond God back then, and not always to be sarcastic. Blond, blue-eyed, square-jawed, muscle-bound, and Pepsodent-smiled — there *was* something divine about Scott. His face seemed to glimmer, all tufts of golden hair and sparkling blue eyes and glistening white teeth. His shoulders were thick and broad under his T-shirt, bulky with muscle, and the pectorals in his chest were so developed as to suggest armor. Scott also beamed an intoxicating charisma. Greeting us at our picnic table, he shook hands all around and immediately swept us up in his current.

"Great to have you here," he said, smiling. "Always good to have more folks around. So the two of you are just learning? Excellent. You'll have a blast. And if you want I can show you a few things. I gotta take it easy this week." He pointed down to his left ankle, swathed in a thick bandage. "I had a little accident a few weeks ago. Nothin' big. Banged it up a little against my ice ax." He grinned broadly and shrugged. "Shit happens, I guess. Didn't hurt that much."

Scott was twenty-two then, making his living as an instructor for the National Outdoor Leadership School. Charming, almost impossibly handsome, wildly energetic, Scott made everything seem possible. Friends gravitated toward him and then hovered expectantly, waiting for something to happen. Around Scott, it usually did. Given a couple of weeks of spring vacation, Scott had gathered a few friends from the NOLS staff and set out for the Zion cliffs. They'd already been there for a few days when we pulled in, so seeing us setting up camp next door, Scott figured he'd do the neighborly thing. Before he left Scott invited us all for dinner. "Come on over a little later," he proposed, flashing that smile and a cavernous set of dimples. "It'll be mellow. Just crack a brew and meet the guys."

We walked over to their campsite after we finished pitching our tent, and as that first night fell we shared their pot of lentils and vegetables. Scott's friends made for a diverse crowd. All six were obviously experienced climbers. Lolling around the campfire, they talked and laughed, speaking in the relaxed shorthand that went along with years of shared experiences. When the talk turned back to climbing, Wes Krause, one of Scott's friends from NOLS, brought up Sink's Canyon, a rocky bowl in Wyoming where they take NOLS students to learn how to climb. In some ways Scott and Wes couldn't have been more different. Scott was rowdy and charming, an audacious product of the upper middle class. Wes came from rural, blue-collar roots in Colorado; his father was a truck driver. For most of the evening Wes had been content to hide behind his thick black beard and shoulder-length hair. He wore a bandanna over his head, and a small diamond flashed in his ear. But when they talked about climbing, Scott and Wes were as close as brothers.

"Well, if we're talking about climbing," Wes said, his voice gaining volume, "why don't you tell our new friends about how you hurt your ankle?"

Scott shook his head. "Boring story."

"I don't think so," Wes said. He looked over at Curt, Evelyn, and me. "He was climbing over in Provo Canyon this winter, on an ice climb called Stairway to Heaven, it's a series of vertical ice steps. Anyway, when Scott got to one of the steps, he found another couple of climbers had just started up that face, so he was going to have to wait for a half hour or so while they went up. Only Scott doesn't like to wait, so he decided to climb around them. Naturally, he was in a hurry to get up and around these other guys, so he's got no ice screws, no ropes. He's climbing without a net.

"Very dangerous, and pretty stupid, but Scott figures he can handle it. He's a pro, so he can handle anything. He gets up about fifty feet, front-pointing with his crampons and planting this little humming-bird ice ax to get handholds. And then right when he's getting ready to cut over to the usual route, he swings in his ice ax, and lays all his weight on it, and it pops out of the ice."

Grimaces, sharp intakes of breath all around the fire. Scott looked down, shaking his head.

"So Scott pops off the ice too, in midair, and then drops fifty feet straight down. And that's painful enough, but when he lands, he manages to put the pick of his hummingbird ice ax right through his ankle. I mean, right *through* the sucker. And that's a hollow point, so when he grits his teeth and pulls it out, the pick removes a core sample of Scott's ankle."

Shaking his head and scratching his thick beard, Wes looked over at his friend. It wasn't the first climbing accident Scott had had. His climbing reputation then was two-sided. People knew him as a hot climber and a dangerous risk-taker. He was trying to change that part.

"You've logged more flight time than an airline pilot," Wes said. "When do you get your license?"

Scott shook his head and reached down, gingerly touching his wounded ankle. "I don't know, man. I gotta cut that shit out."

Looking into their faces and hearing their stories was like entering a new world. Scott and his friends had abandoned the usual social norms for ambitious young people. Most of them had college degrees, but angling toward careers was no longer a part of their game plan. They were still ambitious — hearing them describe their climbing histories or talk about their plans was proof enough of that — but their ambitions had a different focus. Their challenges came in the wilderness, and they found their rewards on the tops of rock cliffs and the crests of mountains. They had their own goals and their own sense of purpose and fulfillment.

And that's what I needed. Lost in college, abandoned by purpose, stripped of goals, I certainly needed something. Sitting by that fire, I stayed quiet, listening to the strong voices, feeling the heat of the embers glowing against my face. These people *lived*. Their lives were adventures. They made their own rules and then rewrote them at will. They had everything I wanted. Everything I was now determined to find for myself.

WHEN Evelyn and I left camp in the mornings, our helmets strapped on, rope, webbing, hexes, and carabiners jingling in the rucksack, we never knew what cliffs we were about to confront, or what it might take to climb them. During the first few days I'd stand at the bottom of a climb, peering up at the crack or series of holds we were aiming for, and feel myself starting to laugh. The proposition seemed so ludicrous — creeping up a crack on a vertical wall, trying to balance my weight on a nubbin of rock smaller than my own baby toe. It was just like climbing that old, hollowed-out tree when I was seven.

I had so much to learn. Both Evelyn and I knew nothing about rock climbing, so Curt had to teach us everything: how to connect a harness, how to tape our hands and wrists to protect our skin from the abrasive rock, why we had to bring water on every climb to guard against the dehydration that sets in so quickly on a hot, sunny desert day. Once we started up a crack, Curt even had to remind me to breathe when I got tense. "You're holding your breath!" he'd call down from where he belayed me, taking up the rope as I climbed higher, prepared in an instant to snap his brake hand and freeze the rope in his carabiners if I fell. "It's okay. Just relax and breathe!"

He taught us the correct way to set protection for a belay anchor, planting nut-shaped hexagonal chocks in cracks, feeding the rope through the connecting carabiners, then using nylon webbing and two central carabiners to connect three hexes into a triangular pattern, thereby balancing the weight they'd bear in case someone fell. We learned the correct way to belay another climber. Once we left the ground, we learned how to find solid fingerholds in hairline cracks, and how to jam our hands, fists, and arms into the wider fractures. We learned how to create footholds, inserting our feet sideways into a crack, then torquing them around to gain a dependable stance.

We moved slowly, frequently getting stuck in bald spots and freezing up when things appeared hopeless. But Curt was a patient teacher, and led us both through each climb step by knee-trembling, sweat-dripping step. He held the belay line and coached us, the sun reflecting off his wire-rim glasses, a few wisps of his black hair and beard blowing in the breeze. I had always thought of Curt as being thin, almost underfed. But on the cliffs I saw how wiry he was, how the muscles on his forearms bulged. He was kind to us, too, and always encouraging, even when we got scared and whiny in a difficult spot.

And the work paid off. The cliffs and cracks came easier after the first few days, and by the end of the week I felt myself gaining confidence. I realized I was strong — I could pull myself up the wall and even hang in place for a while without feeling as if my biceps and calves were catching fire. I liked the mental challenge, too, looking up at a wall and plotting the moves from bottom to top. Each situation presented its own problem, and it felt good to realize I had the mental and physical agility to begin to solve them.

We had planned to drive back to Corvallis after a week, but after seven days it seemed as though we were just getting started. How could Evelyn and I leave now that we were finally making progress? Curt had to get back to school, his duties as a dorm adviser demanded it. But Evelyn and I decided to stay. When Curt left we moved our tent into Scott's campsite and made plans to hang out for another week.

Our first instructor was gone, but now Ev and I could learn from a man who radiated climbing. Born into a suburban family in New Jersey, Scott spent his boyhood playing the usual Little League sports. He eventually grew into a powerful, if undisciplined, high school football player. Scott always had plenty of energy, but as he roared through high school, he seemed to have trouble focusing his resources. Scott could get by on his bright smile and natural charm, but his parents sensed impending trouble for their rangy son. One summer they sent him out west to get a handle on his priorities at the

National Outdoor Leadership School. Scott learned all about discipline and focus that summer, indoctrinated in the standard NOLS program of healthy outdoor adventure, environmental ethics, and decision-making skills. He learned how to climb along the way, and from that point his life was different. After his first summer at NOLS, Scott had gone back to high school in New Jersey, but soon he lost interest in other sports. All he could think about was going back west, back to the wide open spaces and high stone cliffs. He went on to college, but NOLS had been the catalyst for Scott, so he kept close bonds with the school, returning as a student instructor one summer, then as a full-fledged staff member.

Scott took us climbing the next day, up to a thirty-foot fist-and-hand crack that led up to a sandstone bench dotted with sagebrush. The crack wavered between about four inches and two inches, and the wall nearby was almost completely smooth, so there was no way to reach outside and cheat on an external handhold. The only way to climb the crack was by creating finger, hand, and fist holds in the crack itself. Scott flew up to the top and set up a belay for us, but once I started up I managed only about ten feet before I got stuck. Both of my feet were torqued into the crack, and I could fit one hand into the crack at chest level. But just above my head, where I wanted to find my next handhold, the gap suddenly tapered. It was too thin, it seemed, to find a secure hold, let alone jam my toe in for a foothold. I pondered the move for ten minutes, trying a series of finger locks, but when I tested my weight I couldn't get my fingers to stay in place. Finally, with my arms and legs turning rubbery and my feet burning and my mind as blank as the wall around me, I surrendered and let Scott lower me down.

I stood at the bottom, gazing up at the place where I'd gotten stuck. I thought back to what Curt had showed me earlier, the different ways to see a crack, and how to keep your mind flexible enough to work your way through even the most impossible-looking move. After resting for a while, I hitched back on to the belay line and started up again. This time I focused on the crack and my movements around it. I climbed carefully, conscious of my breathing, careful to keep drawing breath even when I was stretching for my next hold. I could feel the dry air in my throat, my heart throbbing, the sweat streaking my brow. I could feel the cool, dusty inside of the crack.

Climbing higher, past the spot that had stopped me earlier, past the midpoint and then higher, toward the top, I could feel my muscles working — the long strands of sinew in my legs, the power running from my arms through my shoulders and across my back. I climbed higher, up to where the breeze was cooler, where it carried the scent of open air, rather than the musk of the ground. When I finally got up to the top, Scott greeted me with a slap on the back.

"Man, great job," he crowed. "You guys are really comin' on here. You're moving up to the big time!"

I realized, I can do this. Evelyn and I climbed by ourselves for the next few days, choosing our own routes and belaying each other, and as each day drew to an end the realization came into clearer focus. I had learned the basics of climbing, and had come to know I was strong enough and agile enough to eventually master the skills. I was surprised and delighted. I'd finally found something I wanted to focus my energy on. Something physical, where I could set goals and achieve things without having to compete with anyone else. Because more than anything, climbing was collaborative.

Learning to climb on the same rope with Evelyn locked our friendship in a much closer bond. She saw the same beauty in the sport, the same potential for personal revelation. With the same commitment, and the same base of physical strength, we worked hard together, coaching, helping, and depending on one another for support. Evelyn and I didn't bother with limitations. Looking to the other for inspiration, we went ahead and learned what we needed to know.

W E had to go back to college eventually. And when we did hitchhike to Corvallis, school life couldn't have seemed more bleak. The weeks dragged. I didn't mean to neglect my studies — I wanted to learn and I wanted to do well. But I had no idea what I wanted to do with my life, and without a goal, school felt pointless. I was in limbo, and I had to get out.

Dropping out of college violated just about every rule of responsible conduct I'd ever heard. You *must* get an education, my mother had lectured time and again. Once my father left, her lectures grew even more adamant. "Without an education," she said, "a woman doesn't stand a chance."

When I confessed my doubts about my academic future, she didn't hold back her opinion of what a college-less life would get me. "You'll always regret it," she hissed, furious.

Images of Zion played in my mind. Those two weeks seemed like a door opening a crack, then slamming shut. I'd seen something beautiful beyond the door, and I wanted to jump inside. It was Curt and Scott's world. The NOLS world. Climbing. The excitement, the challenge, the sense of community. I felt at home in Zion. The people I met there reminded me of the person I always hoped I could be.

If college seemed like a dead end, climbing seemed as though it had endless possibilities. There was so much to learn: the technical skills, the physics and geology that went into the sport. It wasn't a retreat from responsibility, just a different path. You still had to work hard and learn skills, practice and learn how to work with other people. You learned how to gauge risks and how to be resourceful. How to set a series of goals and meet them. Climbing teaches you how to think. And if the experience is removed from the world of bankbooks and office buildings, it can only help you function when you decide to go back.

Walking away from school was difficult, but I knew I had to do it. In the end, I compromised with my mother. When the spring term finally ended, I agreed to take fall off, but then return for the winter semester. A few months spent navigating the cold, cruel world, she figured, would send me scurrying back to college with a much sharper sense of focus. And I did have a sudden moment of focus that summer.

It came on a dry breeze one hot afternoon, standing at the bottom of Smith Rock, a 500-foot chunk of welded tuff rising from the flatlands of central Oregon. Smith Rock and its outcroppings are the climbing capital of Oregon, and I'd spent that day bouldering with Curt, Evelyn, and Chris Mannix, a short, sturdy climber with a thick, blond Amish beard bristling from his jawline. We'd worked up a good sweat in the hot, dry afternoon and, feeling the wind on my forehead, I turned my face upward, letting it cool the sweat on my neck. That's when I saw her poised on Skyline Crack, silhouetted by the blazing sun. She must have been 450 feet in the air then, most of the way to the top of the rock. Seeing her there, climbing in the distance, sent a shiver down my back.

"Who is *that?*"

Curt took out his binoculars and followed my gaze. "It's Shari Kearney."

"Is she from around here?"

"Oh, yeah." He lowered the binoculars. "She's the park ranger." Curt offered me his binoculars, and I peered up through the eye-pieces. On the rock, Kearney was following a crack up toward the summit. When it ended she stopped for a moment, looking around. Finding a foothold to her right, she tested her weight, then made her move, pulling herself onto a small ridge, then jamming her left hand into a wider crack. A few minutes later she pulled herself up onto the top of the wall.

"She's one hell of a climber," Curt said.

And at that moment, that was everything I wanted to be.

3

THE TOP OF AMERICA

I wanted to climb, and not always in the shadow of a better climber. It's easy to let your partner pull you up. If you're with someone who knows what he or she's doing, it's so easy to let that person lead all day, sitting back safely while the experienced climber makes all the decisions and takes all the chances. But that's not what Shari Kearney did. And I wasn't about to spend the rest of my life climbing in the shadows either. The feeling was restless, an itching somewhere in the deep core of my spine. I was ready to push for freedom, the liberation that would come when I could climb either side of the rope. I couldn't spend the rest of my climbing days depending on someone else to lead the way. Eventually I had to throw it all aside and try for myself.

Curt put away the binoculars and nodded to Chris. "You have any preferences?" They looked over to the rock, examining the features of its various faces.

I let my eyes fall to my toes and kicked at the dust. "I'd like to try a lead."

Curt and Chris looked at each other for a moment.

"Are you sure?" Curt put his hands on his hips. "It's not as easy as it looks. You might want to get a little more experience first."

I shrugged. "Now's as good a time as any, don't you think?"

Curt looked at Chris. "Think so?"

Chris shrugged. "Why not?"

Evelyn smiled. "Well, yeah," she said. "It *is* about time we learned how to lead ourselves."

After a few minutes we decided to start on Bookworm, a sixty-foot crack etching a shadow straight up the face of a broken-off slab that leans against the central tower of Smith Rock. As I walked to the base of the climb, my heart surged in my chest. While I roped up, Curt put a hand on my shoulder.

"Are you ready?"

"Yeah." I yanked on the rope to test the knot and looked up. "I'm ready."

Evelyn slapped me on the back. "Good luck," she said. "You can do it."

In climber's parlance, the front end of the rope is the *smart* end. The leader picks the route, locates the best holds, and places the chocks or pitons that stop a falling climber from hurtling into the void. Decisions made by the lead climber have an immediate impact not only on his or her life, but also on the life of the trailing climber.

Approaching the rock, I started up slowly, lingering over my first holds, carefully choosing the next ones, setting a new hexagonal chock into the crack every five feet. Altitude gave me confidence, however, and I developed a comfortable rhythm. The gap was thin at first, a relatively easy jamcrack with plenty of nooks into which I could wedge my hands and crannies to torque my feet into stable holds. But when the crack widened, yawning open into a more difficult off-width gap, my momentum started to waver. I had to wedge almost an entire arm inside in order to brace myself, and by then my balance would suffer. My movements slowed and grew awkward. My mouth became parched, my palms grew slick with sweat.

"How do you feel?" Curt called up from his position beneath me.

"Okay!"

I wiped the sweat from my brow. Curt's voice echoed against the face of the rock. "You're doing great!"

I looked up for my next hold. "So far, so good!"

But not for long.

The next five feet didn't pose much of a problem. The crack was wider than below, but still snug enough to hold the hexagonal wedges I was carrying. But as it widened even farther, I discovered I had only one wedge large enough to fit into the gap.

Clinging to the rock, feeling my left calf turn rubbery with the strain, I knew I'd have to change my strategy. Rather than setting new protection every six feet, as I'd been able to do with the smaller hexes, I'd have to set my one piece, move up a few feet, then reach down, pull it out, and reset it above me. An exhausting and frightening routine, since I was suddenly making complex moves with my closest piece of protection twelve feet beneath me. On the bottom end of the rope, risk is always limited. With someone belaying from above, I might fall all of a foot or two before my partner caught me. But as the leader, I could count only on the protection I had placed myself. I could fall ten or fifteen feet before the rope caught me. And even then, there was always the chance the hexes would pop out of the crack and send me spiraling all the way down to the ground.

That feeling started to drift over me, a thin, cool haze of panic. Even standing securely, I could sense myself slipping. The hard knot in my stomach, the metallic taste on my tongue, the fluttery wings of failure beating against my knees.

I was so close. The lip of the slab, glinting against the empty, light blue sky, was only sixteen feet above me. I swallowed hard and crept upward, jamming an arm in the crack to hold my weight, wrenching my knee into the crack, then jamming my other arm and repeating the process. Every few moves I reached down, tentatively, pulled out the hex, and replaced it above me. It was hot work. Sweat dripped across my brow and down my sides. My arms grew raw and bloody, scraped repeatedly against the jagged rock inside the crack. I kept moving, one foot, then three, then five. The lip drew closer. Soon it was only ten feet away. I was just ten feet from leading my first pitch. And that's when everything went wrong.

I was resting a moment, shifting my weight from leg to leg to keep the blood flowing. Then I reached down to pull out the hex. Only it wouldn't budge. Bracing against the crack, it had somehow locked in to a small internal crag. From my angle, there was no way to jar it loose. My heart drummed against my ribcage.

"It's stuck!" I called down to Curt. Pressed by anxiety, my voice got higher. My shouts were bordering on shrieks. "What should I do?"

Curt thought for a moment. He looked around me, up to the summit of the slab, then motioned me up. "Keep going!" he shouted. "You're okay! Just relax and go!"

I swallowed hard and returned my gaze upward. To calm myself, I thought of Shari Kearney, strong and secure on Skyline Ridge. She could handle this. Just stay cool. I wiped the sweat away from my eyes, took a few deep breaths, and made my next move. Reaching up with my right leg, I searched the interior of the crack for a narrow spot to wedge my knee. But if anything, the crack seemed to widen inside. As the muscles in my left calf turned to jelly, I felt my breath hot against the rock, my heart squeezed tight by adrenaline. I was exhausted by the strain, hands slick with fear, fists seeming to slip, the weight of my body drawn into the void. Spinning with a sudden wave of vertigo, I jammed my knee deep into the crack, wedging it hard against the cool interior of the welded tuff.

I heard my heart rumble.

Curt's voice echoed up. "Are you okay?"

The top of the slab was only six feet away. I had to move again, or risk depleting my muscles. I reached up to jam my arm higher in the crack. But now my knee was jammed so securely I couldn't budge. I strained to free myself, but only gently — the sharp edge of the rock was digging into my flesh. If I pulled too hard, I might lose my balance and go toppling. With my protection already three feet below me, that would mean falling at least six feet, then bouncing against the hard face.

"How are you doing?" Curt shouted again.

"I can't move!" The sweat on my neck had turned icy. I started to tremble.

Then everything exploded. Strangled by vertigo, I stood glued to the rock, too frightened to move. Then my frazzled nerves and deepening muscle fatigue set my knees trembling, and that soon devolved into sewing-machine legs, the wild, uncontrolled vibrating that marks the final descent into full-on panic. I was frozen on the rock, too terrified to look up or down. The edge of my vision blurred, and I stared straight ahead, as if hypnotized by the shadows of the crack. Seeing my predicament from the ground, Chris threw on his rucksack, rushed to the easy side of the slab, and started clambering up.

"Just hold on!" I could hear Curt beneath me, though I didn't dare look down for him. "We'll get you down, just hold on up there!" I tightened my grip and focused on the rock about two inches in front of my nose. Somewhere nearby I could hear Chris running up the face, grunting with the effort, the contents of his pack jangling as he moved. Then I heard him above me.

"Hey down there."

I glanced up, cautiously. He was doing something with a rope, tying it to something, then clipping a carabiner to a knot on the bottom. "I want you to grab on to this line," he said, "and then clip the carabiner onto your harness. Think you can do that?"

"Yeah."

When the end of the rope reached me, I coaxed my right hand free and grabbed for the carabiner. After I clipped in, Chris held the line taut, belaying me so I could feel safe unhitching my knee and elbows from the grasp of the crack. Let loose, finally, and with the line holding me safe from above, I relaxed enough to make my way to the crest.

The paralyzing fear vanished once I had managed to clip on to Chris's rope. Then, after a few moments on top, even the embarrassment faded. By the time Curt climbed up, I was back on my feet, leaning over the edge to greet him.

"Well, *you're* awful chipper now," he said, "for someone who thought she was gonna be dead about five minutes ago."

Actually, I was ecstatic. It seems odd, after such a close scrape, but as we coiled the rope and prepared to head down, I couldn't wait to get back on the rock and try again. I'd felt the freedom of leading. I'd felt how hard it was, and even if I hadn't pulled it off, at least I could see the possibilities. Just as I'd tasted that cold, metallic tang of failure on this climb, I could feel the potential of the future. I could see beyond the mistakes I'd made, and I knew that as long as I kept trying, I'd only get better.

I moved back into my mother's house after school ended. I got my old summer job waiting tables and soon fell in again with my friends from high school. It was easy to be in a holding pattern during the summertime. As long as I lived at home I could bank my entire weekly paycheck — minimum wage plus tips — and save up for my next climbing expedition. My bank account was growing every week, but at such a slow rate I knew I'd never be able to keep afloat on my own. My mother, I thought, was right. Without a college degree or any vaguely marketable skills, I had no future. The summer dwindled, and as the daylight vanished earlier and the nights grew cool my friends started packing up for another year of college.

Fortunately I had one diversion to get me through the last weeks of summer. Evelyn, Curt, Chris, and I had planned to launch their new school year with a week-long climbing trip in Yosemite National Park, and we loaded up Curt's Subaru and drove there together in early September.

Yosemite has some legendary granite faces: El Capitan is vast, vertical, and technical and can require several days to scale. Half Dome is just as spectacular and also takes more than a day to ascend. Climbers in mid-face spend the nights bivouacked in their harnesses, either hanging in slings or hammocks or curled on a rock ledge.

When we got to the park, most of the climbers were settled in a spot called Camp 4, the one central camp in Yosemite reserved for tent camping. With so many climbers sticking around for weeks or even months at a time, many of the campsites became quite elaborate, complete with well-developed outdoor kitchens, dining areas, and fireside chairs. For many of the regulars, the contents of their campsite represented their net worth. For these lean, grizzled young men were Climbing Bums. Their muscular bodies spoke of well-nourished backgrounds, but the dirty knees and elbows protruding from tattered clothes showed these were young men who took their climbing seriously. More seriously, in fact, than they took jobs or money. Unlike Scott and his friends, the full-time Climbing Bums shied away from even part-time labor. Most could barely finance a regimen of rice and beans. The even more destitute resorted to daily visits to the park cafeteria, where they'd stand in the corner waiting for the families to finish eating. Once Mom and Dad had collected the kids and left the table, the Climbing Bums would swoop down like a flock of crows, dueling for the leftovers.

We spent the first few days loosening up on some smaller faces, then got set to make more serious attempts. Curt and Chris had eyes on a two-day ascent of Half Dome. Evelyn and I hoped to work our way up Half Dome's backside, a 1,500-foot face called Snake Dike. The way we planned it, Ev and I would leave the day after Curt and Chris so we could meet at the top, camp out for the night, and then come down the easy side together.

The afternoon before their climb Curt and Chris laid out their assortment of gear — their "rack," in climbing language — and sorted out the hexes, webbing, ropes, and slings they'd need for Half Dome. When they were finished packing, the guys looked up at Ev and me and motioned to the neat piles of equipment still scattered in the rich black dirt. "Okay, girls," Curt said. "Here's your rack. Have fun up there." They left an hour later, hiking over to camp at the base of the cliff.

It was scary to be on our own, and electrifying. It excited me to look at the gear spread on the ground. The carabiners and hexes, glinting in the sun, made it real. We were climbers now. We had our own rack, for the moment, anyway, and now we had to sit down and figure out exactly what to take and what to leave behind. When we left in the morning we'd both wear rack slings, the gear hanging and clanking over our shoulders like bullets and pistols strung on a bandolier. We sorted through the equipment after dinner, stringing it onto our rack slings, and as other climbers passed our camp they watched us with new respect etched on their faces.

Two mornings later Evelyn and I set out for Snake Dike, walking for two hours to the base of the cliff. We chatted nervously as we walked. Occasionally, as we moved through the trees, we'd catch a glimpse of the tower ahead of us. The wall was almost completely vertical and looked so smooth, dark against the bright blue sky. Would Ev and I really be able to climb by ourselves? Trading leads all day on a 1,000-foot wall seemed like a lot for two inexperienced women. And not an easy 1,000 feet either. We could tell this merely by checking Snake Dike's rating, a solid 5.7 on the climber's decimal system.

Climbers rate all the established routes, judging them according to the structured, if wildly subjective, grading system that has been adopted over the years. The ranks, known as classes, start with Class 1, the sort of climbing you might do on a sidewalk, walking to the store to buy an ice cream cone. Class 2 puts you on a rocky trail, and Class 3 throws a few boulders and other obstacles in your way. You won't need a rope here, but you'll certainly have to pay attention to where you put your feet. Class 4 gets more complex, a steep hillside, perhaps, with small stretches of vertical terrain. Still, the climbing comes quickly, with an almost endless assortment of handholds and footholds. Most of the world's serious climbing is represented in Class 5, a grade that is divided into fourteen subsections. Climbs rated between 5.1 through 5.5 require climbers to use ropes and belay one another, but really aren't much harder than climbs on a

Class 4 terrain. The vertical terrain and almost endless combination of footholds and handholds is similar, but the Class 5 climbs are usually more exposed to the distant ground.

Things get more difficult at 5.6 or 5.7, where the routes, like Snake Dike, involve trickier holds and steeper rock. This is generally where most climbers will feel insecure enough to place pieces of intermediate protection between the belay anchors they set at the top of each rope length, or "pitch." A rating of 5.8 or 5.9 means the face is not only difficult, but also has fewer places to rest, and thus requires more thought and greater physical endurance. The rock gets smoother and the cracks tighter through climbs graded 5.10, 5.11, and 5.12, and by the time you hit a route marked 5.13 or 5.14 you're ascending into the realm of miracles. Only a few climbers in the world can master these routes, and they appear to perform something closer to mountainside gymnastics than climbing. So if Ev and I weren't about to blaze any new routes on Snake Dike, we were still well up the ladder from the beginner's runs. Standing at the bottom of the rock, we took a few minutes to drink water and shake out the kinks in our legs. Then, just as the sun crested the cliffs on the east side of the valley, we roped up and climbed onto the wall.

I started slowly, then picked up momentum as we got higher. We switched off leading after every pitch — a distance measured by the length of our 150-foot climbing rope — and after an hour we were looking down on the thick groves of deep green pines on the canyon floor. Yosemite's lush back country rolled off into the distance, and a gentle breeze brushed against my neck. I fell into the rhythm of the climb, and then was part of the wall, prodding its cracks, feeling the mottled texture of its hot, sunbaked face. I listened to the breeze whispering against the granite ridges and dimples and saw the dusty strands of a spider's web woven in the corner of a ledge. Pausing to belay Evelyn, I gazed out into the blue and saw a hawk riding an updraft, floating up in the warm air. Yosemite trembled with life, but Ev and I were alone on the wall, everything quiet and peaceful around us. I heard her breathe below me, and the small grunts as she stretched for a move, the musical clanking of the gear on her rack strap, the rustling of my windbreaker as it shuddered with the breeze. For those few moments, and then as we continued up the warm rock face toward the thin band of blue above us, the world was in harmony. I moved to the vibration, as free as the hawk riding the soft, warm air.

AFTER a few months of rock climbing, I was ready for a mountain. I got my chance in late January, when Curt, Evelyn, Chris, and I set our sights on Mount Washington, a jagged, 7,000-foot peak south of Mount Hood. Mount Washington is one of the shorter peaks in the Cascade Range, but it's steep and rocky enough to qualify as a prodigious climb. Unlike the path to Mount Hood's 12,000-foot summit, which is easily scaled by first-time climbers, the final 300 feet to Mount Washington's sharp, pyramid-shaped peak require complex maneuvering.

We planned for a day-long expedition: driving as far as the snow would let us the afternoon before, then grabbing a few hours of sleep on the roadside before waking early and cross-country skiing to the foot of the mountain. We'd make the summit by mid-morning, take in the view for a while, then hit the down staircase and try to ski out to the car before dark. It would be, Curt said, a quick introduction to the basics of serious mountaineering.

It's hard to predict the winter weather in the mountains, but the day before our climb, it seemed we would luck out. The heavy clouds parted, and as I drove down to meet the others in Corvallis I rode through a crystal winter afternoon, with the pale yellow sun and the mountains white and glimmering just beyond the tips of the fir trees. Night was already upon us by the time we rolled out of Corvallis, so we drove dark highways into the mountains. After finding the turnoff leading to the trailhead, we moved slowly in the heavy snow and managed to drive to within about four miles of the mountain. It was late now, just past eleven P.M. With clear skies above, we laid a tarp on the ground by the car, unrolled our insulated pads on top, and jumped into our sleeping bags. Huddled beneath the clear, star-frosted sky, I dozed off immediately.

It seemed only a few minutes had passed before Curt shook me awake. His stove was already roaring, heating up an aluminum pot of water for hot cereal and drinks. It was just past two. I dragged myself out and pulled a few layers of wool and down over my long underwear. The night was so damp, I wondered what had happened to the crackly dry breeze I'd felt when I went to sleep. It had vanished, and when I looked up into the sky I noticed the stars had, too.

We strapped on our skis and headed up the snowy road. I saw Evelyn's back, a shadow against the white snow, and followed her into the murky night. The warmth from breakfast was already receding in my belly. This machine, I thought, needed to be more fuel-efficient if it wanted to keep up.

We skied out from beneath the trees just after sunrise. At seven we pulled in to the mountain's northeast face, took off our skis, and started climbing. A thick coat of clouds had settled on the mountain, and a stern wind swept hard snowflakes into our faces.

The four of us moved steadily up the north face, slogging through the heavy snow. The clouds swirled in closer, obscuring the top of the mountain. As we got higher, the wind gained in ferocity. The snow came heavier, too, lashing into my face and forming ice in my hair and eyelashes. We kept moving, walking in single file with our heads down, and reached the bottom of the rock just after nine. The wind roared down on us, a frigid, wet blast that sliced through my layers of wool. We stopped long enough to put on our harnesses and rope together, then Chris headed into the rock, setting our route toward the summit. Belaying is safe but slow. No matter how many climbers are roped together, only one can move at a time. So while Chris climbed, the three of us waited on the ridge, huddled together against the wind. After about fifteen minutes Chris climbed onto a shelf in the rock, set an ice screw, and motioned for Evelyn to follow him. I watched her go, shuffling in the snow and beginning to shiver in the cold.

It took three hours to climb the 300 feet to the summit. Three hours of wind and snow and intense, driving cold, of the dull ache that comes before hands and feet go numb, and then the burning pain as they reawaken. Battered by the wind, wrenched by the pain and frustration, I clenched my jaw and blinked back tears. The day had turned into an endurance test. As we crept farther upward, I forced myself to stay calm. *This is mountain climbing,* I thought. *People do this and survive.*

We crawled onto the small summit at about noon. Huddled together for warmth, we shared some chocolate and water. It was hard to talk, with the wind thundering and my lips too numb to form words. Once we finished eating, we spent the next half hour digging through the fresh snow, looking for the metal rappel anchors that had been cemented onto the summit by previous climbing parties.

After we roped onto one, we rappelled about sixty feet down to a ledge where the next anchor lay.

It was a small shelf, perhaps two and a half feet wide — barely enough room for us all to stand in perfect weather, let alone in a blinding snowstorm. We sifted through the snow, each groping silently for the buried anchor, when Evelyn felt something hard beneath the blade of her ice ax. Turning to get Curt's attention, Evelyn saw him bend over, take a step backward, and then disappear.

"Curt!"

It was a thin cry, a dry squeak against the full-throated blast of the wind. But it caught my attention, and I turned around to see Evelyn drop to her hands and knees, peering down. Leaning over, I followed her gaze, and saw Curt sitting about ten feet below us on another, even smaller shelf. For a moment, he didn't move.

Chris leaned over my shoulder and shouted over the wind. "What the hell is he doing down there?"

"He fell!" Evelyn shouted back.

When we all yelled down at him, Curt finally looked up. He waved his ice ax, then got on his feet, a bit unsteadily. Chris dug out the anchor on our shelf and quickly looped our rope onto it. We rappelled down to Curt and found him in one piece, more or less.

"What the hell happened?" Chris said.

"I thought I was a goner," Curt answered, laughing nervously. He'd been searching for the anchor, he explained, and lost track of the edge of the shelf. Thinking he felt his ice ax brush something hard and metallic, he'd taken one more step backward and found himself tumbling through empty air. Until he landed on the shelf right below, he wasn't sure if he was going to fall five, ten, or a thousand feet.

"I could have killed us all," Curt said, roping up to rappel the final pitch to the top of the snowfield.

"How's that?" I asked. "Even if you disappeared we could have found our way out to the car."

He patted his pocket.

"Yeah," he said, a twinkle coming back into his eyes. "But I've got the keys."

WITH the rock behind us, we plunge-stepped down the mountain's steep belly, a slow-motion, stiff-legged downhill run, racing the sun to the dingy horizon, and found our skis at dusk — about three hours later than we'd planned that morning. We strapped them on and skied into the forest, where the trees sheltered us from the remnants of the snowstorm. When we had started out before dawn, it had taken us four hours to ski this path. Now, as the light evaporated from the sky, we had almost twelve hours of work behind us, and at least another four hours ahead. To make matters worse, we had run out of food. Figuring we'd be back well before dinnertime, we'd packed only a small lunch and a few snacks. My hands and feet burned from the repeated freezing and thawing. My legs were tired from climbing and my knees were sore from the plunge-stepping. I was cold and hungry.

For a moment, it caught up with me. Skiing into the deepening black of the trees, I snagged an edge in the snow and reeled off-balance. In that instant I felt myself going over. *I'm going to fall,* I thought. *And if I do, I won't be able to get up.* Just as my legs started going out from under me, I felt a last, blinding burst of adrenaline. My left leg stayed anchored beneath me and absorbed my weight. My right leg came down, knee bent to take the shock. I wobbled back and forth, but stayed on my feet. I kept going.

In the darkness, I concentrated on the sound of my skis scraping the snow. I turned it into a meditation, letting the rhythm fill the void left by my hunger and fatigue. I focused on the moment: the cold air in my lungs, the relentless pounding in my chest.

I felt an odd kind of excitement. The pain, I realized, didn't bother me. If I could just keep moving, if I kept focused on the rhythm of the skis and the sound of my own breathing, I'd make it. We kept moving, slow in the darkness, but the distance gave way. When we got back to the car I collapsed into the backseat, gulping down oatmeal, trying to remember how long we'd been gone. More than fifteen hours, though by then it seemed like days. I was so tired my vision blurred. All I wanted was sleep, but as I leaned my head back against the seat, I felt something stirring inside me. I had pushed myself beyond my own limits, and in the process had discovered something new about myself. Now I knew I had the endurance to climb mountains.

B Y the beginning of spring I had enough money to finance another rock-climbing trip. Ev and I pooled a few hundred dollars and set off for the Portland branch of Recreation Equipment Incorporated, the outdoors store run by Seattle's great climber Jim Whitta-ker, to buy our own rack of climbing gear. We picked out two rack straps, then loaded them up with everything we could possibly need on a rock face: hexagonal chocks, wedge-shaped chocks, carabiners, and slings. We also invested in pairs of lightweight, sticky, rubber-soled climbing shoes, sturdy nylon harnesses, and a 150-foot length of Perlon climbing rope. The new equipment ate up a big chunk of both of our savings, but when we left, clanking across the parking lot with the straps tight across our shoulders, Ev and I felt empow-ered. Now we didn't have to rely on anyone to help us climb. We were serious climbers.

Ev and I climbed in Utah for a few weeks, then went our separate ways. Ev went to work for the Forest Service in Sitka, Alaska, and two weeks later I followed with our college friend Lynn Bornholdt, and soon got a job working on a salmon trawler. Ev and I made money, but climbing was all we really wanted to do. I'd learned ev-erything I knew about climbing with Ev. We owned our rack to-gether. Being together gave Ev and me the energy to do whatever we wanted. We had male friends, male teachers, male climbing compan-ions. We didn't avoid climbing with men, but climbing together meant we didn't have to rely on them, or worry one might question our strength or our ability to climb where only men had gone before. Together, Ev and I could make and live up to our own expectations.

We were planning to make an autumn swing through Arizona, when I got a call from Curt in early September. He'd just finished his master's program, he said, and with no job to keep him busy he was hanging around Corvallis for the fall trying to figure out what to do next.

"Come climbing with us," I said. And that was exactly what Curt hoped I'd say.

E VELYN noticed it before I did. In the dust of the Arizona desert, I kept my eyes on the world around me. For three weeks the three of us hung together, bound by the road and the chase from climb to climb. The year before, Curt had been our teacher and we had followed unsteadily. Now the balance had shifted. We climbed together, trading off leads and belays. No longer burdened by a sense of responsibility, Curt relaxed his tutorial guard and became a friend. And a particularly eager friend, Evelyn noticed, to me.

Standing in the center of the growing tug-of-war, I didn't notice the strain. But Evelyn felt it every time Curt inserted himself into our conversations. Every time he seemed to be sitting with me at the top of a cliff, waiting for Ev to climb up to meet us. Every time she woke up in the morning and found that Curt and I had already risen, dressed, and strolled off to collect water for breakfast. Every time he looked in my direction and just watched me.

Evelyn had never wanted Curt to come with us to Arizona, but she figured he'd probably keep to himself, as he had in Zion the year before. Then she learned she was wrong. The three of us did almost everything together. And when the dynamics of the trio edged one person out, Evelyn found she was usually that person.

But I liked Curt. He was five years older than me, and his age gave him a nice settled-in quality. Where the guys I'd met in college still seemed squirrelly and immature, Curt was dependable. He could treat women as friends, I thought.

Or could he? Ev didn't think so. One afternoon when Ev and I were by ourselves rinsing the dishes under a campground faucet, she told me her suspicions. At first I scoffed. "Don't tell me you think he wants to have an *affair* with me."

"Jesus, Stacy," she sputtered. "Why do you suppose he's been mooning after you all over Arizona?"

"Mooning after me?"

"He's following you like a puppy. Are you waiting for him to send you a telegram?"

At first it bothered me. I had always appreciated that my male climbing partners were buddies, closer to brothers than to lovers. But under the hot Arizona sun Curt came into clearer focus. I had always liked him, after all. He seemed warm and gentle, and he was always full of folk songs and music. Beyond that, I loved what Curt and I did together, his knowledge of the outdoors and mountains, his constant yearning to climb. He could be everything I needed: a climbing partner, a lover, a friend. The axis moved, and Curt and I became lovers. I didn't mean to exclude Evelyn, but now she felt alienated. She packed her things, separated her half of our climbing rack, and left to visit friends in Tucson. From there we went in different directions. I stayed with Curt, and Evelyn went back to school. We kept in touch and even lived in the same house when I made a brief return to school the next winter. But Curt's presence in my life created a distance between Evelyn and me. Our common language broke down. We didn't share a climbing rope again for almost four years.

B Y the time Curt and I got back to Oregon, my shoulders were brown and broad. My legs were lithe and muscular. I walked with a new kind of bounce, and when I looked up at the faces on Smith Rock, I saw so many climbs within my reach. Buoyed by my new abilities, my confidence flourished. When I climbed, I felt part of a different culture. Making my way up the side of a cliff, I didn't have to define myself as a college dropout. I was never a failure when I climbed.

Still, I felt obligated to give college another shot. I went back to OSU for the winter of 1979, planning to take another run at biology. But it took only six weeks for me to realize again that college didn't work. And college can be so competitive, all the students gunning to outdo one another. Combining that pressure with my lack of direction produced an impregnable mental block. It felt as pointless as my last days as a competitive swimmer. I lasted until the end of the term.

After I dropped out again, I moved back to Woodburn and Curt relocated to Portland, where he hoped to find a job as a counselor. He spent a few dismal months working as a janitor before finally managing to locate a counseling job with Tillamook County, a small rural area on the Oregon coast. Moving away wasn't easy for Curt, but little in his life had been. Raised in an ambitious, staunchly Catholic family, Curt disappointed his parents by not becoming a priest. He wasn't an angry person, but he projected an almost palpable darkness.

This changed when Curt was climbing. Being outdoors gave him a sense of serenity he didn't find in the other corners of his life. And Curt encouraged me to seek out that same happiness. Just when I was looking harder at climbing, just as that world was coming into focus, Curt pushed me to stop looking and start doing more. More climbs, harder climbs. I wanted to throw myself as far as I could go. He encouraged me to learn everything I could, so when Chris Mannix and his climbing buddy Bobby Knight asked if I wanted to climb in Alaska with them, I didn't think twice about saying yes.

CURT was committed to his job for the spring, but I had plenty of free time, particularly for a climb in the Alaska Range. Mount Huntington, an 18,000-foot peak in the Alaska Range near Mount McKinley, would dwarf our little day climb on Mount Washington. Even getting to base camp would be an adventure: a commercial flight to Anchorage, then a two-hour drive to the remote town of Talkeetna, where we would hop a Cessna and fly another forty-five minutes to the Tokasitna Glacier, a thin, flat tongue of snow and ice between the jagged peaks of Mount Huntington and Mount Hunter. Once deposited on the glacier, we'd spend the next six weeks in almost complete isolation. A few days of acclimating to the thin air and low pressure of high altitude, then a test run up the nearby mountain called Peak 12,380 to work out the kinks. After that, we'd concentrate on Huntington — scaling the western face and one of its steep ice couloirs.

"It's not going to be a trip for beginners," Curt cautioned before I left, and the gravity of his warnings left me tingling with glee. I was going up into the thin air, up to where the big boys planted their crampons and swung their ice axes into the high walls of the world. This was a new level of climbing. I was ready for everything, and I couldn't wait to get up there and look around.

But first I had to do most of my looking from my sleeping bag. A snowstorm blew in on our heels, so once Chris, Bobby, and I set up camp on the glacier we spent most of our first week tentbound. I'd shared a few climbs with Chris during the last year, but Bobby and I had never climbed together, so while the wind and snow snapped against our tent we played cards and nibbled popcorn and got to know each other. With their scraggly blond hair and thickening beards Chris and Bobby looked like twins. Chris was the natural leader: his entire body seemed to buzz with electricity. His words flowed in a torrent, his eyes gleamed radiant blue. Bobby, on the other hand, could be quiet for hours, and when he emerged from his shell he sometimes reverted to the lecturing tone he'd learned as an Outward Bound instructor.

We enjoyed each other's company, and when the sky cleared we moved eagerly, strapping on our skis and making tracks for Peak 12,380. After six solid days in our sleeping bags, exercise felt like a blessing. The fresh snow was smooth and crisp, and as we slid through the crackly morning cold, the glacier sparkled under the northern sun.

We planted our skis at the base of 12,380's north face and headed up into the first sloping snowfields. We roped together, but less as a precaution than as a way to get used to climbing as a connected unit. And we climbed quite smoothly for the next three hours, hearing the breeze whisper lightly through the rich silence and feeling the pure northern sun beam down around us. It was beautiful, and our only worry was the fresh blanket of snow. Snow on a mountain always comes from a variety of snowfalls, the different layers eventually bonding together to form a cohesive covering. But bonding takes time, and a new snowfall can make the mountainside prone to avalanches, especially during warmer, sunny weather.

By the time we got onto the hill, the fresh layer had had a day or two to settle, but we kept a careful eye on the texture of the mountainside. We even took the time to dig some avalanche pits, poking down to see if the snow was bonding, or if the new snow was separated from the old by a sheet of ice that could keep the layers from joining. Each time, the layers seemed safely enmeshed. But still, our first steps on some slopes would be echoed by the deep *whump* of settling snow. I tried not to worry — surely Chris and Bobby knew what they were doing. And the sky was so blue, the snow so sparkling, it was hard to imagine anything going wrong. Even so, those heavy, adamant whumps sent a chill through me.

I don't remember hearing the whump when Chris stepped into the gully. We were about 500 feet off the glacier by then, poised on the side of a steep, twenty-five-foot-wide gully. Seeing how deep the fresh snow had piled in the furrow, Chris stopped and unhitched the rope from his harness. We knew the line of rocks above us would keep us safe from avalanches coming from above. But we also knew that with all this new snow, we'd still be safer walking across separately. If someone triggered an avalanche, there'd be two others available to dig him out. Gripping the head of his ice ax in his right hand, Chris took a tentative step out into the gully. Then another.

Then the mountain above us seemed to move up. It was an odd sensation at first, the sort of hypnotic, very-fast-but-very-slow effect you get in a car accident. Your eyes open wide, and suddenly you're aware of everything. It was very quiet, almost peaceful, except for the fact that my heart had apparently stopped beating. For a moment I thought of standing on an escalator, heading downward.

"FUCK!" I heard Chris cry out.

I saw him bend his knees and hold out his arms, like a surfer. The wind caught the dirty blond tresses trailing from his hat. Then my feet went out from under me. I hit the snow and started sliding, helpless in the wild current of the avalanche. It was still quiet, the sound of snow rushing against snow, but now the blood was roaring in my ears, a hysterical chorus echoing in my head. *AVALANCHE! What do I do? How do I stop?* Fragments of thoughts rushed past. *Swim with it, stay on top.* Well, I was on top, sliding down feet-first, but completely out of control. *Remember the crevasses!* The seams in the glacier, yawning open below me. But how far down, and how wide open? Would the falling snow sweep me inside one, then down into the bowels of the glacier? Oh, shit, I did not want to get buried.

My arms searched for balance, then flew akimbo in the wash of the snow. The fiberglass shaft of my ice ax, still strapped to my right wrist, whacked against my side. Picking up speed now, I hit the lip of a crevasse and jolted skyward, like a Buick hitting a speed bump at thirty-five miles an hour. I landed hard in the moving snow, then continued down even faster, the blade of my ice ax whistling past my head. *That was close enough.* I did not want to eviscerate myself with my own ice ax, so I wriggled my hand out of the wrist strap. I held it in my hand for a moment, then pushed the ax away. And just then I hit the lip of the next crevasse — like a Buick at forty-five this time. I hit hard, then rolled to a stop at the bottom of the gully, 200 feet from where I'd been standing.

I lay there, still on top of the snow; the silence was overwhelming. After I gathered my wits, I propped myself on one elbow and looked uphill. Chris and Bobby were both standing up, perhaps 150 feet above me, looking down at where I'd landed. Bobby had rolled about fifty feet before he'd stopped. Chris the Surfer had managed to stay on his feet for a twenty-foot ride. It had been a small avalanche, and I had borne the brunt of it.

"Stacy!"

I stood up and dug some snow out from between my collar and my neck. I tested my arms and legs. No breaks. Not even any bruises, it seemed. A little shaken up, but not that bad. I shouted up to them.

"I'm okay!"

Remembering my ice ax, I looked around. I kicked the snow around my feet. It wasn't there. I returned my gaze to Chris and Bobby.

"I lost my ice ax!"

We spent the next two hours combing the slope for it. The three of us traversed the wash of the avalanche again and again, sifting through the loose snow like lifeguards diving for a missing swimmer. We didn't come up with it. It was a long, gloomy trip back to camp.

"It's the one thing you can't afford to lose," Bobby said darkly.

"You never let go of it," Chris added.

Our day's climb was ruined. The entire trip might have been over for me if Bobby hadn't brought along an extra ice ax.

"If you're in an avalanche, I could see how it might just come off," Chris said.

"But you'd never, ever, just take it off yourself," added Bobby.

"No matter what."

"Right." Bobby shook his head. "In no situation. Not even if it might take your whole head off."

"Right."

They were quiet for most of the ski across the glacier. When we finally got to the tent, Bobby dug into his gear and came out with the spare ice ax. Standing in front of the tent, he held it up and placed it in my hands. But before he let go he looked deep into my eyes. "Stacy," he said gently. "Don't let go of your fucking ice ax."

ANOTHER snowstorm blew us off our next attempt up 12,380, and after spending another four days eating popcorn and waiting for the weather to clear, we decided we had better set our sights on Huntington.

The first level of our route up the west side of the mountain took us between two faces of sheer rock, up a long, angled couloir. The gully was icy and steep, and while the weather was lousy we decided to fix 300 feet of rope at the bottom to give us a fast start when we started climbing. From there we'd be on our own, on the stiff angle of the upper couloir, then on to the rough ice above the chute. The entire route would be technical ice climbing, so we figured on taking two days to gain the summit, and then another full day to get back down to the glacier.

We spent most of the next week stranded in our sleeping bags, dodging blizzards as we tried to fix our 300 feet of rope. When the clouds finally broke, we woke to a pink and shimmery dawn, and as the gathering light threw depth and form down to the valley, we traversed our way to the base of the couloir.

I looked up at Huntington, a dark silhouette standing against the incandescent eastern sky. I was determined to propel myself up into the light, and I knew it wouldn't be easy. Even setting the ropes on the gully had been hard for me — Chris and Bobby did all of the serious work, while I watched and tried to learn the principles of protecting an ice climb. Once we set foot on the mountain, it didn't take long for everyone to figure out how far I'd ventured from the fringes of my experience. Climbing a desert bluff on a balmy, windless day was one thing. But on an ice-sheathed cliff swept by stiff, brittle winds, I didn't know what I was doing. Chris and Bobby tried to be patient while we worked on the route. They set the ropes and took up my slack while I tried to get my footing on the mountainside. But as we got ready to set out for the summit, I was determined to get my act together.

At the bottom of our route I hitched myself to the fixed line, took a deep breath, and looked up at the pitch ahead. The ice couloir is a thin, shallow gully on the mountain, the bed of a frozen river that sweeps and tumbles along with the slope of the mountainside. To extend the river analogy, the bottom fifteen feet of this couloir, where our climb began, was a frozen waterfall, a vertical column of ice reaching up to a small shelf, then a long 65-degree stretch. From there the couloir flattened out for a while, then sloped steeply upward again.

To pull ourselves up the steep ice we each carried an ice hammer and an ice ax and strapped crampons with steel toe spikes onto our boots. Thus equipped, we could climb by front-pointing — using the toe spikes to kick footholds in the ice — and planting the picks of the ice tools by swinging them deep into the hard crust.

Bobby and Chris climbed easily, but for me the vertical pitch was slow, painstaking work. The guys were climbing ahead and switching off leads, leaving me to depend on the rope — hooked onto my harness with a jumar, a finger-length metal ratcheting device that attaches to a climbing rope and slides up without sliding down — but the front-pointing was difficult. Even after I reached the gentler slopes of the couloir, each step was tiresome and painful. Kicking and whacking each step, I took a full day to climb the 750-foot couloir. As the hours of effort passed, my arms ached and my calves burned from the constant front-pointing. Being scared didn't help matters either. Drained by anxiety and consumed by frustration, I trailed Chris and Bobby by as much as our rope would allow, working as hard as I could just to keep from slowing them down. When we finally climbed out of the couloir at the end of the first day, I nearly collapsed where they sat, resting on a small ice shelf. By the time I sat down, they were standing up again, ready to go.

"We'll go up and set some lines for tomorrow," Chris said. "Why don't you clear away some space for our tent while we're gone?"

With the daylight still strong on the far end of the afternoon, I swung my ice ax to smooth away the ice beneath our tent. Temporarily relieved of the pain of climbing, I felt some waves of guilt washing over me. I hadn't led a pitch all day, and even as a follower hadn't come close to keeping up. The 300 feet of fixed line would help get the next day off to a quick start. But as I lay in the tent that night, nestled deep into my sleeping bag and still shivering in the cold of the high altitude, I couldn't escape the obvious conclusion: if I wasn't slowing them down, Bobby and Chris would be in a much better position to make the summit tomorrow. My dreams of dashing up the mountain as easily as I had scampered up the cliffs in Arizona were just that: the fantasies of the misinformed.

The next day was just as hard. I didn't quite trust my ice tools to hold me, and the thought of falling kept me rigid with terror. I crawled upward, the muscles in my calves knotting with the pressure. After almost losing my footing twice in the space of three steps, I felt the tears starting to burn down my cheeks. I was so useless. What was I doing here? By the time I reached Chris at the end of the first pitch, I was choked with frustration, tears dripping from my chin. He looked at me as I approached and a smile flickered across his face.

"So, do you want to lead the next pitch?"

My shoulders heaved with sobs. "I can't!" I finally shouted. I wiped cold tears from my chin and looked down at my crampons, glinting against the ice. "I'm scared!"

Chris gave me a hug, but I knew what he was thinking. I couldn't keep up. I'd come to Huntington unprepared, and now he and Bobby had to pull in the slack. From the lost ice ax to my slow progress on the ice, I was little more than a drag on the expedition. I felt humiliated. A little girl bursting into tears.

After a few minutes, Bobby caught up to us. Reaching the top of the rope, he bent over, gasping in the thin, cold air. When he stood up straight again, I noticed how pale his face looked.

"Bobby, are you okay?"

After pausing for a drink of water, Bobby shrugged. "Got a headache," he said. "Dizzy. Been feeling kind of puky, too."

"All day?"

He nodded.

We each knew the symptoms of altitude sickness. Headaches, nausea, dizziness, loss of appetite. He wasn't desperately ill, but it obviously wasn't a good idea for Bobby to go much higher. Still, we were so close to the summit. And after coming this far, Bobby wasn't about to surrender our chance for making the top. He took another drink and then volunteered to lead the next pitch.

The summit was in our sights, about 200 vertical feet away, perhaps a three-hour climb, given the traversing we'd have to do. And if Bobby wasn't going to stop, I sure wasn't going to add to my disgrace by sitting around waiting for them to get down. As long as they kept going, I had to move with them.

Bobby took the lead and after a few deep breaths started up again. He went only a hundred feet before he hit the rock. The tip of his ice ax glanced through the ice and slammed into the rock full force. The impact cleaved the metal tip from the shaft, and as he stood there, numbly holding his empty fiberglass handle, Bobby knew our expedition had just ended. It didn't matter that he'd thought to bring a spare ice ax. I was already using it.

Sitting in our tent that night, back on the glacier, I apologized for being so slow. "You could have done so much better," I said. "I ruined it for you."

"Aw, you didn't ruin it for us," Chris said.

"But I didn't know what I was doing," I protested.

"Forget it," Bobby interjected. "We climbed the couloir, and that's what we came here for. After that, the summit hardly matters. It was just a walk. A formality. Like picking up a diploma. What's more important: going to school or going to graduation?"

I shrugged.

"You got an education," Chris said. "Compared to that, the summit is bullshit. We came to climb, not to stand on top."

After breakfast the next morning I left Chris and Bobby in the tent, put on my skis, and rambled off onto the glacier for a little exercise. The sky was empty and deep blue, and with the sun just cresting the tip of Huntington, the thin glacier seemed to radiate light. Jagged mountains rose in every direction, and in the sunshine the ocean of white pinnacles sparkled. I stopped for a moment and looked around me, into the clear face of the morning. There was no breeze, not even a whisper. Just my own breathing and then, as I swallowed my breath, not even that. I heard my eyelashes flicking against themselves. Alone in the rawest corner of the wilderness, I could finally hear myself think.

I had failed this time, but watching Bobby and Chris, I knew I would succeed next time. And there would be a next time. In the light of the morning, standing alone in the stillness and the beauty, I could finally see what had brought me there, and why I wanted to come back. This was where I could breathe. Where my natural athletic ability merged with my need for challenge, with my love for the outdoors. Out here, I could look for myself, and express the deepest, truest core of myself. Out here I could ignore the limitations others had set for me, and create myself the way I chose.

BACK in Oregon I implemented the lessons I learned on Huntington. I started running in the afternoons, working to build my strength, endurance, and flexibility. When I rock climbed I focused on mastering specific tasks, building up strength and dexterity from my toes to fingertips, learning how to find the most secure route on the worst sections of crumbly rock. By now my ambitions went far beyond rock climbing. Now that I'd been in Alaska, I'd glimpsed the top of North America.

Once you get up to Talkeetna, where the glacier pilots sprinkle climbers onto all the surrounding mountains, it's hard not to talk about Mount McKinley. Tales of the 20,320-foot mountain form a rich legend. McKinley is large in a way few mountains are, enormous at its base and neck-breaking steep all the way up. And it's quite a way up. Although more than 8,000 feet shorter than Mount Everest,

McKinley starts much closer to sea level. So the actual vertical leap the mountain makes from the Alaskan tundra is a full 5,000 feet *higher* than the vault Mount Everest makes from the high Tibetan foothills. And the weather is just as tempestuous. Jutting high into the Arctic air flow, McKinley has winds that blow face-cracking cold and sledgehammer hard. And the news they bring can swerve radically from moment to moment: the view on McKinley can range from endless crystal sky to deadly thick clouds back to endless crystal in a matter of hours. More frequently, the clouds stay on for days, perhaps weeks, at a time, depositing enormous amounts of snow.

For climbers on this continent, McKinley is the place to go. The last rung on the North American ladder, the stepping-off point to the great mountains and legendary climbs in the rest of the world. I had a sense of what the big mountain would throw in my path. And I knew, right now, that I didn't have the skills or strength to pull it off. But I also knew that if I trained hard enough and did my best to learn, if I focused intently enough on this goal, I could give McKinley a run. And if I succeeded, I could go anywhere in the world.

When I got home that summer, Curt and I started planning our climb on Mount McKinley. From that moment, everything we did together was part of our path to the summit. And we wanted more than just the summit. I'd had my problems on Huntington, but Curt figured the experience had taught me enough about ice climbing to move on to more advanced routes. So as we planned our trip, we set our sights beyond McKinley's frequently climbed West Buttress.

"The Butt's a walk-up," Curt said, tracing the route across the map. "No technical work at all. As long as the weather's right, anyone who can climb at altitude can waltz up that route." This wasn't the case with the Cassin Ridge. It was, he explained, one of the mountain's most difficult routes. A 1,500-foot ice couloir, a long knifeblade ridge, and thousands of feet of steep, unsteady glacier. You gain so much altitude so quickly, you have to spend a day or two acclimating in mid-route, huddled on the mountainside in a small bivvy tent. Even in perfect weather it can take almost a week to climb the entire ridge. An entire week spent on the edge, where you have to confront yourself for every step and every breath.

During the next few months Curt and I focused our training on rock climbing. On my own I lifted weights to build upper body power and kept up with my running. Still, with the Cassin Ridge ahead of us, we knew we had to spend some time working on ice. So in July 1980 Curt and I drove up to Canada to climb Mount Robson, an isolated 13,000-foot peak in Alberta.

After a two-day hike to Robson Lake, Curt and I set out for the glacier beneath the mountain. We traveled light in the summery weather, planning to set up our tent and catch a few hours of sleep before starting up the mountain early the next morning. Assuming things went well the next day, we'd make the summit by early afternoon, then retreat down the easier east slope and be back to our tent on the glacier by nightfall.

But the ice face was more difficult to climb than we'd imagined, and it took us more than ten hours to find our way to the summit. By then the sun had started its long slide to the western horizon, and we both knew we wouldn't have enough light to find our tent down on the glacier. Still, a night on the summit didn't seem too awful a fate. With clear, summery skies we'd see a spectacular sunset, then bivouac under the stars. And with a can of tuna, some crackers, and a candy bar stashed in our packs, we'd even be able to have a halfway decent dinner. We ate quickly, exhausted from our climb, then put on our anoraks, pulled our hats down over our ears, and huddled together in a shallow snow pit. As the fireball sun sank into a blood-red horizon, I nestled my head against Curt's chest. My thoughts drifted off into the sky, and I was asleep before the last light faded.

When my eyes fluttered open a few hours before dawn, Curt was already awake. I could feel his arm tight around my shoulders. I could tell something was wrong.

The clouds had descended after we'd fallen asleep. Eventually, snow started falling. When Curt woke up, the wind was starting to blast, whipping the snow into a horizontal curtain. By dawn we were sitting in a full-on blizzard. At first I was almost too shocked to believe it. *How did this happen?* We had always been so conscious of the weather, always ready for anything to happen. Being prepared is perhaps the most important credo for a climber. And we both knew it! You can't take anything for granted in the mountains, no matter how lush and lovely things may seem when you set out. But this one time we took a risk, and now, caught in the bowels of a white-out storm, we had to pay the price.

Our situation seemed bleak. We had no food or water. We didn't have a tent or sleeping bags. The north face was far too steep for us to risk descending in the driving wind and snow. Meanwhile, the heavy clouds showed no signs of clearing, and we couldn't see anything beyond the tips of our own mittens. The temperature continued to drop.

"This is serious trouble," Curt said. Now we were stuck, and for the moment we had no idea if we'd ever be able to find a passable route out of danger. But it's a reality of mountaineering that when crisis hits, you can't let down your guard, can't allow feelings to interrupt logic. As soon as it was light, we scraped our way through the blizzard and searched for a trail down the mountain.

We got one break — in the dull light of dawn we found a faint set of day-old footprints leading down the eastern face. We weren't certain where the steps led, but they were our only hope, our only clue to the way off the mountain. We followed them for the next ten hours, hunkered together against the unyielding winds and hard, stinging snow. When we lost the path, we'd crisscross the slope, bent almost double to search for the slight dimples in the thickening white blanket. But we always managed to find them again, somehow, and in the gathering murk of dusk found ourselves at what we thought was the top of the Kain Face, a 45-degree ice face that stands as the main obstacle on Robson's east side.

As night closed in, we got ready to feel our way down the ice face. The snow and wind had eased in the darkness, but still the clouds swirled around us. As Curt twisted in the first ice screw, I sat on the snow, my arms wrapped tightly against my chest. Hoping to find a hint of a landmark, I strained my eyes for focus and tried to bore through the impenetrable silver blanket. Just the edge of a ridge, the top of a cliff — any clue to tell us where we were on the mountain, where we could find shelter. Shivering and aching with exhaustion, I tried desperately to pierce the fog, but as night slipped up on us, nothing swirled into focus. Dejected and frightened, I looked to Curt for reassurance.

"Are you sure we're headed in the right direction?"

Curt raised his head, pausing, his ice hammer in mid-twist. "No."

He looked down and continued working the screw.

We continued in the dark, wearing headlamps to illuminate our movements. The slim beams of light flew off into the nothingness, but we had to keep going. We had to get off the exposed ridge, down to where we could bivouac for a few hours without facing the killing wind. I down-climbed beneath Curt, moving slowly, kicking for footholds, mustering my energy every time I swung my ice ax. Every thirty-five feet I'd twist an ice screw into the ice, using the pick of my ice ax to twist it in, then stringing our rope through the carabiner. When the wind gusted, I'd squeeze in toward the slope, feeling the cold, bony fingers brush against my sides. The night magnified the tug of gravity. Every step pulled at the tendons wiring my legs, rattled the ladder of vertebrae in my spine. My eyes dimmed, my brain waves seemed to flatten. I hadn't eaten for twenty-four hours. I hadn't had a drink for more than twelve hours. I'd barely stopped moving since dawn. Occasionally the exhaustion would overtake me and I'd twirl off into a weary dizziness. The frigid air and the darkness were seeping inside me. I wondered how much more I could take.

Chunks of ice careened down the slope. Every time Curt swung his ice ax, a bit of the slope would give way, skittering and sailing down on top of me. The shrapnel got larger as time passed. After an hour the ice chunks were fist-sized, falling in abrupt showers that slammed against my helmet and pounded my shoulders. I tried to anticipate the ice, looking up and trying to dodge the bigger hunks. But they rained out of the darkness, and I rarely saw a hunk until it crunched against me.

I moved onward by rote, each motion draining my energy, like a pendulum swinging in ever-smaller arcs. Hearing an oncoming shower of ice chunks, I tried to lean out of the way, but lost a foothold and almost fell. Gasping and clinging desperately to the ice, I tried to reassemble my wits. Shivering with cold and hunger, dazed with thirst, I stood on the slope and waited for Curt. In the darkness below, the face vanished into the clouds. Above me, the rope to Curt faded into the darkness. If I fell, the rope would be the only thing keeping me from the clouds below. The last thin barrier between life and death.

I watched the rope tremble with Curt's movements, and I pulled in the slack as he came closer. I contemplated its flimsy weight. In that instant another ice chunk came cracking against the side of my helmet, an explosion of white light in my brain, another sharp jolt for my body. In that moment I wondered why I was bothering at all. I was so cold and hungry and tired, I had already felt so much raw pain. It was too much. What was the point of going on? In the air ahead of me the rope jiggled again. If I took out my knife, I could cut it in an instant. Then I could jump. No more cold. No more hunger. The misery would end, and then there'd be a blissful emptiness, a world beyond blisters and hunger cramps and parched, cracked lips. I squeezed the rope, stiff with ice, and stared down into the blackness. It'd be so easy to slip away, I thought.

This is not going to happen. The hard shell of resolve re-formed, and I was moving again. When we got to the bottom of the ice face an hour later, we dug a trench in the snow and sat scrunched together, conserving our body heat by folding our knees up against our chests. With the wind roaring and the snow still rushing around us, I'd sink into brief, shallow sleep, only to rattle awake with my own violent shivering. The night seemed to stretch forever. Sometimes I tried to relax enough to stop shivering. I'd curl into myself, limp as a rag, and the vibrating would end. A strange peace for thirty seconds, a minute, perhaps ninety seconds, then my muscles would seize up and my jaw would clatter uncontrollably.

"How do you know when you're going to die?" I whispered into Curt's ear.

"You stop moving." Curt trembled against me. Turning to look into his eyes, I felt his breath against my face. Even that seemed chilly.

"It'd be easy to give up. Just lie down and give in to it."

"A lot of people do," he said. "We'll keep going. Once the morning comes. Can't be much further now." Curt burrowed against me and I felt his head slacken, felt him slip into the blackness for another few minutes. I was alone in the night, sitting on the mountainside in the snow and the wind and the barren glacier. Then he jolted awake and lifted his head from my shoulder. And we sat together, shivering and breathing, waiting for the dawn to come.

And it would come, and we would live to see it. I knew it then, even through the blackness and the wind and the killing cold. I'd made the decision up on the ice face, when the ice was raining down and the rope dangled so thin and delicate. *This is not going to happen.* The moment I snapped awake up there the resolve was even harder and more deeply rooted than it had been before. In the face of everything, I knew I would keep moving. I knew that hunger would pass, that pain would end, and that at some point I'd be able to close my eyes. I willed myself to survive, to keep going, step after painful step, until we got back. Years later I'd realize how often people make another choice. How a struggle to survive leads to a crossroads: life or death, suffering or resignation. You stand there for a moment and make a conscious decision. And at that moment you either sit down and die, or you keep moving.

When it did get light, and we saw how the clouds had lifted from the mountain, we could see the glacier only a few hundred feet beneath us. And right then I saw everything else, too: food, warmth, rest. I saw life. We were back at our tent by one P.M.

CURT and I were bound by our climbing. It was the one thing that gave us a common focus, a language, an ambition to drive us from day to day. And by the fall of 1980 we were two people who needed something to hold on to. Curt was miserable in Tillamook — his disappointment in his counseling job had grown into a real animosity. Meanwhile, my assortment of part-time jobs waiting tables and planting seedling pines in Woodburn left me less than fulfilled. Curt and I decided to find a new life for ourselves. It had to be in the mountains, of course. Even if that meant living in a small town, even if it limited all our job prospects, none of that mattered. Wasn't it time we built our lives around what we loved to do?

We decided on Leavenworth, a small mountain town in the North Cascades of Washington, about two hours east of Seattle. When Curt and I drove into Leavenworth during the middle of October, I felt overjoyed. Soon everything seemed to be coming together: we quickly found jobs at the nearby Steven's Pass ski resort rental shop. And just as quickly we found a rental house, a cozy two-bedroom bungalow on the humble side of town. We had great fun during those first few weeks, but as November turned colder and then fell into December our luck started to run against us. Winter brought the cold and dark, but day after day the skies stayed clear. The winter drought kept the Steven's Pass slopes closed, and soon our jobs evaporated with the tourist trade. Our savings had long since vanished, and in such a ski-dependent community a dry winter made for brutal unemployment. But I hit the streets with a vengeance and after a few desperate weeks of job searching eventually landed work as a high school groundskeeper.

Curt had less luck. After a fruitless month of looking, he settled for a job selling vacuum cleaners door-to-door. It became a bleak winter. Our rented house, once so cozy, turned cramped and dingy, a hole-in-the-wall we could only just afford to rent. Heating oil was way beyond our meager resources, so when the weather turned cruel we tried to stay warm in layers of sweaters and wool hats. When it got really cold, we'd treat ourselves by turning on the oven and propping open the door. We had to be frugal, stocking our kitchen with surplus avocadoes, tortillas, and dry beans that we could buy in bulk. Sitting there one night, trembling in hat and gloves and leaning above the open oven, I felt the last glimmer of romance flicker out of our life. We looked so pathetic, sitting in our own living room swaddled in layers of wool and down. We didn't just look pathetic, we *were* pathetic. I had wanted to be a real climber, but just ended up a Climbing Bum. *A Climbing Bum, for God's sake.* We were just a few steps from those tattered, painfully skinny, torn-denim crows I had seen circling the cafeteria in Yosemite! If our finances continued in the downward spiral Curt and I had maintained this winter, we would have to spend the next year hanging out in the Steven's Pass cafeterias, racing each other to the juiciest leftovers.

I cared about Curt, and I did feel something for him that my twenty-two-year-old self identified as love. At times we had even talked about getting married. And we did have fun that winter, and not just while we were climbing. Curt and I passed many long, dark nights warming each other with folk songs or by reading *Beowulf* aloud. Our joint ambition kept us locked close, but as the winter passed I felt myself preparing to disengage. There was more magic in what we *did* together than in who we *were* together. By the end of the winter the only things holding us together were the rock walls of the Cascades and the big map of McKinley on our bedroom wall, the red felt-pen line tracing our route up the Cassin Ridge.

I knew there had to be more to life. In fact, I was beginning to catch a few glimpses. A few weeks before Curt and I left for McKinley, my old climbing idol Shari Kearney had called. We'd climbed together a few times in Yosemite, and she knew I had started working on some serious climbing in the last few years. Now, Shari explained, she was helping to put together an all-woman expedition into the Himalayas. They were planning to leave that next spring for Ama Dablam, a 22,350-foot peak in Nepal. Would I be interested in going along?

Interested? I could barely contain myself. Of course I was interested.

"I can't guarantee anything," Shari warned me. "But I'll put in a good word for you."

The week before we left for McKinley I got a call from Tanya Erwin, the Ama Dablam expedition's base camp manager. We talked for an hour, and she left me with an enticing notion: "You don't have the high-altitude experience the rest of the team has," she said. "But we're still very interested in you. Call when you get back from Mc-Kinley," she concluded, "and then we'll see how you did at altitude."

The Himalayas! Within my reach! All I had to do was climb Mount McKinley.

W H E N Curt and I finally got to Alaska in mid-May, we loaded ourselves and our gear into a Cessna and took off for the McKinley staging area on the Kahiltna glacier. Flying in, I searched the wild terrain until the mountain finally came into view, soaring up from between the covey of cottonballs hovering around its shoulders. I felt my mouth open, an involuntary breath swelling my chest. As much as I'd read about McKinley, as much as I'd memorized the routes and studied photographs for the contours of its ridges, I was still stunned by how breathtakingly *big* it was. Not only tall — over 20,000 feet — but wide. And steep. Even in Alaska, in that great empty expanse of wilderness and tundra, this one mountain seemed to dominate the sky. The sight made my heart dance.

In the last four years I'd worked my way up a lot of mountains — more than a dozen peaks in the Cascades and the Sierras. I'd made mistakes and had breakthroughs, I'd taken the steps one after another. Eventually I'd turned myself into a serious mountaineer. And at this point it was the one thing I knew I could do, the one set of achievements I could point to as the defining moments in my adult life. And if that was true, if climbing was what I chose to do, I was all the more determined to become a great climber. I'd stood up to a lot of challenges, and now the vast McKinley and its jagged Cassin

Ridge felt like the obvious place to put everything I knew to the test. Because if I could climb the sharp, icy ridge, I'd come away knowing that I could go beyond North America. I could go to Ama Dablam with the other women next year and climb in the Himalayas.

B Y the time Curt and I collected our gear out of the plane and set up our tent, more than a dozen other parties had already staked out turf near the makeshift airstrip. Once we were settled in, we checked in with the camp manager, a young Alaskan woman employed by a conglomeration of Talkeetna Cessna pilots to coordinate the aeronautic comings and goings and keep track of the various climbing schedules and mid-mountain whereabouts. We spent our first week among the crowd on the Kahiltna, acclimating and waiting out a day or two of stormy weather. When the storm broke, we packed our gear and set out for the mountain, skiing toward the immense ridge on McKinley's south face all by ourselves.

We sank our spikes into the 1,500-foot Japanese Couloir just after dawn. The climbing came slow and difficult on the sheer blue ice, and it took nine hours to reach the Cassin Ledge, a four-foot-by-fifteen-foot shelf that marks the top of the couloir. After spending two nights camped on the shelf, taking the extra day in our tent to adjust to the altitude, we headed up into the rocky part of the ridge. Climbing in the Arctic wind with a sixty-pound backpack strapped to my shoulders added an entirely new challenge to the morning. The pack not only threw off my sense of balance, but also caught the wind. The occasional wild gust would shove me sideways, and only a well-placed handhold or two saved me from taking a screamer back down toward the Cassin Ledge. The top of the cliffs didn't offer much safer terrain. Once we scaled the rock pitch we had to traverse Fantasy Ridge, a foot-wide, snow-capped tightrope with heart-squeezing 2,000-foot drops on either side.

Now on a steep glacier, we dug out a small ice shelf and set up our tent for the night. The weather turned by the time we finished eating dinner. Clouds moved in quickly, riding hard gusts of frigid wind. Snow started falling just as the night sank around us. We went to sleep hearing the sides of our tent tremble in the wind, hoping the morning would bring clearer skies and gentler breezes. But the snow only came harder. As the night wore on, loose snow sloughing off the slope — spindrift — glissaded down the icy face of the glacier and started mounting on the roof of the tent. The tent sagged with the increasing weight, and when Curt woke up just after midnight, he found that his side of the tent had collapsed on top of him. He rolled onto his side to prop up the nylon with his shoulder, then gripped my arm to shake me awake.

"We've got a problem."

We dressed quickly, and with our headlamps cutting white columns through the blackness and into the thick feathers of snow, we climbed outside to inspect the damage. The pile of snow on the roof had torn out two stakes, but fortunately the fabric of the tent had escaped with a few stretch marks. It wouldn't take much effort to reset the stakes, but with the snow coming thicker the tent obviously had little chance of withstanding the rest of the night.

We reached for our ice axes and started chopping at the crusty glacier. Working together in the snow and wind, we took six hours to dig out a cave large enough for the both of us and our packs. We finished just after dawn, and spent the next two days entombed in the glacier, waiting for the storm to blow past the mountain. Once the weather calmed enough for us to venture outside again, we spent two more days working our way up the steep ice and rock faces on the ridge. Then another storm blew in, and we hunkered down on a thin ice mantle just above 18,000 feet, tentbound for two more days.

Even with the fits of violent weather, I knew the climb was going well. Curt and I had already spent a week at high altitude, and so far neither of us had developed any physical problems. What's more, I knew the weather could be much worse. Shrieking winds and intense blizzards notwithstanding, we'd managed to avoid the true demon of McKinley: the brutal Arctic cold. We were lucky, so far, and that realization made me nervous. From the moment I set foot on the mountain I was heading into uncharted territory, venturing high into the barren fringe of the atmosphere. I already knew how difficult climbing could be on its own terms. But I also knew that as I wandered farther into the firmament, I was becoming that much more vulnerable to the wind and cold, that much more susceptible to the torments of altitude. No matter how good a climber, I knew a sudden bout of McKinley's notorious cold could bring frostbite sharp enough to steal my fingers and toes. At any moment an altitude-caused cerebral edema could rob me of my senses, and then, almost inevitably, my life. Huddled in my sleeping bag, I could sense the lifelessness around me; the thin, frigid air, the frozen rock, the desolate snow. Again, the realization gripped me, and a sharp surge of adrenaline shot needles through my body. I was out on the edge, farther than I'd ever been before. Closing my eyes in the dark, I could see us against the night, small specks of warmth adrift in the frozen wilderness. Being that alone, that exposed to the forces of a vast, indifferent world, was both terrifying and thrilling. If we were going to survive up here, it was because we were strong enough and smart enough to keep ourselves alive.

As Curt and I toiled on the icy upper reaches of the Cassin, I knew we were gaining momentum. Everything we'd hoped for, everything we'd built out lives around, was coming true. I'd contemplated this moment for months, daydreaming at work or in our living room in Leavenworth. Naturally, Curt and I would be ecstatic, finally sharing the glory we'd longed to reach. But even as the summit drew within our grasp I could feel something looming before us.

It was just a shadow at first. The cool detachment that comes from being preoccupied. But it ran deeper than that. Late one afternoon, when I was leading a pitch on the higher reaches of the ridge, I spent half an hour straining on the end of the rope, combing the rotten ice for a solid spot to plant a piece of protection. I finally gave up, buried my ice ax for a shaky anchor, and belayed Curt around my waist. When he got up to me, he slammed his ice ax with a mighty crunch and exploded with rage.

"What the fuck took you so long?"

I tried to explain, but managed only to burst into tears. Instantly apologetic, Curt reached out to hug me, and for a moment we warmed ourselves. But the surge of affection dried up with my tears, and soon we were silent, climbing on opposite ends of the same rope, both lost in the tangle of our own thoughts. Mount McKinley had given us a purpose. But now, as our tracks climbed the powdery ridge, stretching up almost to the tip of the mountain, I could finally see life beyond McKinley. The expedition to Ama Dablam, and then a different life.

The crest of the ridge was in front of us. A hundred yards away, then seventy-five, then fifty. When I could count the steps, I felt a surge of emotion. Gratitude for being alive, elation from scaling the ridge — it all rushed inside me, and as I stood there, drinking in the cold, empty air above the continent, I felt free. The summit was still fifty feet above us, but that hardly seemed to matter. *We'd climbed the Cassin Ridge!* I had survived! I could let go of everything. I folded my legs and sat down. Curt knelt next to me and put his arms around my shoulders. And we sat there together for a while, looking down at the world stretching away beneath us. Up there, the whole path seemed to present itself in clear, logical steps. If I could climb McKinley, I could certainly climb Ama Dablam. And if I could climb one mountain in the Himalayas, why couldn't I climb something larger — like Mount Everest?

The whole world is out there, I thought. And if I want it, all I have to do is grab it.

4

CHASING DREAMS

THE dreams started in 1979. Hazy images, at first. A man. I'd be walking with him, and we'd talk. I never remembered the conversations or how he looked, but always the feeling. The sense that this person existed and I was supposed to meet him. It would come every few months, and always just before I woke up in the morning. One of those surreal but intense dreams that bridge sleep and consciousness. I'd wake up confused and intrigued.

We'd never been properly introduced, but I did know who my dream man was. It had all started when I'd gone down to Utah to climb in Zion one spring. I'd spent a few evenings hanging out with Randy Aton, one of the NOLS climbing instructors I'd met around Scott's campfire during my first trip in 1977. Randy had recently moved to Springdale, the small desert town near the west end of the park, and was thinking about buying some land to put up his own house. While he looked for his own place, Randy spent a few months house-sitting for a friend, staying in one of the town's nineteenth-century farmhouses, a warm old place with creaky stairs and narrow halls. I was having dinner with Randy in that house one night when I noticed an envelope stuck to the refrigerator. I didn't know the name, Mark Meinert, but I looked twice, for some reason.

"Who's this guy?"

"Mark?" Randy shrugged. "He owns this place. He's working in Alaska this summer."

And that was the end of it. Until the dreams started. I didn't pay much attention at the beginning. I was living with Curt then, and not interested in pursuing the shadowy figures in my dreams. But then it kept happening, and each time I'd wake up a little more curious than the time before.

The dreams became more intense during the weeks after Mount McKinley. Curt and I had already decided to spend some time apart once we'd returned from the mountain. The dreams followed me home to my mother's house, and when I jolted awake one morning I knew I had to do something. I got up and scribbled a letter to Lynn, my old college roommate, then living the rustic life in Alaska. "I'm being drawn . . ." I wrote, then stopped. *Drawn to what?* I pondered this for a moment. Why was I so sure I'd find what I was looking for in Zion? Was it the soul of a man beckoning me, or just the keening spirits in the Virgin River canyon? I considered this, trying to dredge up the fragments of the dream, and I returned to my letter. "I'm being drawn to Zion for some unexplainable reason," I wrote. "Will you come with me?"

Two weeks later I steered my battered Saab into Springdale. Lynn and I spent the night in the Zion campground, then headed into town the next morning to find Randy Aton. The first place we looked was the Bit 'n' Spur, a funky neo-cowboy bar that watered most of the young people in town. Sure enough, we found him kicking back on the front porch. As Lynn and I jogged up to the porch, Randy and Adele Smith, another NOLS instructor I had met with Scott in Zion, leaped up to greet us.

And on the edge of my vision I saw him there, leaning against the railing. I saw his dark hair, the coolness in his eyes. Something hidden just beneath the expression on his face.

Greetings were shouted, cries of surprise filling the dry morning air. He didn't say anything, a stranger to these newcomers, but stood back and watched the reunion run its course. I knew it was him. He was wearing a blue short-sleeved polo shirt and loose white cotton pants. He had broad shoulders and thick arms, I noticed. A longish fringe of dark brown hair, thinning on top, and intense blue eyes. I edged closer. After a few long minutes I walked up to the railing and introduced myself.

"I haven't met you yet. I'm Stacy."

He smiled, leveling his blue gaze at me, and held out his hand.

"I'm Mark."

I felt the weight of his hand, the curve of his fingers, the gap between his thumb and forefinger. So he was real. But where were the sparks? The dreams were always so much more exciting. Randy came up behind me and clapped his arm over my shoulder.

"I see y'all have met. Look, Mark and I have a little business to finish up this morning, but we're planning to climb this afternoon. Wanna come?"

"Sure," I said, and we made arrangements.

"We'll see you at three," Randy called back.

I met Randy and Mark at the restaurant later that afternoon, and we piled into Randy's car to drive into Zion. We parked the car in the Narrows Trail lot and Randy looked up at the canyon walls around us. He and Mark exchanged a few words, craned their necks, and then settled on a spot. Then Randy sidled up to me and put an arm over my shoulder. "Okay, little lady," he said sweetly. "Have we got a climb for you!"

The canyon wall rises from the edge of the parking lot, and Tourist Crack was only a short jog from the car. Standing at the bottom, I looked up at the 120-foot cleft for a moment, took a breath, then started up the smooth sandstone. The crack made for some strenuous climbing — gradually widening from a spidery finger-crack to a gaping off-width — but I managed to scale the wall without much difficulty. When I hoisted myself up to the top, I turned around and looked down.

"Next!" I called out. Randy looked over to Mark and they smiled.

"Very impressive!" Mark shouted up.

"Not bad for a little girl!" Randy added in his Kentucky twang.

Mark came up next, moving smoothly and quickly. When he got to the top, we stood together, watching Randy ease his way up the crack. Relaxing in the heat, Mark hunkered down on his muscular legs, squatting on the warm sandstone. As we talked idly, Mark kept his eyes on Randy, focusing his attention on our friend, now halfway up the crack. *So he's shy,* I thought. But Springdale was a small town, particularly for the younger people, so after we made our way down, we kept running into each other — at the Bit 'n' Spur that night, on a few afternoon climbing parties with Randy or other friends. When I asked about his house, he offered to give me a tour. He'd been working on it ever since I'd first seen it, he said.

"Two years is a long time to spend working on a house."

"It's not all I've done," he said. "My business takes a lot of time."

"You've got your own business?"

"Sure. I do remodels, building, you name it. General contracting." He reached into a shirt pocket and pulled out a small white card. It said *Austin Enterprises* in capital letters.

"Who's Austin?"

"I am. It's my mother's maiden name."

"Why not Meinert Enterprises?"

"Hard to pronounce," Mark said. "Hard to spell. No one gets it right." He was silent for a moment, then shrugged. "Austin's just easier."

A few evenings later, Mark strolled into our camp with a friend, carrying a six-pack of beer. "We thought we might come out and watch the sunset with you guys," Mark said.

We all sat together, watching the sun plunge behind the canyon walls, and as the horizon flared with reds and oranges, Mark and I shuffled off alone. We headed to the sloping edge of the canyon, stepping over the prickly black brush, weaving around the cactus and juniper, the fragrant ponderosa pine. On the edges of the cliffs the sedimentary rock melted time into layers of red, orange, and white. We walked up to the top of a ridge and lay down on our backs, watching the night sky deepen. And as the twilight dimmed, the stars emerged. Then it was night and all of the constellations were there, as close and as clear as I had ever seen them. The Big Dipper, the Little Dipper, the lion and the bull, almost within an arm's reach.

We lay there on our backs, talking about the stars, about the galaxies and the endless universe. I was thinking: *He's going to kiss me.* I risked a glance, out of the corner of my eye, and saw him looking over at me. He moved his head, slowly, imperceptibly at first. The sound of his body moving in the dust. Then he was up on one elbow, hovering over my face and then, tenderly, lowering his lips over mine.

MARK and I were together from that moment. Always trust your dreams, I'd think at night, dropping off to sleep with Mark warm beside me. Sure enough, those bizarre dreams had been right. Mark was the man I'd been looking for. He was an adventurer, but also an adult. He'd been to Africa. He'd built houses in Utah and worked oil rigs in Alaska. He was a pretty good climber and a rugged all-around outdoorsman. While I was drifting in and out of college and having fun on mountains, Mark was *doing* things. He was an artist — a potter and a sculptor. He'd studied theater in California and majored in art at the University of Utah. One of his sculptures, an abstract woman's bust with deerskin stretched over the facial structure, was on permanent display in the Braithwaite Gallery in Cedar City. And he was a man of extreme political passions. As we talked, Mark filled me with shadowy, elusive tales of his environmental activist past. How he'd cut big checks to friends in Earth First!, the army of radical enviro-terrorists. Mark's eyes flashed as he recalled his midnight raids on desert developers. The sugar he'd poured in tractor gas tanks. The earth mover he'd fired up, then steered to make it fall over a 2,000-foot cliff. "The drop was so high," he whispered, "I never even heard it hit bottom."

One day we went together to help gather rocks for a wall he was building. When we got to the particular section of desert he liked, Mark stopped his pickup and jumped out. Large and small rocks lay scattered in all directions, but Mark examined each of them carefully, walking hunched over. We were only after particular rocks, he explained.

"Rocks with character." He held up a head-sized stone with orange lichen swirling across the face. "See? This is a beautiful rock."

We spent two days combing the desert floor. It was a long time to spend gathering sandstone rocks for an ordinary wall, but Mark wasn't about to build an ordinary rock wall. He wanted to build Rodin's rock wall, a wall made from rocks swirling with lichen, rocks with suggestive lips or cracks worn into their faces, rocks with interesting nubbins, dramatic sizes or odd shapes.

"Each rock," Mark explained, "has got to be alive. They each have to look up and say something!"

And that said something to me.

I stayed in Springdale for two months that fall, camped in the canyon with Lynn. But if my evenings were filled with Mark, the days were still jammed with climbing. After a month the efforts of those days got under my skin, turning my forearms to granite, my fingers to rubber bands. My entire body grew taut and honed. I could climb anywhere and spend hours pulling myself up wrinkles in the rock.

There was a reason for this ceaseless regimen. The call had come a few days after Curt and I got back from McKinley. It was Tanya

Erwin, the manager of the Ama Dablam trip. We exchanged hellos, and then I told her about my climb on the Cassin Ridge. "We've been talking about you," she said, and I knew what was coming. "We'd like you to come with us to Ama Dablam."

Everything was perfect. I was spending my days on the magic cliffs in Zion and my nights with Mark. And I loved being in Springdale. During the fall of 1981 it was impossible to go to the Bit 'n' Spur and *not* find a friend to call me over and ask after my most recent adventure. Mark and I went out together most nights, so naturally it didn't take long for everyone to figure out our relationship. About a week after Mark and I got together, Adele Smith sidled up to me outside the ladies' in the Bit. "Hey, Stace," she said. "Want to have breakfast tomorrow?"

"Sure," I said. I didn't know Adele that well, but we had a lot of friends in common and I liked her. There was a clarity in her eyes, a sharpness I associated with strength. When we sat down that next morning, I learned something else was on Adele's mind. "Stacy," she began, "you know I like you." She chose her words carefully. "I think you're a nice person. But I'm worried."

"Why?" I felt my forehead wrinkling. *What's she talking about?*

"I know Mark's a nice guy, and he's a lot of fun." She shifted in her seat. "But he's bad news."

"What do you mean?" I gulped my coffee, feeling the heat burning through my stomach and into my veins.

"You know Mark's already been married," she said. I was listening and dismissing what she said at the same time, but I nodded. "He got divorced and then he was dating another woman for quite a while."

"And?"

"And then he dumped her this spring for some Frenchwoman who was passing through town."

"What's that got to do with me?"

Adele paused for a moment, measuring her words. "He's just not very supportive of his women friends, that's all."

I looked away, pouring milk into my coffee, stirring it. *I knew Mark!* I'd spent almost every spare moment of the last week with him, hadn't I? And no matter what he'd done before, he certainly wasn't going to do it to me now. Seeing the look on my face, the hard shell of resistance, Adele sighed.

"I just thought you should know, that's all."

I picked up my wallet and took a dollar out to pay for the coffee. "Thanks," I said. "But don't worry. It's not that big a deal. Mark and I are just friends."

"All right, Stacy. If that's what you say."

I was too upset to get back into my car, so I walked up the street. The morning air was cool and dry, but I floated through it, unaware. How could Adele be so down on Mark? Everyone makes mistakes, and who could say the problems in his marriage were all his fault? I clomped up the street and found Randy on the porch of the Bit, reading the morning's *St. George Daily Spectrum*. I plopped down and told him what had just happened.

"So what's going on with Adele?"

Randy put down his newspaper. "Let me tell you something." He lowered his voice. "Mark's a great guy. He's a good friend of mine. But you know what? I wouldn't want to be in love with him."

"Why?"

"He has an incredible temper."

"What do you mean?"

"I mean have fun, but watch yourself. Don't get pulled in too deep. Take my word for it, darlin'. There's a lot going on down there that you do not want to get tangled up in."

He stood up, squeezed my shoulder, and walked off. I sat alone, torn between what I knew and what I'd just been told. The man Adele and Randy described bore no relation to the Mark I knew. He wasn't forceful or aggressive. If anything, he was soft-spoken, even shy. And why did it matter to me anyway? I wasn't lying to Adele — I wasn't planning to *marry* Mark. We enjoyed each other's company, I felt happy around him. For the time being, that was all I wanted.

I planned to drive back to Leavenworth during the first week of November. Springdale was fun, my affair with Mark had been good for me, but I knew I had to get my life back into gear. The Ama Dablam trip was looming in early spring, and I had to start making money for that climb.

Then there was the rest of my life to think about. Occasionally I thought about spending it with Mark. I knew we'd only known each other for a few weeks, I knew there were those shadows hovering around him, the things Randy and Adele had said. But I couldn't hold that against him. Mark had affected me more intensely than any other man I'd met. Something in his eyes, the twinkle when he smiled, or the deep intensity when he was serious, cut deep into the soft part of my soul. Being with Mark was like riding a roller coaster. His moods could churn so quickly, darkness rolled across his face like clouds in an unsettled sky. He could be scary at times, but never, ever boring. When I was with him everything seemed possible.

I kept most of my feelings to myself, but on Halloween they burst out. We were in his living room, putting the finishing touches on our costumes. Mark dressed as Medusa, and was endearingly goofy, with a halo of fake snakes around his head. Seeing him there, I walked right up and threw my arms around him.

"Will you marry me?" I heard the words shoot out of my mouth. From the look on his face, Mark was just as surprised to hear them as I was. He laughed and patted me on the back.

"I'll think about it," he said.

Just the same, I had to go. As much as I wanted to stay, I knew it would be better to make a clean break and spend the winter taking care of business. So I set a date, the Monday after Halloween, and on Sunday I went around town to say my good-byes. The next morning I was rolling west on the highway. This is good for me, I thought. Now I know I can have passion in my life, but when I have to cut it off and say good-bye, I can do it. It's just like climbing, a question of control. When you need to move, you have to separate the emotions you don't need, the ones that hold you back, and cut them loose.

A few days after that I was back in Leavenworth, back where my past waited, demanding an explanation. What could I say? As much as I cared about Curt, I knew he wasn't a lifetime mate for me. We separated for good, and I moved into a new house in Leavenworth.

I started preparing for the winter, looking for a job, continuing my workout program for Ama Dablam. Work and exercise would make it a hard, monastic winter, but after my autumn in Springdale, I was ready for the challenge. I continued my self-imposed regimen for precisely two weeks. Then the telephone rang. It was Mark, calling from Boulder, Colorado. In an instant my heart sank and leaped. I was ecstatic, but I didn't want to feel that way.

"Why are you calling me?" I heard my voice against the mouthpiece, admonishing and pleading. Mark laughed. He had just sold his house, he said, and he was spending a few weeks climbing.

"I just felt like talking to you," he said. Then his voice got softer. "I love you."

"What?" My resolve burst like a balloon against a needle.

"I want you to come back to Springdale and live with me."

"Really?"

"But first I want you to come meet me in Denver, so we can do some climbing."

"Oh, Mark." I was shaking my head, pretending I could stop it. "I can't just pull up and leave like that. I have a job and a housemate, I can't just go to Utah at the drop of a hat."

"Why not? You can live with me. You'll get a job down here, or I'll give you a job working with me."

Why resist it? This wasn't climbing, wasn't a life-and-death situation. I didn't have to hide from my emotions just because it felt good to surrender to them. And so I put my belonging back into storage, parked my car at a friend's house, and got on the plane to Denver the next afternoon.

We spent the next month in Springdale. Mark was warm and considerate, even driving me back and forth to the Brian Head ski resort for the days I worked on the Ski Patrol. I didn't want to work there for the entire winter, though, so we'd talk about how we'd make a living after the new year.

"I could teach you about carpentry," he said. "We could work together. And once you learn enough you can go off and work by yourself. You'll have your own career."

And so that was everything: a man, a career, my climbing. This was where all the roads came together. I didn't know what I'd done to deserve the luck.

WE drove to Oregon for Christmas. On our way, I wanted to take a detour to Leavenworth, to pick up my car and some belongings so I could take them back to Utah with us. The North Cascades took us more than a little out of our way, but we weathered the highways well, switching off behind the wheel of Mark's pickup truck. Still, the days on the highway took their toll, leaving us a little weary from the road behind and anxious about the holidays ahead. Things only got worse when we got to Leavenworth.

It started with my car. After standing parked for almost two months, my poor, neglected Saab just didn't want to start. Mark spent two hours trying to fire up the engine, but when the problems proved more complex than a dead battery, we had to punt: rent a tow bar and hitch the car to the back of Mark's pickup. By now it was late afternoon, and a winter storm was settling in over the mountains. Headed for Seattle, we pointed the pickup, with the Saab tugging as a heavy caboose, up into Steven's Pass. And didn't get very far. The truck's engine couldn't pull both vehicles up the steep, slippery highway, and after an hour Mark pulled into a gas station to call for a tow truck. Here our luck grew even darker. "A day like this," the dispatcher sighed, "you're lucky if we get to you by nightfall." So we sat in the pickup waiting for the tow truck to arrive. As time passed and the silence deepened, the tension in the cab increased. Mark's shoulders grew taut. He glared out past the foggy windshield, gripping the steering wheel. "This is fucked," he said. I shrugged and said nothing. What could I say? I already felt bad about my car. Now we were going to be late into Seattle, and all our plans for the evening were ruined. The thought didn't leave me in a sweet mood either.

"Don't blame me," I shot back. "It wasn't my idea to try to pull the car behind your truck."

Then he exploded. Mark pounded the top of the dashboard with his fist and screamed into the windshield.

"Goddamn you! This is NOT how I want to spend my time! You should have got your fucking car fixed BEFORE we got here."

"I didn't know it was broken before we got here."

"You shoulda had someone check it out!"

His voice seemed to pierce my body. Hot tears blurred my eyes. I didn't know what to say. I'd had no idea the car wouldn't start. But for some reason I felt Mark had a point. He was hauling me and my car all the way to Woodburn. He had a right to be angry with me. I shouldn't have let this happen. *But why is he screaming at me?* No one had ever talked to me like that before. I was angry, hurt, terrified. I squeezed closer to the door and leaned against the armrest. I wanted to jump out and run away — but where would I go? In the snowstorm? All my stuff was in the back of Mark's truck, my car was dead. I was stuck.

The tow truck finally arrived to pull my car over the pass to Seattle.

Mark got over his rage, but he turned stony, driving in silence until we got out of the mountains. His mood lightened as the lights of the city drew closer, and by the time we got to Seattle he was back to normal. When we got to my family's house in Woodburn the next afternoon, Mark was polite and charming. He stayed on his best behavior all week, and if anyone didn't like him, nobody mentioned it to me.

When we got back to Utah in January, Mark worked putting a new floor into his parents' house while I trained for Ama Dablam. Together we skied for exercise or took long runs on the empty desert roads. We had time for plenty of adventures, too, going ice climbing in the mountains and taking a long ski trip through the Grand Canyon. When I was with Mark I loved waking up in the mornings. When he was happy his passion for life was infectious. As the winter passed we started making plans for the future. I'd leave for Ama Dablam in early March. Mark would follow in late April, and we'd meet in Nepal at the end of the expedition. From there, we'd travel together for a week or two, taking a leisurely tour of Nepal before returning to Utah in the early summertime.

And then we had to think about our future beyond Ama Dablam. By now we were both talking about getting married, and my mother suggested we make the wedding part of our trip. If we got married in Nepal, she said, we could make the next few weeks our honeymoon, and then when we got back to Utah Mark and I could start our real lives together without any distractions. That sounded fine to us, and in early February we announced our plans to get married in Nepal in May.

"Whatever you do, I'll support you," Randy said to me, whispering at one end of the bar at the Bit 'n' Spur. "But think about it, okay? Just think about what you're getting yourself into."

I thought I knew what I was getting into with Mark. But in the winter of 1982 I was less sure about Sue Giller, leader of the all-woman expedition to Ama Dablam. I had to go to her house for a get-acquainted supper that winter, and though she assumed we were meeting for the first time, it wasn't exactly the case. True enough, we had never been formally introduced. She probably didn't even remember meeting me — I prayed she wouldn't remember — but I had met her. That meeting, collision, really, almost four years past still left me trembling in my climbing boots.

Sue "Killer" Giller is a dynamo. When I happened upon her in 1978, she was already one of the best known woman climbers in America. A blunt, muscular thirty-one-year-old with short brown hair, thick hands, and a solid handshake, Sue was famous both for her gutsy climbing and her regimented style. Raised in a military family, she had a passion for order. Sue knew that climbers had to be allowed to grow and experiment, but she figured it was each climber's individual responsibility to be prepared to meet the challenge. But this didn't always happen, and it wasn't always the climber's fault. Women especially, Sue found, could be maneuvered by others into danger. Particularly women who were climbing with their boyfriends. The combination of impatient men and intimidated women often resulted in foolish accidents, and when Sue first laid eyes on me, she was certain the same fate was about to befall me.

I was with Evelyn and a friend named Todd Diffendurfer, bouldering in Eldorado Canyon, a climbing nook just south of Boulder, Colorado. Working out some moves on one of the larger rocks, I got stuck about fifteen feet off the ground, unable to move up or down. Sue happened upon us just as Todd was talking me down, shouting instructions to lead me from one hold to the next. When I finally made it back to terra firma, the short, muscular woman walked up to Todd with blood in her eyes.

"That was really stupid," Sue said.

Todd's face froze in a kind of dull, uncomprehending look. "Pardon me?"

Sue, perhaps five feet three, glared up at the solid six-footer and took another step in his direction. "It's obvious," she hissed, "that she's never done this before. And you let her go much higher than she should have."

"Well," Todd began. He made a hollow laughing noise. "I guess I didn't know she was going to have that big of a problem."

"Maybe you should think about it next time," Sue snapped. Then she spun around in the dirt and stalked off.

Todd looked over at me, still getting my bearings on the ground. "Holy fucking cow," he said. "What was that?"

That, we learned, was Sue "Killer" Giller: backwoods feminist.

I laughed when I heard Sue was leading the trip to Ama Dablam. But by the time I was at her front door to meet her, somehow it seemed less funny. What if she recognized me? *Oh, you're the feeb from Eldorado Canyon!* I rapped — tentatively — on the door and tried to smile. Inside, I heard her footsteps coming closer.

Of course she didn't recognize me. We shook hands, Sue ushered me in, and then it was all smiles and compliments. "We wanted to give a young climber a chance to go," she said, dishing out a plate of her own vegetarian lasagna. "And you were on the Cassin Ridge? A helluva tough route. Ama Dablam shouldn't be much of a leap for you."

The biggest leap I had to take, it turned out, was adjusting to Sue's super-organized leadership. It was so impressive. Schooled by her career army father, Sue had plotted out the expedition like a general sending the troops into Normandy. The group's finances and equipment procurement schedules were measured on charts. One set of graphs tracked each climber's work days and rest days on the mountain. Another set showed the progress of the team as a whole — the equipment being hauled and the food and supplies needed along the way.

As a latecomer to the expedition I didn't have many pre-climb responsibilities. I volunteered to track down a few dozen pairs of polypropylene long underwear, however, and to work on a little fund-raising for other last-minute expenses. Most of the executives I spoke to were happy to donate a few dollars to something as novel as an all-woman expedition. Only one fellow didn't seem to understand the spirit of the expedition. He was interested in donating, though, and we had quite a few conversations before he called to finalize the offer.

"Just one last thing," he said. There was a silence, and then he cleared his throat. "You gals will pose for pictures on the mountain with our logo, right?"

"That's part of the deal," I said. "And if everything goes right we'll even do it on the summit."

"Oh, good," he said. "That's excellent. Exactly what we were hoping." A pause, then another ahem. "But, uh, what do you usually wear when you take the pictures?"

"What do we *wear*?"

"I mean . . . you pose in bikinis, right?"

We decided we could probably get by without the benefit of that particular donation.

THE expedition left the United States in the beginning of March, flying from Chicago to Germany, then to Delhi and finally to Kathmandu. Just stepping out of the airplane and onto the tarmac, I could feel the Third World brushing against me. The sun was strong and the heavy air thick with a sweet, pungent smell: rotting vegetables, the remnants of the wandering sacred cows, the sour odor of poverty. On the steps of the airport we found lines of beggars — the crippled and the maimed, legless men pushing themselves on plywood boards equipped with rusty wheels. The suffering was hard to watch, but away from the airport the city was alive and exciting. The streets were narrow but jammed with people, the men in grimy T-shirts and shorts, the women in colorful cotton saris. The entire city seemed to be late for an appointment, everyone tearing around on bicycles, bells chiming and wheels clanking on the pavement.

We spent a day or two resting in Kathmandu, then rode a creaky bus up into the hills, out to where the road ended. From there we launched a hundred-mile trek on winding mountain paths. Springtime was beautiful in the hills of Nepal. The mornings were cold and crisp, the sky a deep royal blue, and the rolling hills velvety with green vegetation. The day would warm as the sun rose, and with our small army of porters in tow we'd troop up dusty paths and across thin footbridges. Up past the terraced farms that carved the hills into green stairsteps, across the silver streams knifing down the valleys, beneath the thirty-foot rhododendron bushes, all bursting with bright pink blossoms.

The ground turned rockier and the terrain less luxurious as we gained altitude. After sixteen days we reached our base camp, just beneath the base of the mountain on a desolate plateau at 16,500 feet. We set up our tents on rocky, subalpine land, next to a small, glacier-fed pond. The terrain was gaunt and brown in the early spring, but still nourishing enough to help support the local yak population. The huge, furry creatures were regular visitors to our camp, pausing to drink from the pond or nibble at the sparse grasses sprouting from between the rocks.

I already knew the reputations of most of the women on the expedition, but I got to know them as people while we set up our base camp. All of them were experienced climbers. Shari Kearney was in her late twenties by then, and had climbed her share of big mountains, as had her new housemate from Montana, a lanky six-footer named Lucy Smith. Ann MacQuarie, a twenty-five-year-old ranger at Yosemite, was just as strong and experienced, and had bigger things in her future: she and her husband held a permit for Everest in 1983. Jini Griffith, a thirty-year-old builder from Idaho, was a generous, though very independent, climber. Susan Havens, a thirtyish physical therapist from Alaska, was quiet and graceful. Our doctor came from Switzerland: Heidi Ludi was the only non-American in the group and at thirty-six was also the senior member of the expedition.

Seen from its base, the top of Ama Dablam appears almost vertical. The peak, a face of snow and ice-covered rock, is jagged, a razor of ice scraping high against the firmament. The mountain has a distinct presence. The routes are steep and very technical, and rarely climbed. We were only the third modern expedition to climb on Ama Dablam — the Nepalese government had kept the mountain closed until 1980.

Our route, as traced on Sue's various charts and graphs, took us up the mountain's southwest ridge. Most of the climb followed the ridge itself, a thin knifeblade of rock rising from the snowy face of the mountain. Snaking between climbable pitches on both sides of the ridge, you have to cross over the ridge several times, along the way taking in some extreme rock climbing, technical ice climbing, and then, on summit day, a long 45-degree snow slope.

The complex climb was made even more challenging by the pressure of altitude and the burden of the thin, thin air. In Kathmandu we encountered more than one local expert who would only shake a head at our plans. *So technical up there . . . are you sure you women can do it all yourselves?* Well, why not? Back when Sue started climbing, just the concept of an all-woman expedition in the Himalayas would have been unthinkable. In the early seventies the majority of male climbers were up-front about their sexism. Women, they said, just didn't have the muscle power to take on the big mountains. That attitude had dominated mountaineering since the sport's beginnings. Only a handful of Western women ever ventured onto mountain terrain in the nineteenth and early twentieth centuries. Marie Pardis climbed Mont Blanc, a 15,771-foot Alp, in 1808. The first significant climbing by an American woman was done by a New Englander named Annie Peck, who climbed the Matterhorn in 1895 (when she was forty-five) and then thirteen years later climbed Huascarán South, a 22,205-foot peak in the Peruvian Andes. Women didn't climb to 8,000 meters — a mark hit by men in 1950 — until three Japanese women climbed Manaslu in 1974. Another Japanese woman, Junko Tabei, summited Everest a year later. Even so, Western men remained stubborn about including women. When Arlene Blum, a climber from Berkeley, decided to lead an all-woman expedition to Annapurna in 1978, the American Alpine Club hemmed and hawed about making the recommendation the Nepalese government required for admission, even after Nepal's climbing ministry said they'd be delighted to host the group.

Blum's expedition had been successful, despite two deaths. An all-woman climb on Dhaulagiri the next year was less successful, and lost one climber. Sue had been a member of the Dhaulagiri team, and although she had enjoyed the climb she had not thought of leading her own all-woman team to the Himalayas until a climber named Annie Whitehouse called late in 1980, offering her a permit for Ama Dablam in 1982. Sue agreed to take over Annie's permit, then started pondering climbers. She knew mixed climbs usually worked better, since the varied physical abilities and character traits of men and women can make a more complete team. But an all-woman team had its benefits, too. Raising money, Sue knew, would be much easier for an all-woman expedition. And with so few American women ever having climbed in the Himalayas it was always good to give as many women as possible a chance to climb there. Each woman who did could be a role model for women climbers who had only dreamed of going.

The sexual politics of the climb held little interest for me, but once we got to the mountain it was fun to be in a group of women. When men are on the team, it's easy to defer to their strength. If the going gets really tough, a woman knows she can hang back and let the more muscular men take the lead. A group of women doesn't have this luxury, which is both sobering and freeing. We had to do everything for ourselves.

Which we did quite smoothly. With Sue's careful planning, our weeks of mountainside preparation and route-setting went off like clockwork. We carried the loads up the mountain on schedule and worked and rested according to our preset agendas. Throughout, Sue was a model expedition leader. Although in peak climbing shape and itching to work on the mountain herself, she spent most of her time in base camp, sitting in a lawn chair with her charts and a bowl of popcorn, peering up at our progress through a powerful pair of binoculars. Sue oversaw each step from a distance, allowing each of her climbers to take turns leading the way up the mountain.

When we finished setting the route, stocking our camps, and anchoring the rope up the steep flanks of the mountain, we split into two summit teams and prepared to make our move for the top.

Setting out from base camp on the first summit team with Shari and Lucy and Susan Havens, I pressed up the ridge toward the summit, feeling strong and confident. I was sure of myself on the ice. I had no problem on the steep rock pitches. I was even relaxed most of the time — in itself an improvement over the tense week and a half I'd spent inching up Mount McKinley. I was finally comfortable at altitude, understanding I could survive in the thin air. There had been only one moment of doubt when we were setting the route, back on the first night I spent above 19,000 feet. I woke up in the middle of the night wondering who'd pounded the ten-penny nails through my skull.

I was reeling with dizziness. There were the nails, of course, plus the vise tightening around my skull, pressing the hemispheres of my brain together, squashing my fragile hypothalamus. I knew exactly what was happening. Altitude sickness. Too panicked to be polite, I sat up and screamed. Shari, huddled deep in her sleeping bag next to me, lurched up in the darkness.

"What's the matter?"

"I've got to get down," I wailed. "Right now!"

She looked up from between the folds of her bag, mumbling through a fog of sleep, "Huh?"

"I've got a headache."

"A headache?"

Now she was awake. She repeated what I said, only without any tangible concern in her voice.

"You've got a *headache*?"

I listed the rest of my symptoms. Or rather, the lack of my other symptoms. No nausea. No gurgling. No hypoxia. Just the headache. A *terrible* headache, I added. Something had to be really wrong, right? Shari sighed. She reached into her pack for her first aid kit. She held out her fist and dropped two aspirins into my open palm.

"Swallow these," she said. "And then go back to sleep." She dove once more beneath the surface of her sleeping bag. I woke up the next morning feeling fine.

EVEN as Ama Dablam's summit drew closer, one thing loomed above us. The same peak that had captured my imagination from the moment I set foot in Nepal. No matter how much we sweated and strained to pull ourselves to the top of Ama Dablam, Mount Everest dwarfed us. She was an elusive giant on our side of the mountain, hidden behind the summit we were now trying to climb. Even when we got higher, the peak of Everest usually vanished into the cloak of puffy white clouds gathered around her shoulders. But I could see it in my mind.

I could always sense Everest's presence. We could all feel it, and we all knew who was on that mountain, too. A woman named Marty Hoey was part of that year's American expedition up the North Ridge. Marty was a fairly experienced mountaineer, but according to a few women on our team, she was far from the ranks of a technical climber. Even so, if she made it to the top, Marty would be the first American woman to summit Everest. To some American women climbers the distinction wasn't that important. But then again, we had to admit that getting an American woman to the top of Everest *was* important. Once a female counterpart to Jim Whittaker presented herself, she'd become a natural focal point for all American women climbers.

Marty was the first and only American woman even to climb on the mountain. But next year was going to be very different. Ann and her husband, Chas, had a permit for the 1983 climbing season and were planning to bring at least three or four women. Assuming Marty didn't make the summit, their primary goal would be to deliver the first American woman to the top of Everest. As our expedition went on, base camp conversations focused increasingly on Ann's Everest expedition. Most everyone wanted to go, and Ann knew it. In the end she invited Shari, Lucy, and Sue.

I wanted to go, too, but I didn't dare say anything about it. I couldn't imagine asking, for one thing. I was so young, still so inexperienced. I hadn't even finished climbing my first Himalayan peak, so it seemed terribly presumptuous to imagine I could take on Everest.

But I did make it to the summit of Ama Dablam. And I stood there alongside Lucy and Shari and Susan, gazing up through the clouds, which parted momentarily to afford us one long look at the crooked rock pyramid cresting 6,678 feet above us.

"That one's next!" Shari said. The others murmured, or laughed, but I was lost in my own thoughts. Standing up there, I realized Everest was no longer out of reach. I'd have to work hard, but it was possible to go. I had a long way to go — anyone coming near the mountain has to know that. But I also knew I was strong enough to try. Even after the clouds closed above us again the others continued dreaming aloud, pondering the routes. Everest was everywhere around us, but I kept my thoughts to myself.

W E left Ama Dablam's summit and got down to Camp 1 just after noon on the day after we summited. We were preparing to spend the night there, giving ourselves an afternoon off on our way down the mountain. But when we called in our position to base camp, Tanya had a special message for me.

"You've got a surprise waiting." Crackling over the thin radio channel, her voice had a singsong tone. "I won't tell you what it is, but he's got blue eyes!"

Mark.

I hoisted my pack right back onto my shoulders and headed for base camp. I saw him a few hours later, walking just above camp. He waved, and I broke into a stiff-legged run, the contents of my pack bouncing and clanking with every step. He ran up to meet me and we collided in each other's arms.

"You did it!" He held me against his chest and spun me around gently. "Congratulations!" Mark kissed me, then pulled back, still holding my face between his hands. "You look great." He hugged me again, wrapping his arms around my shoulders. "I love you! I love you!"

We walked back to base camp and spent the next two days together, talking and sleeping and sitting in the sun and listening to progress reports from the second summit team. When Sue called down at the end of the second day, she had great news: they'd all made it to the top!

Mark and I planned to get married in Nepal. It had seemed such a romantic idea back in Utah, although we had no precise idea where we'd have the ceremony or even how to go about arranging for one. But then Pasang Timba, the head Sherpa on the expedition, overheard me talking about the wedding, and offered to let us use his house in Namche Bazar, a small village in the Khumbu region of Nepal.

"It would be an honor," Pasang explained. "A celebration for the entire village."

The local Ringboche — the ninety-year-old high priest from the Buddhist monastery — agreed to perform the traditional Buddhist rites, and after three days of preparations we were ready. Early in the afternoon of May 4, Pasang's family, a flock of the townspeople, and all of the expedition members gathered in the small communal area of Pasang's house. It was an old structure, a two-story wood house with a steep ladder leading from the lower-level barn area to the main living quarters upstairs. The communal area was dark, with only a few small windows and two bare light bulbs hanging from the rafters. When I climbed up the ladder on a bright afternoon, it took my eyes a moment to adjust to the dark. The big fireplace in the corner, used for heating and cooking, had no chimney. The walls, I noticed, were blackened with smoke. The furniture was sparse. Wooden benches lined the walls and a few low stools were scattered on the floor. The only wall decoration was three or four rice-paper hangings, all printed with images of Buddha.

When the ceremony began, the men gathered on the right and the women sat on the left. Mark and I stood at the front, holding hands and dressed in traditional Tibetan Buddhist wedding costumes. I wore a gold silk cape, brocaded with dragons. We both wore ceremonial snow leopard skin hats and yak skin boots, complete with elf-style curled toes.

We knelt on the floor while the Ringboche stood above us, reciting prayers and invocations in Sherpa. Pasang, meanwhile, stood in front of us, whispering an English translation. I glanced over at Mark, kneeling on the floor, his eyes shut, his face turned down. The ear-flaps from his leopard hat dangled against his cheek. Tears welled in my eyes, seeing him there. It was surreal, and yet so perfect. I'd never heard of anyone being guided into marriage by Sherpas. But then, I'd never heard of anyone who had the thrilling bond Mark and I had. We were soulmates. Just being together gave us power, and now that we were joined together forever I knew we could have everything we wanted. We could invent our own lives — working for ourselves, doing good work, and always being free enough to take off and have adventures.

As the ceremony came to a close, Mark and I sipped from cups of rakshi, a grain alcohol. Then the Ringboche, with a fatherly smile splitting his withered face, stepped forward.

"He will bless your fertility," Pasang whispered.

The Ringboche dipped his fingers into a cup and rubbed something into my hair, and then into Mark's. Something foul. I reached up and dabbed a little on my own fingers and waved them toward my nose. Catching the vapors full force, I imagined I might topple over.

"What is it?"

Pasang smiled.

"Yak butter."

Then the reception began. Vats of chang, the local beer, and bottles of rakshi were opened and quickly drained. Tables were hauled out, then loaded down with great bowls of momos (dumplings with meat inside), potatoes, yak meat, rice, and dal, a spicy lentil stew. The expedition members supplied a wedding cake — produced from a few leftover packages of dehydrated cheesecake mix — and someone cranked up a boombox for dancing. And as darkness fell on the hills of Namche Bazar, the B-52s wailed "Rock Lobster," many Americans fell victim to the potent wiles of Nepalese rakshi, and Mark and I, holding hands, stumbled up the hill to our tent and the beginning of married life.

BACK in Utah that summer Mark and I moved into a house in Rockville, a small town about three miles down canyon from Springdale. All our friends were just a few minutes down the highway, and the cliffs of Zion only a couple of miles beyond there. I thrived on Mark's energy — his charisma, his free-wheeling creativity. And I knew he needed me. I could feel it in the way he touched me, gently. The way he'd reach for my hand while we walked down the street, the way he'd catch my eye across a room. I loved Mark, and I knew

I could make things better for him. There was so much that could be better for him.

Mark did his best to avoid it, but there had always been darkness in his family. It was a weakness, and Mark hated it. If we visited his parents and found his mother had been drinking, Mark would turn on his heel and head straight for the door. "Stacy, we've got to leave right now." As an adult Mark learned to depend on himself. He knew how strong he was, and physical power gave him independence and a sense of mastery. He could do anything with his hands. Everything except control the darkness inside himself. I'm sure he tried, on some conscious level. But it was deeper than that, a fissure buried somewhere beneath the foundation of his spirit.

Barry Sochat knew Mark's moods better than anyone. They'd grown up together, close friends since before high school. And Barry looked up to Mark, to his charisma and artistic skill and his endless ability to dream things up and get them done. Mark and Barry were very different. Barry worked as a nurse, and he projected that Jesus-hippie look, with his wispy beard and shoulder-length hair and gentle manner.

Mark could be a generous friend, and when Barry wanted to build a house in Rockville, Mark insisted on volunteering all of our services. He even spent his birthday pouring cement for Barry's foundation. We worked on Barry's house through the summer of 1982. Barry's land was a short walk from our house, and we went over just after sunrise. Barry would fix breakfast for us at his tent, and we'd all sit for a while, watching the morning light paint the canyon walls. When we got to work, Mark served as principal builder and chief instructor, giving us both a step-by-step tutorial in house construction. Mark was a brilliant craftsman, but as a teacher he got frustrated easily: once he explained something, he didn't like to repeat himself. At first Barry absorbed most of Mark's abuse. I'd be hammering away on something, and hear Mark's voice echoing over the site.

"Come on, man, don't be so fuckin' stupid!"

Looking over, I'd see him grab the hammer or the saw or the level Barry was holding and shove him out of the way. The sight made me cringe, and later, when I'd find Barry alone, I'd tell him to stand up for himself.

"Don't let Mark talk to you like that. It's not fair."

He'd shrug.

"That's just Mark."

"Well, it shouldn't be."

But I knew what Barry meant. Mark could be so warm and generous, but everything he gave came with one unspoken caveat: you had to play by his rules and put up with his moods.

When Mark taught me how to run the table saw, he made a special point of showing me how to stand — always to the side of the machine, never behind the blade. You had to do it that way, he explained, because if the blade catches on the wood, it'll kick the board right back into your gut. But one day I got careless and when I fed a short two-by-four into the saw I stood directly behind the butt of the board. The blade caught, and when the two-by-four kicked out it hit me square on the hip, sending me flying backward into the dirt. My tool belt took most of the impact, but when Mark saw me lying on the ground, he blew up.

"Jesus fucking Christ!"

He flew across the field and turned off the saw. "If you can't learn one simple thing about the table saw, I don't want you using it again!"

From across the house the sharp impact of Barry's hammer echoed through the air like rifleshots. Sitting on the ground, the dirt hot with the afternoon sun, I tried to explain — I'd done it right before, I'd just screwed it up this once — but Mark didn't care. He stalked off without looking over his shoulder. "You heard me," he said. "Now don't go near it."

I sat alone for a moment, watching Mark's back, feeling ashamed, then angry, then furious. I didn't have to take this. I wasn't going to, either. Standing up, I tore off my tool belt and threw it into the dirt. I started for the road, walking at first, then running in the heat, the dry summer air burning my face. I ran as fast as I could for a hundred yards, until the tears and sweat stung my eyes. Pausing to wipe them with my shirt sleeve, I started walking again, sucking in the hot wind, sweat trickling down my sides. Then I heard the slap of Mark's boots on the road behind me. I turned around, not certain what to expect. But as he drew closer I saw his eyes were clear and open. A crooked grin lit up his face.

"I'm sorry," Mark called. "Come back, Stace, I didn't mean it."
His strong legs made up the distance and soon he had me in his arms,
damp with sweat, holding me close to his chest. "Come on," he said.
"I just didn't want you to get hurt." He cradled me, rocking me back
and forth.

I held on to his back, my face pressed against the bits of sawdust
clinging to his chest. I leaned against Mark and rubbed my wet
cheeks against his shirt. I knew I needed him. I loved Mark, and I
needed to feel his strength around me. I'd have to make some sacri-
fices, but you never get anything you want without giving up something else. I wanted us, that feeling of security and power I had when
we were together. I pulled away and looked up at him.

"I'll come back . . . but only if you'll let me use the table saw."

He sighed. "All right, all right."

Mark took me by the hand and we walked together back to the
house.

SOMETIMES we seemed golden. Late in the fall we climbed
West Temple, one of the rock peaks in Zion. The air was dry and
cold and very clear, and when we got to the top Mark and I sat on
some Thinsulate pads and ate a tin of oysters and some cheese and a
loaf of fresh bread. When we were done eating, we looked over the
canyon, the rolling gray hills and jagged brown cliffs stretching out
into the distance, and talked about the house we wanted to build.
Our land was close to the park, on a ridge about 300 feet above the
floor of the canyon. We'd make our own house, then raise our family
inside the walls we'd built.

One day that winter we drove up to look at the property. Mark
had already started sketching his ideas, and as we walked around the
site his hands flew through the air, describing the angles of the living
room windows, how we could set the entire house to frame the view
so perfectly. His visions came in sudden bursts, clear and logical before he even committed them to paper. It was a cold afternoon, the
sun pale and low on the horizon. We got into Mark's pickup and
started down the gravel road for the highway. He was excited, and
his words flowed out, leaving me silent against the barrage. Finally I
found a gap in his monologue and inserted myself in.

"I've got nothing to say about this?"

"What?"

"You chose the land. You paid for it, and now you're drawing the plans, and I don't have anything to say about anything. It's not *our* project. It's *your* project."

It happened in a blur. I saw the highway beneath us, empty blacktop stretching out in either direction. In the foreground I saw the dirt on the dashboard, the grains of dust on the windshield. I didn't see his fist. It came on a sidearm blow, arcing like a pendulum through the air. I didn't see it, but the impact was solid and hard, a deep thump against flesh and bone. My lungs emptied with surprise, and then his voice came at me, deep and hysterical.

"Don't say it's not your fucking house!"

My left shoulder burned. My right hand flew to the spot, prodding gingerly, feeling the heat of impact. I was terrified — Mark was out of control. Would he hit me again? Try to kill me? I had no idea, and no way to protect myself.

"Stop the car!"

"Shut up!"

We were at the highway now. Mark jammed his foot down on the gas and spun the wheel to the left. The truck rocketed out onto the pavement, tires spinning in the loose gravel. When the wheels gripped solid road we dug in and flew away from town, toward the Zion gates and the empty park beyond.

"Let me out!"

"Stop crying!"

"You can't hit me, you bastard!"

We roared into the park. I scrunched up against the door, terrified of Mark, wanting to jump. But he was going too fast. Outside the window the rocks and brush flew by in a blur. Mark jerked his head back and forth, glancing at me, then the road. He knew he couldn't drive forever, he had to do something.

"I'll stop, but don't jump out!"

He started to slow down, edging to the side of the empty road. I didn't say anything, too scared to know what to do. He looked over again and shouted above the sound of the engine, the rattle of the gravel.

"Promise me you won't jump!"

"Okay, okay . . . just stop the fucking car."

Mark steered the truck onto the gravel shoulder. It jerked to a halt, throwing us both forward. The instant we fell back against the seat I wrenched the door handle. In a heartbeat I was out on the road, running fast. Behind me I heard Mark curse. Then his door opened and slammed shut. Mark's footsteps hard behind me, I swerved off the highway, flying down a hill, frantic, tripping on the loose rock, dodging the knee-high cactus and the mounds of sagebrush. I had to get away. I couldn't let him catch me. But there was nowhere to hide, and then Mark was right behind me. He slammed against my back, his hands grasping for my waist. His weight sent me flying, and we rolled together down the hill, banging against rock and black brush. When we stopped, Mark wrestled me onto my back. He was sitting on my chest and pinning my arms over my head. The backs of my hands scraped against the cold desert rock.

"Don't hurt me!"

I tried to squirm away from Mark's grasp, but he leaned more weight against my wrists, jamming them against the sharp pebbles on the ground.

"Shut UP!"

I struggled against him for a moment, but I knew it was useless. Mark's hands pinned my arms, the weight of his body held me helpless against the ground. I went limp, dissolving beneath him into the dusty ground. When he felt me give up, Mark's hysteria subsided. His fingers loosened around my wrists. He let out a deep, trembling breath, then leaned down toward my face. I turned away, closing my eyes, and felt his lips brush against my cheek. Then his voice, soft and quavering.

"I'm sorry."

When I looked up, Mark's face was soft. His hair flowed across his brow, still wild from the running.

"I love you. I'm sorry," Mark murmured gently, leaning up on his haunches, releasing my wrists. He climbed to his feet and dusted himself off; then he took my elbow and helped me stand. When I was on my feet, he cradled me in his arms, swaying gently back and forth.

"I'll never do it again . . . I swear I'll never do it again."

Holding my hand, he led me away. I felt hollow, as if my mind had switched off. I didn't think, I couldn't think. I was in shock, my eyes open and seeing nothing. We walked back to the pickup truck and went home. We fixed dinner, Mark whistling around the kitchen as if nothing had happened. Later I sat on the couch and read *Time* magazine until bedtime. I went from page to page, reading every article, focusing on every photograph. The real world was out there, I could see it here in the news. I didn't have to let Mark warp me, I could leave. I had to leave. The next morning, after Mark went to work, I made a plane reservation, packed a duffel bag, and drove my car over to where Mark was working. I found him standing by his truck, bent over some building plans. He looked up and smiled when he saw me coming.

"I'm going to Oregon," I announced. His smile faded and he shrugged.

"Fine. Do what you've got to do."

I was still angry in Oregon, but revived. I stormed around for the first few days cloaked in righteous indignation. No one was going to hit me, not even Mark. Especially Mark. At first I wouldn't take his calls, then I spoke to him coolly, businesslike. I'm not coming home, I said. Not the way it is. Get some help, then I'll think about coming back. My fire lasted a week, then cooled. My entire life was in Utah now — my friends, my career. My husband. And where would I be without him? I had to go back to him.

After a week Mark agreed to call a therapist, and then I agreed to come home. "It's okay," I told my mother. "Things are going to change now. We're both committed to this, and everything's going to be much better."

"Stacy, are you sure?" I could tell she wasn't convinced, but I nodded my head and felt my eyes sparkling. The credulous smile of the true believer.

Mark did make an appointment, and when I came back we started seeing the therapist together. The doctor was a Mormon, and his office was as prim and starched as a stockbroker's. He perched behind an epic desk, wearing a white shirt and a tightly knotted blue tie.

"A husband tends to react to the way his wife behaves," the doctor explained. "So, Stacy, you need to ask yourself: what am I doing to make Mark so angry?"

The sessions ended after a month. We've got everything under control, Mark assured the therapist.

NOTHING was under control. By now the pattern was established. The pressure between us would build for weeks or even months. Then Mark would explode in a hail of verbal and sometimes physical abuse, and then he'd feel guilty. He'd be full of love then, the poor, anguished boy trying to make things right.

I lived with the pressure. There were always projects keeping us busy during the week, then our own house going up slowly on the weekends. Every day of the week, it seemed, we started early and stayed late.

Eventually I couldn't even find the time to climb anymore. The days flew by in a blur, and then I'd realize it had been months since I'd even driven into Zion. Randy would call sometimes, asking me to go with him on one climb or another, but Mark would shake his head and I'd say no. Between our projects and our own house we never took a day off.

One day I insisted. Mimi Stone, a friend of Adele's, was in town and looking for someone to climb with for a day. I hadn't been on a rope for six months, so I told Adele I'd go. The next morning, as I dug through our closets looking for my climbing shoes and the pieces of my rack, Mark paced our bedroom, coffee cup in hand, and glowered.

"Don't you think you're being kind of selfish?"

"No." I found one shoe, tucked deep in a box. I dug for the other, and didn't look at him. "I haven't climbed since summer, and there's nothing at work today that can't wait until tomorrow."

"Nice fucking attitude." Mark slammed down his coffee cup on a bedside table and stomped out to his car.

It was a beautiful day and I loved being back on the cliffs. The sun and the dry desert wind stroked my back, and I couldn't believe how light I felt on my feet. After six months away I was a little weaker, but I could still move on the rock. I felt so free up there, like a bird released from a cage. Mimi was planning a month-long trip to Peru that spring, and when she invited me along, I said yes, eagerly, then thought better: "I should ask Mark first." When I mentioned it to Mark at dinner, the blood left his face.

"If you do that," he said, "we're finished."

OUR relationship consumed me. When we were together, we were together for virtually every waking moment. From the moment I opened my eyes in the morning, Mark would be there. We'd go running in the dawn, then shower together, grab a quick breakfast, then go to work. We worked shoulder to shoulder all day, then came home and made dinner together. We had the same friends, went to all of the same parties. Mark and I were lovers and partners and friends. Sometimes we seemed like Siamese twins — everything about our lives seemed to go in tandem.

There was always that promise, those golden moments when we were in control and everything seemed to be going our way. We could do anything then. But then there would be an argument. I'd see the blood drain from his face, and then I'd feel the weight of his hand hard against my cheek. An explosion in my head, the roaring of molecules as my body re-formed itself on the floor.

And sometimes I could play him, too. In an argument I would spin on my heel and walk away. No words, no expression. Just silence, and it drove Mark wild.

"Don't ignore me."

Nothing.

"You can't fuckin' ignore me!" He'd be on my heels now, his hot breath on my neck, a hand darting out, pushing my shoulder.

"Don't push me." For a moment I had perspective. I could see us from above, and what was the point? It was so draining, just trying to keep this relationship on an even keel. What, really, was holding me to it? How long, I'd ask myself, can this possibly last? For that moment I'd wonder, and begin to see another life. Then Mark would be back again, charming and gentle, the Mark I loved.

"Please, Stace?" His eyes glinting hopefully, that boyish pucker on his forehead. "Can't we be friends again, please?"

And then I was gone again. I did believe what he said about me. *You're ruining my life!* There was no point looking further, because no one else would ever love me. Why would they? I could barely function as a builder, I was forever making mistakes at home. I was, as Mark had put it so many times, *fucking worthless.* So I was with Mark. There was nowhere else for me to be.

5

DEATH AND SURVIVAL

CLIMBING Mount Everest was my idea. I'd brought the notion down from Ama Dablam, but Mark was eager to be included. While we were working so hard, we'd go for weeks or even months without talking about the mountain. But that image was always in my mind. Sometimes, lying in bed before I fell asleep at night or while I had a chance to daydream at work, I'd see myself on the mountain, climbing higher. The wind would be rushing around me, and I'd have to lower my head, but I'd keep going, plodding higher on the hard snow. When I got to the top — I always got to the top — Mark was never in sight. It was the independent me again, Stacy Allison.

EVEN if Mark didn't encourage me to keep climbing, he was an integral part of my Everest plans. He wanted to climb the mountain, so, except in my dreams, we planned to do it together. And even though we had signed up for our own permit we started looking for someone who already had one. This was a challenge. The Tibetan side of the mountain was almost impossible to climb, and during the mid-eighties the Nepalese government put severe limits on the number of expeditions operating on their side of the mountain. One way to shortcut the government route was to locate a small expedition with a large permit. If a group had fewer climbers than the permit allowed, the leader could go into business, either charging individual climbers to join the expedition or selling portions of the permit to one or more independent groups who then would hitchhike to the mountain on the first group's paper.

We didn't have much luck until Randy Aton mentioned my old

friend Scott Fischer. "He just got a permit for the North Face," Randy said. That was the steep, rocky Tibet side of the mountain. Scott had been offered the permit a year earlier and turned it down. No one had ever managed to climb the North Face, so what was the point of raising all that money and hustling for all that gear if you were pretty sure the task ahead was impossible? But then in 1984 an Australian group managed to get three climbers up the North Face and then onto the top of the mountain. The climb hadn't been easy — one of the Aussies lost most of his fingers to frostbite, while another climber nearly lost his toes. Still, the Australians had broken the North Face barrier. Fortified by that success, Scott called the Chinese government and told them he'd take their permit after all. Now he was set to hit the mountain in the fall of 1987 and trying to put together a strong team to go with him.

Scott and I had lost touch over the last few years, but I always remembered what a great climber he was, and what a fine mentor he'd been during my first days on the cliffs in Zion. And Mark was a friend of his, too, back when they were both new to Springdale. Randy gave me Scott's number in Seattle, and one evening I picked up our telephone and dialed. "Well, sure," Scott said, after I'd asked him. "I'd love to consider you guys." A few weeks later Scott called back with good news: we were invited. Scott set up a meeting in Springdale that fall to distribute the fund-raising and equipment-gathering duties. Mark and I volunteered to serve as equipment directors. We also agreed to accompany Scott and a few other expedition members on a practice climb that next spring, a month-long trip to climb Pik Kommunizma and perhaps a few other mountains in the Pamir Range in the Soviet Union.

Now that Mark and I were actually going to Everest we juggled responsibilities. Rather than working full time, I'd focus on gathering equipment for the Everest expedition while Mark supported us. He had a lucrative project to work on — an intricate restaurant remodeling job up in Salt Lake City. He'd have to live in an apartment provided by the restaurant's owner while he was out of town, but that was a sacrifice Mark figured we could make. We'd be able to spend a few weekends together, whenever I felt like driving up to see him.

He loaded his tools into his pickup truck a few days after Christmas. "Next year at this time we'll have finished our own home," he said, kissing me and pressing me against his chest. "And then we'll go to the top of the world together."

He kissed me again, and I believed every word he said. I knew we'd had hard times, we'd even skirted destruction. But I could feel him now, he was holding me against him and I could feel his arms, I could hear his heart drumming inside his ribs. We were bound together, and it would always be that way.

ALONE, I filled the empty hours with work. Mark told me not to start any major projects when he was gone, but I got lonely by myself, and when the silence in our half-finished house became too dense, I'd break it up with my tools. I drilled holes for expansion bolts in the concrete walls, then bolted two-by-two spacers to hold the Sheetrock. I hammered in the shake roof, wearing a wool hat and gloves while I worked in the crisp winter air. Some days I'd get so excited about what I'd done I'd pick up the telephone to tell Mark. You're not going to believe this place when you get back, I'd say.

Or I'd want to say it, but frequently Mark wouldn't be there to listen. I'd hear the ringing telephone, I'd count to five, ten, fifteen, twenty, then hang up. He was working long hours, Mark would explain when I did manage to reach him. Curtis, the restaurant owner, kept him hopping. Sometimes he didn't get home until very late.

"I called you until three A.M. last night," I said one afternoon. I didn't mention that I had spent the night with the lights on, hoping desperately to hear his voice. "You weren't working that late, were you?"

"Of course not," Mark said. "I was sleeping in my truck."

"Your truck?"

"Yeah," Mark said. Then he sighed deeply. Aggravated with me, or just tired? I chose the latter. "Curtis left another load of receipts on the couch. He's doing his taxes or something, and he gets pissed when I move things around. You know, I don't think he really wants me in that apartment after all."

That excuse seemed plausible enough. So relief flooded in and I felt myself relax for the first time in days . . . but wait a second. This was January. It was below zero at night.

"Didn't you freeze?"

"I wore a hat," he said quickly. "If we're going to climb Everest we've gotta get used to sleeping in the cold, right? And how's that going? Everest, I mean. Have you worked out who's gonna supply the stoves yet?"

Just after Valentine's Day I drove up to Salt Lake for a weekend visit. While I was there, I spent some time helping Mark with the paperwork from the project, sorting through the pile of bills and invoices he hadn't found time to organize. We were driving through Salt Lake in Mark's pickup when I opened his leather briefcase to look for an address. Sifting through the drifts of paper and carbons, I noticed a box of expensive licorice. Mark loves licorice, and most of the candy was gone, but I reached in for a piece. Taking it out, I saw the card attached to the box. My heart sank. *Thanks for being a good friend,* it said, in rolling, feminine handwriting. *Diana.*

Diana?

I snatched the card out of the briefcase and held it out to him.

"Who's Diana?"

Mark looked over and shrugged.

"It's nothing," he said. He cleared his throat and shrugged again. "Diana's just a waitress at Ruth's. She's breaking up with her boyfriend, so she talks to me."

Oh. Okay. Blood still boiling, I put the card back in Mark's briefcase. If he's cheating on me, I thought, I'm gonna . . . what? The emotion receded, a wave draining off the beach, and I felt naked again. If he's cheating on me, I realized darkly, then there's not a lot I can do about it. Two days later I was back in Springdale, hanging on to the endlessly ringing telephone. Now Mark was just as elusive as before, only when we did manage to get in touch, something seemed different. At first it was hardly noticeable, the hollow distortion of the long-distance wires. But even as we spoke from the same telephones, we seemed further apart.

"I've been talking to Curt Hill," Mark said once, mentioning another carpenter in Springdale. "When I'm through up here, I think we're going to do a project together."

"Oh, great," I said. "Curt's a nice guy. It'll be fun working with him." Mark was quiet for a moment. Actually, he said, he wasn't thinking about the three of us.

"Maybe it's time for the two of us to work apart for a while."

"Work apart?" Without Mark I couldn't work at all. I wasn't even close to having my own contractor's license. If I didn't work with him I'd have to find someone else willing to hire me. Not an easy prospect when so many men were out of work.

"I don't want you working as a builder anymore," Mark said. "You know we fight all the time, and it always starts at work. It'll be better for us if we have some space."

Better for you, I thought. Now what was I supposed to do? I hung up and lay back on the bed. Mark was pushing me away, and it wasn't exactly a spontaneous move. Mark had never really wanted me to become a builder. At least not an independent one. The summer before, I had been approached by Jimmy Jones, an artist who was looking for someone to frame a wood post-and-beam house for him. Mark was too busy to take on the project, but Jimmy asked me to take the job. He'd pay me by the hour, he said, so I wouldn't have to bid on the project. There was no way we could lose money on the deal, but Mark still tried to dissuade me. "I just don't think you've got enough experience to do it alone." But this only made me more determined to do it, and so I called Jimmy and accepted the job.

"Excellent!" he crowed. "When can you start?"

Immediately, but here was my more pressing concern: when would I finish? Mark was partly right. It *was* a complex project, and deep down I wasn't sure I could pull it off. Framing a house in the standard style is one thing, but working with mortises and tenons — no nails, no visible screws — was all that and much, much more. Here I had to make precise measurements of every post and beam. When you work with a woodcarver, each notch in the posts and each crosshatch on the beams has to meet in exact accordance. An eighth of an inch too much or too little can set the project back by weeks.

While I worked on Jimmy's house on top of his mesa, Mark worked on a house at the bottom of the mesa. During the days, we could actually see each other and hear each other banging around. And although I was supposedly working by myself, the job gave me plenty of opportunities to seek Mark's counsel. Whenever I got lost or confused I'd grab my plans and tear down the road for advice. Most of the time he'd make the imposition all too obvious. "If you don't know what you're doing," he'd complain, "you shouldn't be doing it." But I still got his attention.

And the posts and beams went up, and eventually the frame of the house stood on its own. When I was finished, Mark came to inspect my handiwork. Finally, he seemed proud of me. He ran his hands along the beams, checking the strength of the joints. "You really did it," he said, letting a smile crease his face. "Nice job, too."

But when I took another job later that summer, his smile faded. If he was proud of what I'd done on the first house, Mark didn't want me to go on from there. He didn't want to be bothered by my questions, didn't want to have to deal with my schedule or my pressures, didn't want to feel responsible for what I did. Finally, Mark told me to get out of the business entirely. You should focus on getting equipment for the Everest expedition, Mark said. Unable to work for myself, unable to find work in other construction companies, I hung up my tool belt.

MARK had been home for a week when I found the second card. It was in his briefcase again, along with the receipts and contracts. Did he really think I wouldn't see it? I knew what it was before I read it. Something in the weight of the envelope, or the flowing handwriting that spelled out his name. I stalked into the living room, anger rising in my throat. Mark didn't look up. He was sitting on the couch, slouching back into the cushions, reading a magazine. He probably looked up when he got this card. *I'll miss you*, it said. *I love you, Diana*. I held it up and stood in front of him. I wanted to roar. He wasn't going to do this to me. Not without a fight, anyway.

"Mark, what the fuck is this?"

When he looked up and saw the envelope, his expression froze. For a moment he was ice. Finally he snapped back into life, looked up and smiled, a little too warmly.

"It's nothing," he said. "A note from a friend."

He flipped the pages of his magazine and kept reading, the pages not quite blocking that small smile.

"Nothing?" My face had gone red. "No one says 'I love you' for no reason!"

He sighed. The magazine drooped and he sank deeper into the couch. My eyes burned into him, and for a moment I thought I was losing my mind. I was shocked, but somehow not surprised. Of course Mark had betrayed me. How could I imagine he wouldn't? But he wasn't going to get away scot-free. I was going to make him admit it.

"Are you having an affair?"

Silence. The clock ticked in the kitchen. Outside, the wind pushed against the windows. Mark stopped smiling. He avoided my smoldering gaze. "Yes. But it's over."

"It's over?"

Now Mark was losing control. He leaned forward and put his head in his hands. His shoulders trembled. When he looked up, two thick tears tumbled down his cheeks.

"She doesn't mean anything," he cried. "I swear."

"Fuck that," I shouted. But my words were braver than I was. Seeing him sniffling on the couch, I felt weak. Then I was sitting next to him, on the couch, into his arms, then we were holding each other. And then the anger washed away and what remained was so familiar, so reassuring, so easy. How could I blame him for wandering when I knew our relationship was such a mess? Deep down, I knew I had to blame myself, and so then everything was normal, and surrendering was the natural thing to do. And so I gave in.

WE continued our lives. Waking up in the morning, going for a run, then driving over to the Driftwood Inn to meet our friends for coffee. The texture seemed normal enough, but just beneath the surface loomed something harder and uglier. I froze to his touch. I saw shadows in his eyes, coldness in his expression. The furrows in his brow that once seemed so boyish now revealed calculation. Mark was always calculating something. How much wood for this project? How much longer can I stay with Stacy? His brow furrowed, and I never knew what the numbers were, or how the balance was shifting. I felt as if I were spinning endlessly, tumbling through empty air. I was flailing, but unable to curl a finger around anything solid.

When I felt blind I called my mother. She tried, but eventually could no longer counsel a sightless person who also refused to listen. "Don't you know what this is doing to me?" she would plead over the phone. "He hits you, and you still won't do anything about it. If you won't do anything to help yourself, how can I help you?"

I did help myself once. One day when Mark was gone I found a check for $2,000 in a filing cabinet. It was dated a few months earlier, from one of our projects, and somehow it had fallen into a folder of receipts. The check was meant to cover a business expense, but it was made out to me. I held it in my hand for a moment, my eyes locked on the numbers. It was business money, bound for our joint account. But Mark controlled that account. In fact, he'd kicked me out of the business. If I put it in there, I knew, I'd never see it again. I folded the check in half and stuck it in my wallet. It was dishonest, but honesty hardly seemed the governing factor in our relationship. If Mark wasn't expecting this check, he certainly wasn't going to get it. I drove downtown, walked into the bank, and opened a savings account in my own name.

We played at normality, but I knew I couldn't ignore what happened. Not after I'd grown up swearing it wouldn't happen to me. I had to ask the questions my mother never could: What's she like? What was so wonderful about her? Mark would entertain no questions. It's over, was his standard, gruff reply. Forget it. But I kept pushing. We were in the truck, driving home from the Bit 'n' Spur. *You were the one who was screwing her,* I said. *You tell me what was so great about her.* He shouted at me, I shouted back. Then he was beyond words and it happened again: the explosion in my head, the burning pain, then the deep quiet. The roar of blood and surprise and shock.

When I woke up the next morning, my left eye was swollen shut. Mark grimaced as I came out of the bathroom. "Christ, you've got a shiner," he said. "You better not go out today."

I shook my head. "I've got work to do. There's no way I can just hang around."

"You can't tell anyone how it happened."

"What am I supposed to say?"

Mark thought for a moment. "Tell 'em you were working with the big Milwaukee drill," he said. "You had the big bit in there, and it caught on the wood and jumped up at you."

I shrugged, and walked toward the shower. Was I actually going to lie for Mark? Of course. Our problems weren't anyone's business anyway. We set out on our daily routine — coffee at the Driftwood, errands in town. *A little workplace mishap,* Mark said. I played along. This was our business. We would take care of it ourselves. And no one seemed to suspect anything different until I bumped into Adele in the post office.

When she saw me, Adele looked into my face, frowning darkly.

"What happened to your eye?"

I started telling her about the drill, but Adele shook her head.

"Bullshit," she said. She leaned toward me and whispered, "Mark hit you, didn't he?"

I stared at her, not sure what to say. Adele knew! I felt so ashamed. Ashamed and relieved. Now I wasn't alone. I nodded, then looked away. "Yes." She made a face, and reached out for my shoulder. I felt her arms around me, warm against my back. After a moment she led me outside, out to the sidewalk and the gold light of morning. We were by ourselves out there, and I told her everything — the insults, the beatings, the affair. It was like a breakdown, an eruption of rage, welling up and finally bursting out. Adele shook her head and paced back and forth.

"That bastard," she said. Then she looked into my face again. "What are you going to do about it now?"

"I don't know."

A few weeks later Mark decided not to go on the Pik Kommunizma climb. "We're in the middle of a project," he reasoned. "I need to stay here and keep it going." It only made sense, he added, if we were going to spend three months in Nepal next year.

So I was going to fly out of Las Vegas alone, and Mark drove me down there the day before I left the country. We spent the night in the desert, woke up early in the morning, and went for a walk. It was warm and very still just after dawn, the new sun peering over the edge of the horizon. Mark and I walked hand in hand, between the rolls of spiky sagebrush, the cactus, the small tufts of dry grass. And everywhere the deep, pungent smell of yerba santa. Mark reached down and picked off a small branch.

"I'll be with you," he said. "Every step." He squeezed my hand and I smiled. He held up the stem of yerba santa and pressed it into my hand. "Keep it with you," he said. "And whenever you smell it, you'll know I'm right there."

AFTER gathering in Seattle, the expedition team flew into Moscow, spent a few days sight-seeing, then took an all-night flight to Osh, a small mountain city in the south of the Soviet Union. From there we joined another group of mountaineers, these from Czechoslovakia, and together we piled into a cramped propeller plane that buzzed us to a gravel airstrip high in the Pamir Mountains. A small detail of uniformed Soviets helped load our gear into two trucks, and then put the crowd of us in three run-down school buses that rumbled up the dusty high plain to Achik Tash, the government-run base camp for visiting mountaineers.

We spent four days adjusting to the altitude, then loaded our gear into two huge army helicopters and flew up to the Pik Kommunizma Advance Base Camp, a stretch of rocky moraine at about 14,000 feet, just beneath the mountain's first glacier. This was another military-style camp, a bleak assortment of canvas tents and one wooden privy. We all ate in a central mess hall, a large tent with a dirt floor and long, communal wooden tables. For the next few days we organized our gear and adjusted to the altitude. The Pamirs are on a high plateau, a range of huge mountains running for 150 miles across west-central Asia, connecting the Hindu Kush and the Tien Shan mountains. The Pamirs are a beautiful range, remote and wild, in the upper reaches of the earth. But weather in the Pamirs is notoriously rotten, and the perpetually heavy snow blanket makes for unremitting avalanche danger. Even the drier climbing season does little to stabilize the terrain. All the mountains wear thick coats of glaciers, and all are lined with yawning crevasses. And beneath the glaciers the land itself is riddled with faults, rendering the entire plateau subject to sudden, violent earthquakes.

Dangers aside, Pik Kommunizma is still a breathtaking mountain. Jagged-peaked with razor cliffs on all sides, the tallest of the Pamirs towers over its corner of Eurasia, cresting just under 24,600 feet. Remembering how huge McKinley seemed from below, I found it sobering to realize that Pik Kommunizma dwarfs North America's largest peak by more than 4,000 feet.

Our eleven-member team was made up of two groups. Scott had originally envisioned the Pik Kommunizma trip as a training run for the Seattle-based 1987 Everest crew, but when some team members had to back out, he called Mark Udall, a friend from Colorado who was planning a major 1987 expedition to Cho Oyu, a Himalayan peak close to Everest. Mark, the tall, amiable thirty-five-year-old son of Congressman Morris Udall, decided that was a fine idea, so he signed up along with his wife, a Sierra Club lawyer named Maggie

Fox, and his equally tall younger brother, Brad. The Udalls filled out their Colorado-based group with two climbers they knew through some other friends. Steve Monfredo was a true backwoods bohemian — a stunning athlete and concert-caliber pianist in his early thirties who lived in a mountain shack without running water. Fredo, as his friends called him, brought along a buddy named Mike Carr, a quiet, moody twenty-eight-year-old.

The six climbers in our Seattle delegation were all headed for Mount Everest. Wes Krause, Scott's old NOLS friend and business partner in their Mountain Madness guide service, served as deputy leader. Still more reserved and conservative than Scott, Wes was a moderating force when his friend strained to roar into the great unknown. Geo Schunk, a thirty-two-year-old lawyer from Montana, was as disarmingly handsome as Scott, but his charm was cooler. Geo's smile seemed elusive, like a mask. Liz Nichol, who ran a health food store in Colorado Springs, was easier to get to know, as was George Karhl, one of the Bit 'n' Spur owners. George was the youngest and least experienced climber in the group — just twenty-four years old — but he had the right attitude. He was just out of Harvard and ready for adventure.

Scott was the linchpin for both expeditions, the visionary who dreamed up the climbs and the organizer who made them reality. Scott's work as founder and president of his own adventure service had rendered him a seasoned leader and guide. Given a dozen wealthy but soft middle-aged travelers, Scott could navigate them through the bureaucratic maze of the Kathmandu airport, lead them through a two-week backcountry trek, pull them up a crevasse-mottled mountain, take their picture on the summit, and *then* lead them back down again without losing a customer to exhaustion or frustration. Leading adventures was Scott's daily life, his career. So he got us into the Soviet Union and to our final base camp without pausing to roll up his sleeves. But from here, Scott figured, we could lead ourselves. He was still the leader in name, but in name alone. We were a democracy, a group of equals.

Using a relatively lightweight approach, we planned to climb the mountain's Borodkin Ridge as quickly as we could, carrying all our gear on our backs and moving our camps up the ridge as we progressed. The lower part of the route poses little challenge — a small, dirty glacier, then a long stretch of loose, crumbly rock as we traversed the mountain to the bottom of the Borodkin Ridge at 17,000 feet. The ridge itself is steep snow and ice, a 3,000-foot slog straight up to a crest that overlooks a deep notch in the mountain. This notch — the floor of which is 1,000 feet below the apex of the crest — is the mountain's greatest eccentricity, a mile-long valley of flat snow and ice called the Pip Plateau. Beyond the plateau the route turns steep again, slightly more than 4,000 vertical feet scaled mostly by kicking steps into a stiffly angled slope. Calculating in a few rest days and at least one snowstorm, we figured the entire climb would take ten days, or perhaps two weeks. And eager to escape the gamy Soviet food at base camp and our concerned yet imperious hosts, we loaded up our freeze-dried food and drinks, packed in some tins of Russian caviar, hunks of cheese, and a few loaves of their good black bread, and fled for the freedom of the hills.

We were climbing again! Scott and Wes were in famous spirits, parading in the middle of the pack and having a ripsnorting old time, sucking in that golden air and pushing against the hot white pillars of the sun. The Udall boys were like matching machinery, those long legs pumping evenly, both sets moving in almost perfect rhythm. And I was with Fredo, walking fast, the two of us pushing the front edge of the expedition. We carried our loads up to our first camp, a short haul to the top of the dirty glacier, just above 15,000 feet, only 1,000 feet above base camp. A short hike, but plenty of time to talk. Fredo, I learned, was a character, a hippie mountain man from the far-high reaches of Crested Butte, where he lived in the shack he called Cow Camp. He was also an experienced climber, an avid kayaker, and a skier who entered hot dog contests and won them easily.

Day one made for swift walking, and our momentum carried us into the second day, for another glide up the glacial moraine. Then the traverse across the mountain, up a gradual 2,000 feet to the base of the Borodkin Ridge at 17,000. Here we dumped some equipment, then scampered back down to 15,000 feet, giving ourselves a chance to acclimate to the thinner air before heading up again. We retraced our steps the next morning, across the rocky face one more time to our camp at the base of the Borodkin. I passed Fredo on the way up, and gave him the high sign as I went past. How's it goin' today? He smiled and waved. "Doing okay," he said, his vowels just a little

wheezier than they had been the day before. "A little tired, but okay."
I nodded, and kept going.

The thin atmosphere at 17,000 feet sapped a lot of the life force.
Mike Carr and Maggie Fox both became nauseated and headachy
that afternoon and decided to retreat to base camp for a day or two
of rest and acclimitization. Fredo still looked peaked, but he opted to
keep going with the group. The next morning we all strapped on our
packs to make a carry straight up the Borodkin, climbing 3,000 vertical feet to the top of the crest. Looking down on the Pip Plateau,
the floor of the notch 1,000 feet below, fired up Scott. He looked at
us and motioned down. "Who wants to keep going?" The Udalls,
Geo, and George shook their heads. Too long a day, they said. Wes,
Liz, and I decided to go with Scott, and we moved on to establish our
camp on the Pip.

I worked to keep up with Scott and Wes, wanting to see how I'd
do on a mountain with them. And the guys moved quickly, but as
long as I concentrated on limiting my movements — not swinging my
arms, not swaying from side to side, but focusing all my energy on
climbing up — I did fine. Finding that sense of concentration was the
hardest thing. Once my thoughts wandered from the task at hand,
back home to Utah, I could feel them splintering, my energy waning.
I'd think of Mark and I'd be spinning again, gasping in the thin air.
He'd promised to be faithful to me, he made such a point of it. Sometimes I'd reach into my pocket for that twig of yerba santa and hold
it close to my lips, hearing his voice. *I'll be with you every step.* But
was he really? I wanted to believe him, I wanted to believe us. But it
took so much energy . . . tears would swim in my eyes. Just summon-
ing the effort it took to focus on the mountain drained me.

THE next morning's report from Soviet base camp was ominous. "A storm moving in," the thick voice intoned in a monotonic
Russian accent. "Heavy clouds and snow. Perhaps several days. We
recommend immediate descent."

"Oh, I don't think so," Scott muttered, and turned off the radio.
He looked over at Wes. "What do you make of these Commie
weather reports?"

Wes peered out of the tent, past the liquid blue sky and out to where a few clouds were scuttling on the horizon. "Hard to say," he mused. "There's something going on out there. But a week-long blow? Maybe not."

Besides, we had food and good tents, we could survive a long time on the mountain if we had to. "We're goin' up," Scott announced to our Soviet mentor, and then we did, climbing back up the Borodkin to the snowy crest, then down the 1,000 feet to the floor of the Pip Plateau. Here we set up our tents, and as the sky grew darker and the wind whipped up and the storm bore down on us, we climbed into our sleeping bags and prepared to wait it out.

The storm kept us tentbound for three days, the nine of us huddled on the Pip Plateau while Maggie and Mike waited it out down in base camp. When the winds finally subsided a bit on the morning of our ninth day on the mountain, Scott called down to base camp for our daily check-in. To our surprise, our Soviet climbing coach had revised our plans.

"Your time control plan has expired," his voice crackled through the radio. "The winds are too high and you must come down immediately. Over."

"What?" Squatting outside his tent, Scott shouted into the microphone.

Another burst of static. Then the stern voice again: "Do not climb higher. Return to base camp."

Scott shook his head. "No fucking way," he said, laughing. "Over."

A shriek of feedback. Then: "Repeat?"

"I said" — Scott held the microphone very close to his mouth now, and beneath his turtleneck the veins bulged from his neck — "no way. Fuck you. We're going up to do what we came to do. If you want us you have to come and get us. Over. And out."

We didn't actually leave the plateau that morning — the clouds were still too low on the mountain, the winds still gusting, sending heavy clouds of powder roaring up into the sky. But the storm was waning, and Scott figured the next morning would be clear enough to offer safe passage to our next camp, an exposed hillside roost at 21,000 feet. Not everyone agreed. The new snow on the mountain, argued the Udalls, hadn't had a chance to settle yet. And waltzing up an exposed face with a ton of new powder on it could stir up a major avalanche.

"I think," Mark said, speaking for the entire Colorado contingent, "that we're going to wait for another day." He didn't trust the snow. And besides, Mike and Maggie were still way down the mountain and needed to catch up. Scott nodded and shrugged. Everyone had to make his or her own decision, and that was fine with him. But he was still going up. Watching him jitter and squirm in the tent, I could see why — he just couldn't bear to lie in his sleeping bag for another day. Then Wes spoke up. "I want to go, too." There was silence, and they both looked around, gauging the faces. We had only three-person tents, and a limited supply at that. To take one of the tents up to 21,000 they had to find one more person to go with them. After a moment I raised my hand.

"I'll do it."

Scott smiled and squeezed my shoulder. "What a woman," he said. "Stacy, you're such a champ."

The sky was clear the next morning and we set out after breakfast, climbing carefully through the fresh snow. Scott led the way, pausing occasionally to dig a pit down through the layers of the snow, making certain the cover wasn't too top-heavy. It looked fine, and we continued up, pushing ourselves higher on the mountain. I could see the summit, a sharp line of icy rock against the deep blue sky. It seemed so close now, deceptively close, just beyond the top of this snowfield, just around the next cornice. But it was never that close. I could always read distances in the mountains. Looking up, I can see beyond the false summits and phantom ridges. I can anticipate the work ahead, the sweat and effort. I focus on it, and reel it in one step at a time.

We got to 21,000 feet by late morning and spent an hour digging out a platform for our tent, then setting it up and getting situated. The three of us spent the night, then stayed put for the next day, digging out tent platforms for the others while they caught up. They all arrived by the middle of the afternoon, including Mike and Maggie, a little tired from their dash up the mountain, but in good shape from their days at base camp. The next morning we all got up early to head to our last camp, another exposed perch on the ridge at 23,000 feet. By now the altitude was becoming extreme — we were already above the top altitude of Mount McKinley. I got a slow start in the morning, leaving after most of the others had already packed their tents and taken off. Fredo had managed an early start, but then faltered. I caught up to him after forty-five minutes, when he had stopped to rest. He was standing still, paused just to the right of the stairs kicked by the climbers ahead of us. Even with the exertion his cheeks looked waxy, and I could see his chest heaving beneath his parka.

"You okay?"

It took a moment for him to answer. "Yeah." He breathed for a few more beats. "No problem. Go on."

"Sure?"

"Just a little tired."

We climbed to 23,000 feet, dug out platforms, and set up our tents on the ridge, and by late afternoon started melting snow for dinner. Scott made the rounds of the tents to get out the word for the summit attempt. The wake-up call would come at two A.M., he said. Anyone who felt like getting up was welcome to go. I ate dinner and then huddled in my sleeping bag. Exhausted from the day's climb but apprehensive about the coming morning, I sank into shallow, restless sleep. Swerving in and out of consciousness, I swam in my sleeping bag, hearing the wind and loose snow blowing against the tent. I woke up briefly and glanced at my watch. It was just after midnight. Then I was asleep again, deeply this time.

I was dreaming. The same dream I'd been having for the past three nights, ever since we were stranded on the Pip Plateau. It was an odd, frightening scene. I was on the mountain with Fredo, and he was suffering from pulmonary edema, the worst kind of altitude sickness. He had rales, an edema-related condition in which his lungs filled with fluid, drowning him in his own body. Each gasping breath sounded like a death rattle. But I helped him down, my arm around his shoulder. I led Fredo back to base camp, and then he was fine. Each time it came the detail of the dream was intense, like a technicolor movie. When I woke up, it left me wondering. Was someone looking out for him? I had watched him down on the plateau — Fredo had been faltering, but he said he was fine. A little sluggish, it was obvious, but Fredo knew about altitude. He'd climbed McKinley and Annapurna II. He didn't need babysitting.

But something poked at me. We had climbed quickly and made good time, even given the four-day storm on the Pip Plateau. We hadn't had any injuries or illnesses — calamity hadn't visited us yet — but somehow I could feel it hovering nearby.

WHEN Scott made the rounds of wake-up calls at two A.M., we all got ready at our own speed. Geo left first, then Scott and Wes. I was slinging on my pack and just about to leave camp when George Karhl leaned out of the tent he was sharing with Fredo and called me over. They were both in their sleeping bags.

"We're not going," George said. "Fredo's got rales."

My dream.

"Does he need help getting down?" I peered in at Fredo, huddled deep in his bag, panting lightly.

"Naw," George said. "He's not that bad off, and we've got enough people here to get him down to the plateau."

Fredo looked up at me and I waved. "How you doing?"

"Okay," he said. Fredo's voice seemed thick, but he was coherent. "I'm fine except for the rales," he rasped.

I gave him a long look and nodded. If Fredo said he was fine, then he was fine. "Okay," I said. I turned around and headed up after Geo, Scott, and Wes. Mark Udall came a few minutes later, followed by Brad and Liz. The others stayed in camp. Maggie was feeling the altitude again, a squeezing headache that sapped her strength and left her dreaming only of lower terrain and richer air. Mike felt the same, while George, already thousands of feet higher than he'd ever been before, decided he had also seen enough, thanks anyway. The four of them would form at least two parties, it seemed, and everyone would have someone else to descend with, Fredo especially, since he had the first signs of pulmonary edema. Someone would certainly be descending with him.

But then it didn't work that way. Fredo left first, alone. George followed, figuring he'd soon catch up and be able to watch Fredo the rest of the way down. Then Mike and Maggie left together. All of them were bound for our camp on the Pip Plateau, thinking they'd be there by late morning. By then the lower altitude would stave off the sharp claws of Fredo's edema. Maggie and Mike would have clearer heads. If they had the energy, they might even go down farther. But as dawn lit the sky, George never found Fredo. His tentmate wasn't on the route, nor was he waiting in the camp on the plateau. How could it be? As morning turned to afternoon, George's concern took on an edge of panic. Fredo was missing. Maggie and Mike were also overdue. Calamity had stalked us for days. Now calamity had struck.

Up above high camp I caught up with Geo, Scott, and Wes after a few minutes, and we continued unroped on the steep ice faces, moving slowly in the predawn blackness. The wind whipped around us, a constant thirty-mile-per-hour howl that occasionally roared into wild gusts. Once, when I stopped for a breather, a sudden blast of wind caught the side of my pack and blew me in a semicircle, rotating helplessly around the ice ax I'd just planted in the hillside.

Eventually some fragile rays of light climbed out of the eastern horizon. The sun rose from between the neighboring peaks, but the weak light did little to soothe the gnawing windchill. Whenever I stopped to rest, or to get a drink of water, I had to swing my legs to keep blood moving through my extremities. Even in my heavy boots, with layers of wool and polypropylene socks on, my feet never got warm enough to get beyond feeling numb. After a while the lifelessness in my boots sounded an alarm: numb toes, I knew, are freezing toes. Unless I found a way to encourage blood back into the freezing tissues I could lose bits of myself to frostbite. And I wasn't the only one having trouble. Brad Udall got so cold he just turned around and headed back to camp. And the frigid air continued to take its toll from everyone who remained, so when we found a sheltered spot just forty-five minutes from the summit, we sat on our packs, stripped off our boots, and held our stockinged feet against the warmth of each other's bellies. It took about twenty minutes for the blood to start flowing again.

Then we were climbing, traversing the perpendicular ridge of ice that stretched to the summit. Up higher, creeping up the shocking white of the snow, pushing our heads against the luminous cobalt sky. I was with Geo, Mark, Scott, and Wes step for step, climbing smoothly, feeling good in the thin air. Everything was going well now. I took a turn breaking trail and soon I could see the summit, the last shock of white against the blue. I turned around to check on the guys below me and Scott gave me a thumbs-up. Now it wouldn't be long.

I turned back to the mountainside and took another step. I could feel everything now. The blood swishing through my veins, the cold, dry air in my lungs. Everything was working perfectly. I took another step, felt my crampons bite solidly into the brittle crust of the snow. This was what came naturally to me. The work and the reward added up. I could come to the mountains, I thought, and no matter what happened I knew I would never regret being there. It was the only place I knew I would always have a voice — my voice.

We pulled ourselves to the top just before noon. I hugged Scott, Wes, and the others, and we stood there together for a few moments, passing a bottle of water among us and looking down as the Pamirs spilled into the rest of the continent. The tip of Pik Kommunizma was the top of the Pamirs, so the Soviets had taken pains to mark the spot. A placard stood anchored to a rock, a metal signpost engraved with Russian characters and a portrait of Lenin. But the glory of the Soviet Union was the furthest thing from my mind. For the minutes we stood up there, and then as we started down for camp, I glowed with a new sense of awareness. Or an old sense, perhaps reborn. Knowing that I was strong and capable, that I could not just keep up with my friends, but help lead the way.

W E started back down after only a few minutes, but with the steep approach to the summit and then the deep snow below it took until four P.M. to reach the safety of high camp. By then we'd been climbing for twelve straight hours. We were all exhausted, dropping our packs and retreating into the warmth of sleeping bags, but still elated by our successful climb. The feeling wouldn't last.

Scott picked up the radio at five P.M., eager to spread the good news to our teammates below. But when he roused Brad down at the plateau, Scott's smile faded.

"We've got problems," Brad said. As his voice crackled through the static Scott's head tipped forward, his eyes squeezed tight. At first he peppered Brad with questions — Is there a rescue going? Which doctor is there? Does he have the right equipment? — but as the litany went on Scott's replies turned monotonic. *Uh-huh, uh-huh. Right. Jesus.* When he signed off his face was ashen.

"We're fucked," he said.

The trouble had started just after dawn, when Fredo left camp by himself. As it turned out, he was in worse shape than he had let on. The ravages of altitude had fogged his judgment and stolen his sense of direction. What should have been a four-hour descent straight down to the plateau turned into a solitary nine-hour ordeal of wrong turns and desperate traverses. By the time he stumbled onto the plateau, Fredo was exhausted and barely coherent. And even after his 3,000-foot descent his rales were as bad as, perhaps even worse than, they'd been that morning. After putting him to bed, George sent out an emergency call. Soon an Austrian doctor and a few Soviet rescue climbers came onto the scene, but they didn't have all the medical equipment needed to stabilize him. All they could do for Fredo was help get him down to base camp, and they couldn't even start doing that until the morning.

Our problems didn't end there. Descending through a rocky patch about 1,500 feet below our high camp, Maggie caught a crampon and tumbled forward, off-balance and splayed far enough to shatter her leg. Alone and far from help, Mike tried to build a splint for Maggie, hoping just to immobilize the fractured leg before he left her to go to the plateau for help. Luckily Brad happened upon them just then, descending from his aborted summit attempt. Brad helped finish the splint, then jerry-rigged a sled out of a pack frame, and the two men worked together, helping to lower her slowly down the steep face toward the plateau.

Maggie was in pain — she'd suffered a particularly nasty spiral break of her tibia and fibula — but Fredo was desperately ill. Sprawled in his sleeping bag, lapsing in and out of consciousness, he withstood the night on the plateau without getting worse, but without improving, either. The Austrian doctor tended him as best he could, but without a pressurized Gamow bag or any of the medications that relieve high-altitude sickness, he could offer little more than shots of antibiotics and cortisone until it was light enough to move. As dawn approached, the Soviets rigged a sled from a pair of old wooden skis, strapped Fredo on top, and started pulling him toward the crest above the plateau. Fredo was conscious — he was complaining that the sled was irritating his back, which he'd hurt in an avalanche a few years earlier — but he was still groggy.

Up above, Scott and Wes packed up and left at daylight, tearing toward the plateau in order to help carry Fredo down the mountain.

They caught up to the rescue in three hours, and from there helped pull Fredo's sled down from the top of the Borodkin. While they descended the ridge Fredo's condition seemed to improve. His head was clearer and when they hit some easier, flat terrain he could climb out of the sled and walk. The group spent the next night at Camp 1, at 17,000 feet, and as the night passed, Fredo gained more strength. He was rational, talking about his condition and eating and drinking. He was still shaky on his feet, however, and when they set out for base camp the next morning, the group took turns helping Fredo down the ridge.

Finally Scott could breathe easier. Fredo had had a close call, but the rescue had kicked into gear in time. They'd already lowered him far from danger — they were more than 6,000 feet from where he'd become ill, and even the most radical edema usually clears up after a 3,000-foot descent. Three hours into the day's descent, Scott was taking his turn with Fredo, walking slowly with his arm around his shoulder. They were just beneath 15,500 feet now, and the snow on the ridge was shallow, the pitch not very steep. It was easy walking, but Scott was taking it slow, letting Fredo set his own pace. No need to rush now, they were only a few hours from base camp, and from there a short helicopter hop to the hospital. Scott was peering down the slope toward base camp when he noticed Fredo slowing down, teetering slightly.

"Okay, Fredo?" Scott looked over at him.

"I've gotta stop."

Suddenly Fredo seemed about to collapse. Scott grasped his shoulders with both hands, holding him up. Something squeezed his heart, and he felt his own knees go slack. But he held on to Fredo and tried to keep him on his feet.

"You can't stop," Scott said. "You've gotta keep on."

Fredo shook his head. "I've gotta."

Fredo sat down on the snow, then toppled over onto his side. Scott looked down the slope and shouted for the others, walking a few yards ahead. It took only a second, Fredo had been on the snow for a heartbeat, but by the time Scott sank to his knees and rolled him onto his back, Fredo had stopped breathing.

"Goddammit, no!" Scott looked up for an instant and saw Wes and the Soviets running toward him, just a few feet away. He leaned down, listened for a heartbeat. Hearing nothing, he jerked upright. The two Soviets dashed up. "Help me!" Scott shouted. They threw off their packs and fell to their knees, the three of them working together, blowing in air, pumping his heart. *Come on, Goddammit.* But Fredo just lay there, his face empty, his arms askew. Scott worked his chest frantically, leaning in to check for a heartbeat, hearing nothing, and then pumping again, muttering as he worked. *Come on, Fredo, you're almost home, man, come on!* Fredo's hat had fallen off, and a few crystals of snow had gathered in his hair. He almost looked, Scott noticed, like he was playing games. Like a boy who had fallen backward to make an angel in the snow, and then became hypnotized by the falling snowflakes. It was very quiet.

LATER that afternoon I was walking down the mountain with Brad Udall, descending the steep pitch just beneath the crest of the Borodkin Ridge. Maggie was ahead of us, getting hauled down to base camp in a rescue sled fashioned from half a plastic water barrel. Brad and I had stayed behind, gathering the last pieces of the plateau camp. Now we were finally moving, looking forward to getting down the mountain and catching up to the rest of the crew. We didn't know much, but we'd heard things were looking up: Fredo had left the 17,000-foot camp that morning, he should be in base camp by now. We could see Maggie in the sled ahead of us. When one of the Soviet doctors came toward us, headed up the mountain, we stopped him for news.

"How is our friend?"

The doctor's face turned grim and he waved his right hand across his chest, making the sign of the cross. Brad looked at me, his eyes empty, face blanched with shock. He turned back to the doctor.

"*What?*"

The doctor shrugged, looking for the words. Finally: "He is dead." I reached for Brad's arm and held on tight.

FREDO was dead. Scott stood, started to walk away, then came back, staring down at the body as if he still wasn't convinced. He swore, then spun around again, pacing out and back in small, jerky steps.

"Dammit, Fredo. Goddammit."

They wrapped Fredo's body in a nylon rainfly, laid him in the toboggan, and started down again, walking slowly toward base camp. When they came within a short walk of camp, they dug a shallow grave in the snow, just enough to cover him. When they were through, they marked the grave with the skis from the sled.

BRAD and I continued down the mountain, and by dinnertime we joined the rest of the team at base camp. I went up to Scott and gave him a hug. His eyes were red. "I don't get it," he said. "I just don't fuckin' get it."

Scott was incredulous. They had hustled Fredo down after he got sick, literally thousands of feet beyond the point where an edema should clear up. And he was improving! He was walking and talking and doing fine, and then he just keeled over. But it wasn't just his sudden downturn that puzzled Scott. How had he gotten so sick in the first place? We could all see that Fredo wasn't in top form when we got above the plateau. But whenever anyone asked after him, Fredo shrugged and said he was fine. At least, that's what he'd said until the rales had kicked in.

But fatal edemas rarely happen overnight. If Fredo's edema was really that bad, he had to have been feeling awful for days. He never told us, but we knew this for certain the morning after he died. Someone had fetched his journal, and sure enough, the entries started reflecting his problems two days after we left base camp: "This hypoxia," he wrote, referring to brain-related oxygen deprivation, "is the best drug I've ever had." Fredo knew hypoxia was an early sign of altitude sickness. Why didn't he tell anyone? Did he really think it wasn't important, or was he too excited about climbing the mountain to turn back? Did he make a conscious decision that the summit was worth risking his life? Or did he just assume he could get away with it?

We spent a gloomy night at base camp, then early in the morning a helicopter roared in to take Maggie and Mark to the hospital in Osh. When they were gone, the rest of us gathered for a memorial ceremony. We were all at a loss. Except for Mike, none of us had really known Fredo for more than two weeks. Even the Udalls, who had invited Fredo along, had only known him through mutual friends. So we sat on a few boulders, eight of us gathered beneath a glorious lemon sun, a cloudless sky, and the endless Pamirs, and tried to find words for a man we'd barely come to know. I sat quietly, but torn by my own thoughts. Why hadn't I paid attention to my dreams? If I'd helped Fredo descend, as I had in my dreams, maybe he would have gotten down sooner and had a better chance of surviving. Instead, I'd gone to the summit. Fredo stumbled down to the plateau alone, and now he was dead.

The helicopter came back a few days later to take us down to the Achik Tash camp. Several days after that it came again to carry Scott and Wes down to Osh for Fredo's autopsy. According to the Soviet doctors, Fredo's pulmonary edema had been the least of his problems. His heart was enlarged and elasticized, they said. His lungs were scarred by a bout with pleurisy he'd suffered years earlier. Fredo didn't belong in the mountains, one of the doctors said to Scott. Our usually unflappable leader was still shaken, trying to recover his balance after witnessing the autopsy, and the doctor patted him on the shoulder. "The man was headed for disaster," the doctor said. "It couldn't be helped." Even so, Scott wasn't convinced. Too upset to return to Achik Tash, he and Wes flew straight to Moscow and waited for the rest of us to join them there. We gathered our things and piled them on the next helicopter, then wended our way back to Moscow and the next flight back to the United States.

On the airplane heading home, watching the lights of Moscow trail off behind us, I felt subdued. Still numb about what had happened to Fredo, still worried about Maggie, who was holed up in the hospital in Osh. But also a little sorry to be leaving so soon. It was ironic that at the same time Fredo lost his life I had started rediscovering mine. Whatever the true cause — an edema or an already weakened cardiovascular system — the siren in Fredo's ears had led him past the threshold his body could stand. He loved climbing, and all the time he was climbing higher, pushing himself through the weak air, growing more dizzy and frail with each hour, Fredo must have heard a voice telling him to turn around. He knew what was happening . . . *this hypoxia is the best drug I've ever had* . . . he knew the altitude was stalking him, had him in its sights, squeezing the trigger. But he kept going.

At first I thought his death would make our success seem hollow, but it didn't. I knew Fredo wouldn't want us to feel that way. Seeing it happen, being a part of the tragedy, made the entire mountain experience feel different. Not worthless, and not foolish. But more serious. And more integral to the rest of my life. When I climbed, I felt courageous, strong, honest. Once I managed to get beyond the problems I faced at home, I had felt as free on this mountain as I'd felt in years. I even stopped thinking about Mark, after a while, and started thinking about life without him. It was possible. It was scary, but it could happen. When I was on the mountain, I could see myself living without him. If I could climb a mountain I could certainly make a living, find my own friends, even go to Mount Everest. All it would take was courage, a little emotional strength, and honesty.

We flew back to Seattle, and when I cleared customs I walked through the glass doors and found Mark standing in the international arrival lounge. He saw me coming and came right for me. In an instant he was wrapping me in a long hug. At first I felt wooden against him. Then he loosened his grip and pulled back, holding on to my elbows.

"We heard someone died on the trip," Mark said, all in a rush. "But we didn't know anything else. I was so worried about you!" He threw himself against me again, and now I reached out to hold him. Feeling his warmth, his need, I weakened and dissolved. We were back together.

Scott had planned an Everest expedition meeting in Seattle, so we stayed in town for a few days, then Mark and I went on a vacation to New York City. We were relaxed and happy, our days filled with museums, restaurants, and plays. But back home in Springdale when the carnival was over, I finally had a chance to sort through the months of battered gear and dirty laundry. And I found my real life just where I'd left it. In the Soviet Union I'd climbed a mountain and left feeling renewed. But back home nothing had changed.

IN the Soviet Union I'd thought about changing my life — ending the cycle, leaving Mark, starting on my own. *I didn't have to be helpless! I could learn to do things for myself again!* But New York was so much fun, and then in Springdale I fell back into the usual rhythm and reached out for Mark to dance along in our standard pattern. He reached back, but now it seemed his grip wasn't as tight. We'd be in town, running errands, and he'd glance at his watch, then start edging away from me. I started wondering.

"I've got to make a phone call."

"To who?"

"Oh. Business. It's nothing. Back in a sec." Then he'd be gone, and I'd be wondering. Before I went to Pik Kommunizma Mark swore he was finished with Diana. I believed him then, and I still did. Sort of. If I wanted our marriage to continue, I didn't have a choice. But what were these telephone calls all about?

One night we met at the Bit 'n' Spur after work and had dinner. When we were leaving, we headed for our cars and Mark shouted after me, "Go ahead — I'll be right behind you." I pulled out onto the highway and headed for our house, out toward Zion. I slowed for the turn-off, flicked on my brights, and rumbled up the dirt road. It was a warm summer night, so I sat out on the steps, waiting for Mark to drive up. When he didn't show up after ten minutes, I got back into my car, started the engine, and drove back into town.

I didn't pass him on the highway, and back at the Bit I could see the empty space where Mark had parked his truck. So he'd certainly left the restaurant. But to go where? I turned around and got back on the highway, driving toward our house. He was probably back home now. Maybe he saw someone and stopped to talk. Maybe I'd missed him on the road. Anything could have happened. But when I got to our turn-off, I kept going straight. Something had struck me: there's a pay phone at the visitors' center in the park.

When I pulled into the parking lot, I could see Mark's truck, parked next to the telephone booth connected to the near side of the visitors' center. I turned off my headlights and drove to the far end of the lot, near the far side of the building. I got out of my car, clicked the door shut, and crept around the building. Even from a distance I could hear his voice, a deep murmur against the night. As I got closer I could make out the words.

"Did you tell your parents about us?"

I crept closer, my shoulder pressed against the brick wall. I stopped short of the corner. Mark was just on the other side, perhaps five feet away. When he was quiet I could hear him breathe.

"They were delighted, right? You seeing a lowly carpenter." Mark laughed. He kicked at a pebble on the pavement, then shuffled his feet.

I had to hear it. My heart was pounding, and I was glued against the wall.

"No," Mark said. Then again. "No way. It's over." Then Mark sighed. "Listen. It's over." His voice was gentle and patient, the way I used to hear it. "I don't love her anymore. I love you and I don't want to be with her."

I stood upright again and took a step. My foot brushed against the pavement and I sent a few pebbles skittering away. I moved in a daze, like a puppet with her strings slashed. He did it, I thought. I felt disemboweled — even the part of me that wanted out didn't want it like this. Leaving on your own steam can be liberating, but being betrayed is ridicule. A loss of control. Abuse. Mark slapped the receiver back into the cradle and I took a step around the corner. When he saw me, appearing suddenly on the edge of the pool of light from the parking lot, Mark jumped. Then he squared his shoulders.

"How long have you been there?"

I made a hoarse laugh.

"Long enough."

"Goddammit."

Mark backpedaled on the pavement, searching for the next thing to say, but I shook my head and glared at him. I wanted to hurt him, wanted to launch myself at him and dig my nails into his throat. But I kept still. He'd kill me, I thought, the moment I touched him. Instead I lashed out at him with my eyes, blazing up in the darkness.

"I guess I'll go see my attorney."

Mark shrugged. "Fine."

I found an attorney the next afternoon. He scribbled half a legal pad of notes during our conversation, then explained the procedure. "Patience," he said. "It'll take weeks just to draw up the papers." But when I got home Mark met me in the bedroom and handed me a completed set of divorce papers. Then he reached down and picked up a duffel bag. "I'm going away for the weekend," he announced. "See you in three days."

I was numb. How could Mark already have divorce papers? The truth settled on me, cool and surreal. *Mark had started seeking a divorce when I was on Pik Kommunizma.* I felt a hard laugh escaping from my lips. *Mark said his spirit would be with me . . . but meanwhile his mind and body were with his lawyer.* I sat down to read the settlement Mark's attorney had written. According to Mark, I was supposed to move out immediately and leave him with our house and all our common possessions. My God, I thought, he's throwing me out without anything. I called my lawyer in a panic and flew down to his office for an emergency meeting. He took the envelope from me, and opened it, and after ruffling the first few pages he looked up and smiled.

"This dog ain't gonna hunt," he said. "Don't move anywhere."

I stayed put. Mark came back after the weekend, then moved out to house-sit for some friends in Springdale.

Mark couldn't shake me that easily. My attorney went to work on his attorney, and eventually they negotiated a settlement for the years I spent with Mark, a chunk of cash to help me start another life.

But I couldn't shake Mark that easily either. Mark had been the centerpiece of my world for so long it was hard to imagine standing upright without him. We'd been so close, and his rages had made us even closer. That's the cruelest irony of abuse — it's so shameful, it becomes a secret that only spouses share. It stays tucked away, putting on weight and adding gravity until it pulls you away from the rest of the world. Soon you're governed by the abuse itself. It's scary enough when there's two of you. Then what happens when you find yourself floating there alone? Your abuser is gone but his voice echoes. *You're ugly. You're stupid.* It was the law of the universe, and so I believed it. And now that I'd lost Mark who could ever love me? And even if I found someone how could I be sure he wouldn't be worse than what I'd already had?

WE signed the divorce papers on December 16, and I left a day or two later, driving to Oregon for Christmas. After the holiday I drove back down to Springdale to pick up the rest of my stuff and move back to Oregon for good.

6

THE ROAD TO BASE CAMP

AT first I denied there was a problem. "I can handle climbing with Mark," I told Scott. Who was I kidding? Not Geo Schunk. Even in Montana the lawyer/climber could smell the sulfur rising from my exploded marriage. When he heard the news, Geo fired off a letter to Scott: *There's no way Mark and Stacy can both go to Everest.* Once he thought about it, Scott agreed. After that he scribbled a pair of notes, one to me and one to Mark: *I cannot let your personal problems disrupt our expedition,* he wrote. *Figure out what you want to do and let me know.*

I wasn't about to let go of my slot on the expedition, but I sure wasn't going to be the one shoving Mark aside. We'd both anted up nonrefundable $1,000 deposits to the expedition. The last thing I needed was to have Mark accuse me of pushing him off the trip. I called Scott and tried to be casual. "Whatever you decide is fine with me." Hardly. In the beginning of 1987 climbing Everest was the only thing I had. Whether I was writing letters on team stationery or going running in a team T-shirt, the mountain on the team's logo gave me the only sense of purpose I had. I was going to climb Mount Everest — the highest mountain in the world. That *meant* something to people. It meant everything to me. I certainly wasn't going to drop out.

Then Scott called. "Hey, man, what's with your ex?" I didn't know. What did he mean? "I keep writing him letters and trying to call him, and he never calls me back."

I was noncommittal. "I don't know," I said.

"Well, fuck," Scott replied. "I guess he's telling us something, then. I think I'm going to ask him to resign."

I lived in Seattle for the next two months, staying with my sister Wendy and her husband, John, and spending the days at Scott's office in West Seattle, helping to rope together gear and money for Everest. Even nine months before we boarded the airplane, we were already more than a year into our campaign to raise money, pull together equipment and food, and choose our last few team members.

Sometimes separate tasks could dovetail. When we decided to reduce the size of the standard crew of paid Sherpa help for a larger team of American climbers, Scott made sure to increase the team's financial base by choosing new members who had money, or access to money and/or gear. Experience and climbing ability were still key factors, but other things could tip the balance of Scott's judgment. Peter Goldman, a twenty-nine-year-old appellate prosecutor in Seattle, had little mountain experience, but he did have quite a lot of family money. Before he signed on to the team as a support climber, Peter signed over a check for $20,000.

Resource-tapping wasn't new to any of us. Most of the original climbers already had some specific connection or expertise to offer that went beyond their climbing ability. Liz Nichol, for instance, who owned a health food store in Colorado, had solid contacts to food suppliers. Ben Toland was marketing director for Sierra Designs, an outdoor gear manufacturer. As an attorney, Geo Schunk could draw up contracts and help guide us through the federal tax system. And Dr. Dave Black, an orthopedic hand surgeon by trade, could be counted on to tend to sick or injured climbers once we got to the mountain.

As equipment director, I had to create two master lists of gear and clothing. The first was the group equipment list, which I computed from the top of the mountain down. How many tents would we need in each camp? How many sleeping bags, stoves, fuel canisters, pots? How much rope, how many ice pickets, ice screws, and carabiners would we need to connect the camps? I figured for dozens of other items to stock base camp: batteries, spatulas and silverware for the kitchen, tarps to cover boxes, hundreds of plastic containers to store food and equipment, a pump for kerosene.

Meanwhile, the second list tracked each climber's personal gear — everything from polypropylene socks to thermal underwear to wool mittens to thick pile hats. Also toothbrushes, toothpaste, tampons, headlamps, ice axes, crampons, thermal sleeping pads, down climbing suits, harnesses, thermoses, and leather bota bags for beverages.

We needed an incredible pile of gear, and all of it had to work. There's no point in lugging a stove to 23,000 feet if its fuel lines clog at high altitude. So when I sent out my detailed list to each climber, I included a questionnaire: What companies make the best gear? What designs or brands must be avoided? There's always room for disagreement — if anything, climbers are opinionated, and everyone has had his own experiences and come away with his own idea of what works best. Even so, compiling a wish list for fifteen climbers is the easy part. What's harder is trying to convince manufacturers to give us everything we want for free.

It's a standard ritual in the elite expedition world. Everything about climbing screams for big money — from the airplanes that transport you to far-flung continents to the staff the local governments require you to hire, the packets of high-carbohydrate dehydrated food that sustain you, the clothing that shields you against the elements, and the boots and crampons that finally bite into the surface of the summit. And scrimping on even the smallest details isn't a good idea, either. There aren't any mountaineering supply stores at 25,000 feet. If you didn't bring it, you won't have it. And sometimes not having it can mean losing the summit. Or your life.

The budget for our entire expedition was only $250,000 — some groups spend as much as a million dollars getting themselves ticketed, transported, and dressed for Everest — and almost half of our money would go straight to the Chinese government for our climbing permit and related bureaucratic expenses. Yet we needed at least $100,000 worth of equipment. If we were going to stay anywhere near our budget, I'd have to convince manufacturers to donate at least 70 percent of our gear.

Collecting the quarter million in cash would be an even stiffer battle. As expedition leader, Scott took the lead on raising money, but we were all expected to pitch in, and we all had a keen sense of motivation: the more donations we raised, the less we each had to pull out of our own pockets.

In the mountain-climbing world, raising money is a lot like scaling a sheer rock face. You work your toes and fingertips into the smallest wrinkles, and then try to creep a little higher. More than anything, you have to make a potential donor feel the poetry in the climb. No matter where you're going and what you hope to achieve when you get there, your ultimate goal in fund-raising is to prove that your expedition transcends sport, that the climbers' teamwork, strength, and endurance represent the courage and commitment of the community as a whole.

It's always a challenge, but in 1987 we had a few points in our favor. Scott knew enough about fund-raising to make sure we looked like a professional outfit. All the people we solicited received our pitch in a white two-pocket folder imprinted with our custom-designed 1987 American Everest North Face Expedition logo. Inside, they found a color photograph of the mountain, thumbnail bios of the climbers, a fact sheet about the North Face route, and instructions for donors.

For just $25, you got the regular Friends of AENFE Newsletter, plus the promise of a personal postcard sent to your home from a climber at base camp. A hundred bucks bought all that plus a photo of the climbers on the mountain. Two hundred and fifty earned a replica of the expedition's summit flag, while any $500 donor received all that plus a photograph of the actual load-bearing Tibetan yak temporarily renamed in the donor's honor and wearing a hand-painted plaque to that effect.

We wooed the corporate dollar with a two-pronged assault. Advertising was the obvious hook — the prospect of having a corporate name and/or logo connected to something as dashing as an Everest climb. A company could also use the climb as an internal motivator, using our model of teamwork and risk-taking as a kind of living parable for their employees. Tangible rewards varied according to the company's level of commitment. In our strata of corporate sponsorship, donors could earn everything from official expedition photos for their advertising to having their logos sewn on the group's backpacks and parkas to a post-climb visit and slide show presented by an actual climber.

I had started targeting equipment manufacturers before we went to Pik Kommunizma. My first stop was the Ski Industry Association/ Outdoor Industry Show, a massive fashion show and flesh-pressing party held every spring in Las Vegas. With every major outdoor product manufacturer in attendance, the booths and displays filled the convention hall. Legions of buyers prowled the building, fingering the products and scheduling appointments with the salesmen. The hype came from all directions — the Gore-Tex Company even paid for a lavish private party, an open-bar affair with Chuck Berry performing live. Glitz and hype were everywhere, but even so, the most ambitious salesmen might have been the climbers, all making the rounds to talk up their expeditions.

I worked the floor with Scott and Ben Toland, chatting up manufacturers and trying to nail down donations. Tales of our upcoming voyage to Everest netted a good reception, and so we came home with some new contacts. My most fruitful connection was with Ditrani, an established Canadian ski clothing manufacturer. I had spoken to the company's clothing designer on the telephone before the convention, and during the weekend I had six hours of meetings with the company's sales rep. In the end they decided to sign on as major donors. Ditrani not only provided us with all of our down climbing suits, waterproof pants and jackets, down jackets and mittens, but also designed each piece specifically for our needs.

Equipped with a pared-down list of manufacturers, I fired off a series of detailed cover letters and AENFE folders to the marketing directors of each company. A few days later I followed up with a telephone call. When I got a marketing director or some other executive on the line, I'd point out the benefits we could bring them — how they could use us in their advertising, and how we'd be able to give them in-depth feedback on how their water bottles or sunscreen or tents actually worked in extreme conditions. Assuming the products worked well, we could then write testimonials — another feature for their advertisements.

Understanding how the benefits of the deal could go both ways, they frequently thought donating was a fine idea. We got our $70,000 worth of equipment.

W E also found the money we needed, thanks to a creative assortment of ways and means. We held our own auction in Seattle, in which an experienced auctioneer sold off a list of goods and services that had been donated by friends and local restaurants and merchants. We solicited small donors by promising to put their names on a strip of microfilm that would be left on the summit. We enticed larger donors by selling spots on a high-country trek through Tibet to base camp. We sold AENFE T-shirts. Without any major corpo-

rate donors, we played every angle we could imagine to entice individual contributors.

By the end of the winter we had recruited the balance of our
climbing team. George Karhl had decided to drop out after Pik
Kommunizma, and so the final team included Scott, Wes, Wes's
twenty-six-year-old girlfriend, Melly Reuling, Q Belk, Geo Schunk,
thirty-four years old now, and assistant attorney general of Montana;
Dave Black, a thirty-four-year-old hand surgeon from Longview,
Washington; Michael Graber, a thirty-five-year-old professional pho-
tographer/mountain guide/ski instructor from Mammoth Lake, California; Ben Toland, the Berkeley-based thirty-eight-year-old director
of marketing for Sierra Designs; Liz Nichol, now thirty-eight, and her
forty-year-old lawyer boyfriend, Bob McConnell; Mimi Stone, the
twenty-seven-year-old medical student from Seattle who had taken
me climbing against Mark's wishes that afternoon in Zion; and Peter
Goldman, the twenty-nine-year-old prosecutor from Seattle. When
I had a chance to suggest climbers, I had two excellent candidates:
Evelyn — at twenty-nine still my best climbing buddy, now living in
Utah — and her avalanche forecaster husband, Rick, thirty-one. Both
were experienced climbers, so Scott and the others agreed happily.

It's always great to have good friends on an expedition, so adding
Ev and Rick was special. Even though Ev and I had kept our distance
for a few years when I was with Curt, our friendship had revived
during the mid-eighties. She and Rick had moved to Salt Lake when
I was living in Springdale, and so it was easy for us to keep in touch.
Occasionally we'd take a few days to go climbing or skiing together.
And I still loved climbing with Ev. After sharing ropes for most of a
decade, we had an intuitive feel for each other's strengths and weak-
nesses. We'd learned so much together, had so much fun together, it
was great to imagine the two of us reaching the summit together.
Even if that didn't happen, I was reassured to know Ev would be
there to lean on if the climb became a trial.

LATER that spring we had to package the food and gear into
small portions, seal it up, and ship it off for Tibet. The boxes had to
weigh sixty-six pounds or less, so with 30,000 pounds of food and
equipment, we ended up with 460 wax-coated cardboard boxes, each
of them two feet wide by four feet long and one foot high — the size
most easily carted by yaks.

Six weeks before departure the group got together for a final pre-climb meeting in Seattle. Scott led us through the last series of details — the money we'd raised, the tasks we still needed to perform. And in the end Scott made one thing clear. When we got to the mountain, he wanted to stop being expedition leader. It was the same arrangement we had made on the Pik Kommunizma expedition. He'd still be designated the leader, for official purposes, and still take the lead in unraveling the red tape on our way up to base camp. But when it came down to making everyday decisions about setting the route or planning summit attempts, he would wield no more authority than anyone else. We were all experienced climbers, no one needed to be led by the hand. What's more, we were all friends. Most of us had known one another for years, we'd climbed together for years. If we couldn't run a democratic expedition, who could? That very question, as it turned out, would return to haunt us.

Working on the expedition gave my life a direction. After I left Springdale for the last time in January, I split my time between Woodburn, living in my mother's house again and working construction for my uncle, and Seattle, where I stayed with my sister Wendy and spent the days working on the expedition at Scott's Mountain Madness office. The days passed faster in Seattle — there were fewer memories there. But no matter where I was, I always felt myself facing Mount Everest.

I knew the mountain would transform my self-image. Even if being the First American Woman on Everest didn't mean I was the best climber in the nation, I knew being the First American Woman would give me permanent stature, a title I could take to my grave, like a Medal of Honor. I saw it just like that — a medal, a crutch, a shield. Once I had it, I believed I would become immune to my own insecurities.

THERE'S always something surreal about setting out on a long-planned journey. You think about it for so long, but so much work separates you from the trip. Finally, though, four of us gathered at Sea-Tac International Airport on July 22. The rest would come later — we were heading to the mountain in different groups — but the departure of the first group marked the start of our climb to Everest. The first Kathmandu-bound group included me and Wes

Krause, his quiet girlfriend, Melly, and Bob McConnell, a balding, bearded grizzly bear of a man. Together, the four of us would organize the fresh food and buy other last-minute supplies. Scott and Liz flew directly to China to get the gear we'd shipped. Peter Goldman, Evelyn, Rick, Ben Toland, Q Belk, Mimi Stone, and Geo Schunk would meet us in Kathmandu four days later, while Dave Black and Michael Graber would hook up with us at base camp.

Above Kathmandu we descended through heavy clouds and landed in a thick curtain of rain. We got our visas, then collected our baggage and passed through customs. By now the rain was over, the sun pierced the layers of clouds, and the steam rose off the street dense with the ripe odor of the Third World. Walking out into the street, we stood on the curb for a moment, watching a knot of Hindu women swish past in their saris. Then the porters descended, coming in a swarm like a legion of feeder birds. The bus to the hotel was just across the street, but the porters — wiry, hungry-looking men in blue cotton shirts — insisted on helping us from here to there. Eventually we managed to get everything to our temporary storage space, the back room of Yager Mountain Guides, a locally based guide service Scott had hired to ease us through Kathmandu and escort us through Nepal to where we'd meet him at the Tibetan border.

After dumping our gear, we moved into the Kathmandu Guest House, an old colonial building in the Thamel part of town. Once we settled in, we spent the next few days filling in the gaps in our expedition supply list. Bob and I hunted down most of the fresh food, sitting in an open-air market to negotiate for garlic, potatoes, cabbage, onions, and mangoes. We also picked up bushels of canned fruit, spices, curry, salt, and sugar. We spent about $1,000 on the food, then started loading up on kitchen gear and some extra climbing supplies. We bought about 1,100 feet of Perlon climbing rope, several dozen propane/butane fuel canisters, and enough pots and pans to stock the main kitchen at Advance Base Camp. We also rented three sleeping bags for a rupee a day, or $45 each for the three months. The director of Yager Mountain Guides helped us find two Sherpa helpers, Ungel and Renge, both experienced expedition cooks. Finally, we rented a bus to take us toward Tibet, and hired a scout to work the road ahead of us, locating and hiring porters to haul our loads across the landslides that divided the road.

We rented bikes to transport ourselves around town, cycling through the churning mobs in the street, dinging our bells and swerving to avoid the cows and people. One afternoon Wes, Melly, Bob, and I pedaled out of the city, up the windy roads to the Swayambhunath Temple, an ancient monastery perched at the top of one of the deep green hills just outside Kathmandu.

When Peter, Evelyn, Rick, Ben, Q, Mimi, and Geo arrived at the Kathmandu airport four days later, they found us ready to go. We'd finished all our chores: the fresh food was packed and waiting, the equipment was parceled up. Scott and Liz were probably settling accounts with the Chinese government even as we spoke, and would soon be waiting for us at the Tibetan border. Beyond that, we were burning to get out of the city and start making tracks for the mountain. We would spend one more night in Kathmandu, we proposed, then start trekking in the morning. It sounded like a swell plan on our end, but the new arrivals gaped in horror.

"Are you nuts?" Q shook his head. "Come on, man. We just spent eighteen hours on an airplane. Don't we get a little downtime before hitting the road again?"

So we cooled our heels in Kathmandu for another thirty-six hours, then loaded the gear into trucks and early on the morning of July 29 set out for the Tibet border. The road to Tibet heads up into the foothills, a thin road winding through the lush vegetation, past the terraced farms on the hillside beneath us, and tall crystal waterfalls falling from the cliffs above, and a roadside chain of small, dirty villages, all ripe with the sour odor of decomposing garbage and human waste. Throughout, the going was slow. Every monsoon season unleashes a few mudslides over the road, so until the government highway crew repairs the damage in the dry season, auto traffic on the Nepalese highway is limited to the distance between washouts. Hitting an impassable point, we hired porters to ferry the loads until another truck could resume the trip. Truck drivers who find themselves stranded between washouts can earn a good living working their own section of the highway, ferrying loads and passengers back and forth until the government clears away the rock and mud.

We drove only for a few hours before we hit the first landslide, an enormous stretch of eroded highway near Llamasangu, a small village about twenty-six kilometers from Kathmandu. Our scout had already put out the word for porters, so when we stopped our truck we were surrounded by dozens of eager villagers. Bob threw open the back of the truck and stood on the tailgate with our two Sherpa cooks, trying to distribute loads as fairly and evenly as possible. The throng grew and pushed close to the truck, a riot of chattering dark-skinned men with thin mustaches and crumbling white teeth, most wearing topis, multicolored cotton hats perched high on their heads. Bob distributed the loads and gave marching orders to the troops, sending out fifteen porters with every two expedition members. We tried to be efficient, but with the constant negotiating and organization the process used up the morning and then stretched into the afternoon. By the time the last of our ninety-two porters were sent up the road the front of our expedition was almost two hours ahead of the rear.

Chaos reigned. With the group trailing out over the hillside, our lines of communication dissolved. I walked near the back of the line with Bob and Ben, and when we finally got started we managed to travel for only half an hour before the daylight started to fade. We stopped for the night in an army camp in Langasangua. It had been a long hot day, and when we settled in, a friendly officer escorted me down to the open shower area to clean off. It was dark by now, and I used my headlamp to find my way down the stairs. The soldier left me alone to bathe, and when he was gone I switched off the light, in efforts to secure a little privacy before stripping off my dusty clothes. It was quiet and peaceful in the dark, and the cement floor was cool under my sore toes. While I waited for my eyes to adjust to the dark, I listened to the sounds of the night. The soft breeze tickling the bushes, the chirping of insects, the chatter of our porters, cooking their dinner on the hill above. It was dark and peaceful, and I was happy to be alone.

Scott met us at the Tibetan border, and once we passed through Chinese customs we started up the road again, heading for the high Tibetan Plateau. When we found Xegar, a small village with a military outpost, Liz was waiting patiently. Once there, we spent the next three days resting and adjusting to the altitude. By now the land had turned barren and desertlike, a dry, windblown landscape, all dust and rocks and arid mountain air. We stayed at the army camp and it was the dreariest of places, an array of squat, concrete buildings. And every day began with the morning's Communist propaganda piping out of the camp's network of tinny loudspeakers. I got sick in Xegar and spent most of my time sweating and trying to sleep on my hard little military cot. I tried to eat, although the local cuisine did little to encourage my appetite. For a while it seemed as if time had stopped.

I mounted a slow recovery, and soon our parade of trucks and climbers set out again, rumbling across the dusty roads, up the plateau toward the crooked, snow-covered pyramid we could now see ahead of us, standing above the mouth of the valley. The mountain Westerners call Everest, its neighbors Chomolungma, the Mother Goddess of the Earth. The sight of it! Just a few more days, I thought.

We rode in our slow parade, wearing masks against the dust, pile jackets against the chill, hats, sunscreen, glasses, and umbrellas against the strong, burning rays of the sun. The cool winds are deceptive at 15,000 feet. Even bundled up, you have to remember to drink your fluids, or else the sun and parched air will sap you dry within a few hours. We passed through the towns — small congregations of short cement buildings, some ancient stone ruins, a few tractors parked outside — and brought out crowds of townspeople. Small, Mongolian-featured people, coughing from the smoke and dust they inhale all day, ears glinting with the turquoise baubles dangling from their lobes. Jewelry is a key tradition for the Tibetans, who see earrings as more an expression of humanity than a fashion statement. Either pierce your ears, they believe, or come back in the next life as a donkey.

Traveling was easier on the dry, rolling hills in Tibet, but our road to base camp still had obstacles. Loaded into three rented trucks, we traveled only for a day before one of the trucks broke down. With the nearest replacement parts something like two weeks away, we unloaded our gear while Scott spent the next three hours negotiating with a farmer to use his tractor and trailer.

We rumbled into base camp late in the afternoon of August 8, unloaded the trucks, and bid good-bye to our drivers. Now we were heading straight up into the throat of the mountain. We'd have to rely on yak power from here, hiring village yak herders and their animals to carry our equipment up to Advance Base Camp (ABC).

Base camp on the Tibetan side of Everest serves mostly as a drop point for the trucks. The camp area is on the floor of a glacial valley, a flat, barren expanse between high, sloping walls of crumbly gray scree. The glacial moraine — the field of dirt, rock, and assorted crud displaced at the front end of the moving glacier — is gray and dusty, like a high-altitude granite pit. Close to 17,000 feet in elevation, base camp is a good spot for upward climbers to rest for a few days, pausing to adjust to the thin air while they double-check their gear. So we spent the next two days preparing for our journey to ABC. A few other North Face expeditions had already set up their own tents across the moraine. A group of Japanese climbers had stowed their gear close to ours. A French expedition had set up a storage tent just over the hill, and Misha, a solo German climber, was off in his own corner, resting up for his attempt on the summit.

The day after we arrived we spent hours organizing the equipment boxes — distributing personal gear, putting aside the things we wouldn't need for a while, setting up storage tents, and negotiating for forty yaks to carry the rest of the gear up to ABC. Later Scott and I went over to say hello to Misha, and he seemed delighted to see Americans moving into the neighborhood. Misha offered us some advice to take up the mountain. Go slow, he said. Go high to acclimate, but then come down to get strong again. We nodded.

"See me?" he said. "I'm getting strong now. You do the same. Everest is a patient mountain. And only through patience will you reach the summit."

We nodded. Later, I inscribed everything he said in my journal. "We will listen," I wrote. We should have.

Now it had been more than two weeks since the first group landed in Kathmandu. We'd made the trek all the way to base camp, and we were poised to move onto the mountain. However, the expedition was still missing something — the distinct sense of togetherness that is needed to bond a group of individuals trying to collaborate. We still weren't all together. Dave Black and Michael Graber were trailing us by a few days. We'd been with Scott and Liz only for the days since we'd crossed into Tibet. As a result, the closest members were probably the ones who had been a part of the first group to arrive in Kathmandu.

During our next-to-last dinner in base camp Liz and I told the others we were thinking about taking the forty-five-minute walk to the Rongbo monastery the next morning. I'd been through the blessing ceremony once before, on the Ama Dablam trip, and I think it's a good tradition to follow when climbing in the Himalayas. Having it not only shows respect for the local culture, but also puts the Buddhist Sherpas at ease. What's more, it gives the American team members a chance to do something meaningful together before the climb — a moment of focus that transcends the relentless grind on the mountain.

But the response was silence. I looked over to Scott. If he decided to go I knew he could get everyone else to go too. But he shrugged. "Go for it, if you want," Scott said.

When Liz and I left the next morning, carrying our expedition flags, all of our teammates stayed in camp, absorbed with their own concerns.

The monastery was an old whitewashed structure surrounded by the remnants of bombed-out outbuildings. It had been gutted by the Chinese when they invaded Tibet in 1959. For centuries, the Tibetan landscape had been filled with large, opulent monasteries, but during the invasion the armies went from monastery to monastery, collecting gold and jewels and slaughtering the monks. Once Rongbo had had 200 monks. When we got there they were down to ten.

The walls outside were stark and dusty, but inside the rebuilt structure the monastery was clean and elaborately decorated. The altar was covered with photographs of the Dalai Lama, prayer scarves, handwritten prayers, and folded-up tangles of cash.

The monastery's Ringboche, the head lama, wasn't at the monastery when we arrived, but the senior lama let us in, bowing and smiling, pointing us toward some cushions on the floor. All monks wear sacred maroon robes, but up in the mountains they wear their robes beneath a few layers of warmer clothes. The lama, an older man in a red wool cap, wore his robe beneath a thick orange parka. The younger monks, sitting in a line to his right, looked like mountain climbers, dressed in layers of T-shirts, sweaters, and jackets.

Liz and I sat with the monks for a while, drinking salty black tea and negotiating a price for the blessing. We placed the money on the altar, then handed the lama our expedition flag, our American flag, prayer flags, prayer scarves for each climber to wear, and some rice and popcorn kernels to be blessed during the ceremony. The lama started chanting and sprinkling the rice and popcorn on the flags. Two nuns came in, kneeling down and joining in the chanting. Then the lama walked over to the altar, took up a ceramic vial of blessed water, and anointed the flags. Moving in our direction, he poured some of the water into our cupped hands for us to drink. Throughout the service, the other monks fed us sampas, balls made from barley flour, and continually filled our teacups. Eventually the chanting slowed, then stopped. The monks sat quietly for a moment. The service was over.

When we got back to camp, Ungel set to stringing up our prayer flags. The flags come in five colors — orange, red, white, blue, and green, signifying the five elements of life — and they have to be sewed together in a particular order. Each is covered with the same prayer, *Om mani padme hum,* "Hail to the jewel in the heart of the lotus."

The next morning I carried my first load up to Advance Base Camp. I didn't want to push myself too hard on the first day, so I loaded a day pack with some containers of water and food, and set out with Mimi. We talked for most of the way, looking up at the mountain in the clouds and pondering the mission ahead. As we walked the clouds sank onto Everest's foothills. The sky grew gray and featureless, covering the mountain at first, then sinking down on us. The wind blew up, and then snow started to fall. I turned my head down against the wind, drawing my neck into my coat and peering down to find my footing in the loose rock. Climbing higher, I could feel the altitude clutching at me. Even on this simple terrain my heart pounded and my lungs burned with effort. I moved more slowly, stopping to watch the yaks carrying our loads.

Everything about yaks is amazing: their long, doglike faces, the set of curvy horns poking up from their foreheads, their broad shoulders and bowed spines, their shaggy black fur coats, and the combination of bells they wear, the big ones clonking and the lighter ones chiming with every heavy step. It's quite musical when the herd of them moves together, especially with the yak herders — we called them yaksters — walking behind them, hands tucked behind their backs as they sway from side to side. The yaksters supervise the creatures with a secret yak language of chants and whistles, occasionally punctuating the conversation with a stone hurled from a leather slingshot. Then there's more music: the sling whistling in the air, the sharp crack of release. The yaks don't much care for the flying rocks, so the sound of the slingshot is usually enough to send them scurrying back into line.

Advance Base Camp for North Face expeditions is on a patch of glacial moraine just beneath the Rongbuk Glacier at 18,500 feet. A steep ridge of loose rock — a collection of mountain sediment coughed up by the glacier — separates the camp from the snowfields. A stream of glacial runoff flows down the ridge and into a shallow bowl, feeding the small pond at the marshy end of the valley.

Again, a few other expeditions had claimed their own turf in camp, but we found a nice spot on the sheltered end of the bowl, close to the pond. Once we established our space, we spent the next two days running loads back and forth, organizing the gear, and setting up our tents. We put up a large tarp for the kitchen, with a big kerosene cookstove and boxes piled sideways to double as shelves and walls. Next to the kitchen we pitched a huge Coleman tent to serve as our dining room and communal area. Inside, we used a sheet of plywood for a table and short wooden stools as chairs. We used one far corner of the tent as an equipment storehouse, with boxes of clothes and gear stacked neatly. There was also another big supply tent and a scattering of small dome tents for the climbers.

We spent the next two days at ABC fulfilling one of our pre-expedition promises. It's long been one of Everest's great paradoxes that the earth's wildest, most isolated mountain is also one of the most abused spots on earth. Some climbers call Everest the World's Highest Garbage Dump. Even the top of the mountain is strewn with empty oxygen bottles and other ditched gear. Some climbers have made a habit of throwing their garbage or unneeded equipment into the mountain's glacial crevasses, perhaps imagining that years spent under the churning ice would break down anything into tiny bits. Unfortunately, everything that goes into the glaciers ultimately gets spit out at the other end. But because climbers spend more time at the ABC level, that part is worse. Tin cans rust in piles on the rocks. Yellow and white cigarette butts dot the grayish moraine. Gobs of pink and white toilet paper mark where climbers have relieved themselves over the years.

Before we left the United States we had committed ourselves to living up to a different standard, not only to clean up after ourselves, but also to do a little janitorial work for those who preceded us. We spent two days going over ABC, gathering the tin cans, spiking up the clumps of toilet paper and the cigarette butts. We burned what we could, and did our best to hide what we couldn't pack out. After the two days our site was noticeably cleaner. And in the years since then other expeditions have followed suit: Bob McConnell and Liz Nichol have led three Everest Environmental Expeditions to the base of the mountain, working with the Chinese government to recycle the debris that can be reused and have the rest hauled off to established garbage dumps in nearby villages.

After the two snowy days at ABC, the weather calmed and we could focus our attention on the mountain above us. Dave and Michael had finally arrived, so now we were together, all focused on the mountain and feeling ready to climb. The real work would finally begin. It was an exciting feeling, standing on the edge of Everest, having it all just ahead of us. It was Wes's thirty-fourth birthday, so we made a huge dinner and had Ungel bake a cake in a modified pressure cooker. Once we finished eating, the bottles of bourbon and vodka came out in force. Then things got wilder. The trek receded behind us, even the mountain ahead seemed to vanish in the night. We cranked up the boombox and the music joined us together. Soon the walls of the tent were vibrating with climbers leaping around and passing bottles from hand to hand. After a few hours Scott went out to take a leak, then came back with a bunch of yaksters. At first he'd invited them in for a drink, but then they developed a taste for the Talking Heads and stayed to dance.

It's important for expeditions to feel bonded, and before we left, we'd always boasted about how cohesive our group was. So many old friends, so much common history, shared victories, shared lessons. Ironically, it had taken a while for the group to come together after we left home. But here we were, dancing and singing, a chorus of wild voices carrying into the empty Himalayan air. The noise from the boombox faded, and then we were outside the tent, all of us, standing together and looking up into the star-crusted night, faces all turned in the same direction. My throat was sore from singing, my feet sore from dancing, my head a little fogged with firewater. But so what? Now we were truly a team, and on the eve of the greatest climb of our careers. We all agreed: it was time to stumble back to our tents to rest up for the first equipment haul to Camp 1.

It might have been the last time we all agreed to do anything at the same time.

7

STRANDED HOPES

LEAVING Advance Base Camp after breakfast next morning, all fifteen of us set out in walking shoes, moving across the rocky glacial moraine. The yaks and the yaksters followed, carrying the gear to the spot we had established as our equipment cache. We walked alongside the bottom slopes of the Rongbuk Glacier, past the wall of ice towers built against the scree by the constant rolling pressure from above. After forty-five minutes we came to the equipment dump site, a flat, safe stretch where we could stack boxes of food and gear before returning to haul them up the mountain on our backs. After we each picked out likely-looking loads and covered the remaining boxes with waterproof tarps, the yaks turned around to start back for base camp. We headed upward with our loads and our cross-country skis, walking another twenty minutes before stepping onto the glacier. Here we traded our walking shoes for boots, strapped on skis, then started up the glacier for Camp 1.

It's an easy ski at first, up a few rolling hills and across a long, gentle slope. After a while the glacier arced higher, and we traversed the broad, steep snow face in a series of switchbacks. From there we skied up to the right, heading to the center of the glacier in order to avoid the lips of the deep crevasses ruffling the snow around the edges of the slope. We followed the glacier left, then skyward again, up a stair-step valley of slopes and plateaus. We stopped there, after almost two hours of skiing, and set up our first camp at 19,300 feet, a little more than 800 feet above ABC.

Everest is full of extremes, and when the sun comes out in the afternoon, temperatures on the Rongbuk Glacier can soar to close to

100 degrees. By mid-morning heat steamed my glasses and I could feel sweat tickling my sides and drenching my polypropylene underwear.

We got to Camp 1 at midday and spent a couple of hours pitching the tents, stowing gear, and eating lunch. By early afternoon we turned back, skiing down the glacier to the edge of the dusty moraine. We spent the night in ABC, then repeated the process the next day, rising early to carry loads up to Camp 1, then turning around and skiing down.

During the next few days the loads went up the mountain in a scattershot pattern. When morning arrived, anyone who felt like going would eat an early breakfast, then set out for the equipment dump out on the moraine. Once there, you could grab anything that caught your eye, load it into your pack, and then set out for Camp 1. Load weight and content varied according to the climber and his or her mood. Most expeditions have specific load agendas, the expedition leader making certain the appropriate gear gets up the mountain at the appropriate time. But neither Scott nor Wes had bothered with constructing anything so formal. We'd already decided to work as a democracy, and we'd all climbed on big mountains before, so the attitude became *go with the flow.* Everyone had the same goal, we all knew what had to be done.

In that spirit, while the rest of us were playing it safe and following the rule that it's best to not begin a climb with a massive altitude jump, Scott and Wes decided not to turn around the day we first established Camp 1. Their feet got itchy, standing on that snowy slope beneath the gleaming white North Face. Sure, it was only our first day above ABC. But with the sun beaming down and the breezes so light, you couldn't ask for better climbing weather. It was too perfect *not* to go. So knowing that the lines to Camp 2 had to be fixed eventually, they headed off, hammering in three-foot aluminum ice pickets to anchor about 800 feet of line onto the lower reaches of the North Face. Down below that afternoon, we weren't really sure what had happened to Scott and Wes until they called down from Camp 1 just as the afternoon faded to twilight. "We're going to spend the night up here," came the radio message. Most expedition-style climbs tend to move in small increments, like a caterpillar. You push ahead inch by inch, building a solid base of stocked camps and fixed lines as you go. Now it was becoming clear we'd abandoned any semblance of having a plan. I remembered our climb on Pik Kommunizma. Here we were again, our first day on the mountain, and already it seemed as if we were playing catch-up. Our co-leaders were gliding up the mountain so fast the rest of us had to hustle just to keep them in sight. We always seemed to be in a hurry, even when we weren't quite certain where we were going.

WE stocked the lower camps through late August and early September, gradually carrying our entire store of food, gear, and oxygen to the supply stations at Camp 1 and Camp 2. In an expedition-style climb, the lower camps on the mountain serve as way stations for climbers and equipment headed up the mountain. On the North Face of Everest, Camp 1 sits just below the start of the steep part of the climb, the last refuge before the cliffs and avalanche chutes. Although Camp 1 was only 800 feet above ABC in elevation, the journey across the flat, hot glaciers could take three or four hours and was exhausting under the scorching sun. From there carrying loads up to Camp 2 presented a different series of problems, as the route turned sharply upward on avalanche-prone terrain.

We made dozens of trips during the first few weeks, climbing the route until the contours of the ridges and snowfields seemed as familiar as the streets of home. But if the trek to Camp 1 grew into a routine, the climb to Camp 2 always put me on edge. To avoid the avalanches, we knew we had to climb up and down before peak avalanche time in the heat of the day. Sleeping at Camp 1, we'd set our alarms for two A.M., then switch on headlamps to climb in the dark. We could ski for a while, up the steep slope directly above our camp, then on the gradual uphill that leads to the avalanche cone at the base of the North Face. Then we'd set our skis a safe distance from the constantly shifting debris, strap on crampons, and start on foot, walking through the darkness, up the center lane of the avalanche highway. The avalanche cone sloped up gradually, an open area directly beneath the throat of the Great Couloir. The chunky avalanche debris fanned out at the far end, growing more dense as it rose to meet the bottom of the couloir. Walking through the debris gave me an eerie feeling, particularly in the dark, when vision ended with the headlamp's faint thread, and everything beyond was little more than a dangerous mystery. If you look at a couloir like a gumball machine, the cone is the slot at the bottom. It's almost inevitable that every avalanche in the immediate vicinity will run through it, and for the twenty minutes it took to climb the 300 feet of snow and ice I was on tenterhooks. In the darkness the slightest breeze sounded like a roar. But the cone was our only way onto the North Face, the only conduit to Camp 2, and then to the rest of the route. Every time I passed through, I crossed my fingers and tried to walk fast. And lightly.

The bergschrund, a three-foot slot in the ice wall at the bottom of the couloir, marked the top of the cone, as well as the start of our fixed lines. At the fissure in the ice, we hooked on our jumars, reached for a handhold, and hoisted up over the crack. Once on the slope we kicked steps in the steep snow and ice, following the lines straight up the face for more than two hours, heading for a dark outcropping of sedimentary rock. The lines run straight up the vertical pitch, and at the top of the rock we moved up a 200-foot knife-blade ridge, a long, steep climb overlooking the Great Couloir on the left and another deep gully on the right. The sun would be rising by now, and behind us the peak of Changtse would be glowing pink in the thin morning light. Just above, the snow cave we called Camp 2 sat at the end of a flat section on the ridge, pecked like a woodpecker's nest into the bottom of the next vertical rise.

The familiar climbs could get tedious, but as I went back and forth I had a chance to climb with different groups, each time measuring my expedition mates' speed and skill — just as they were measuring mine. The early part of an expedition can seem like an Alpine version of "The Dating Game." Ferrying loads and setting the ropes, everyone keeps an eye on climbing partners, gauging abilities and personalities, searching for the two or three partners who would be the best companions for a summit attempt.

Climbing between ABC and Camp 1, I did most of my carries with Rick and Evelyn. After a decade of shared climbs I was already familiar with Ev's steady pace. She can handle anything in her own sweet time. Rick is a phenomenal athlete: a short fireplug of a man, all chest and pythonlike arms. An avalanche forecaster for the Salt Lake Department of Transportation, Rick is an expert on snow textures and conditions. On our first few days I spent hours quizzing him on the terrain. Is the windpack solid? How old are the layers, and are they bonding safely? How thick is the ice covering the snow?

While Ev can be extremely assertive in a social situation, Rick can seem withdrawn around some people. But when he feels comfortable, he can hold forth not only on snow, but also on a legion of arcane philosophers, the latest climbing trends, or obscure rock 'n' roll bands. Still, he can be moody, and while the other climbers were busy feeling each other out and trying to appear strong and impressive, Rick sat back with a passive grin on his face, listening.

But as the days passed Rick didn't have a lot to smile about. As we pushed our route higher on the North Face, both he and Ev were getting sick — a flare-up of his chronic intestinal problems and a bout with pleurisy for Ev. Weakened, both of them were quickly nudged to the background. I could see it starting to happen one bitterly cold morning, on the route between Camps 1 and 2. Climbing with Mimi, Michael Graber, and me, Rick could manage only a slow pace. Sapped by weeks of diarrhea, he lagged on the rock chimney, spending more than half an hour negotiating the brittle rock and ice. Meanwhile, we had to wait for him at the bottom, swinging our legs and clapping our hands to try to keep the blood flowing. As the minutes dragged, Mimi was beside herself.

"What the hell is his problem?" She shot a dark look up to Rick, still twenty-five feet from the top of the cliff. "Jesus Christ, already. I'm freezing my ass off. If this guy can't hack it up here, he oughta stay down below."

In some ways I knew Mimi was right. Rick's strength was vanishing, and unless something miraculous happened his time on the mountain was just about over. But the resentment flashing in her eyes revealed something else to me, too. *Mimi doesn't have any patience for weakness*. In some ways I could understand her frustration. I was cold, too. But I'd climbed with Rick so many times before, I'd seen how fast and strong he is. Now he'd been weakened, but he was still trying. Mimi's nastiness made me mad. It's one thing to have doubts about your climbing partners. Making them so clear to everyone in such a public way seemed gratuitously mean.

As the weeks passed Mimi seemed less and less team-oriented. In the early weeks of the climb she had formed a bond with Michael Graber, and from that point the two of them became inseparable. I could see the attraction. As a free-lance photographer Michael lived a dashing, adventurous life. He was the sort of hip young photographer you might see in whiskey ads, the handsome, devil-may-care fellow who lives for the moment, traveling light and moving fast through the world. Michael had done it all, and he could be quite charming.

Sometimes it seemed Michael and Mimi were their own expedition, a separate entity in the midst of our larger group. One night, several weeks into the expedition, I shared the snow cave at Camp 2 with them. While the two of them melted snow on the stove for breakfast, I went outside to pee. I assumed they were making enough for all of us, but by the time I got back to the cave, they had used all the water for themselves. "We didn't know when you'd be back," Mimi explained. But my pack and all my gear were still in the cave. Where could I possibly be going?

Everyone seemed to approach the mountain with a burning impatience, and Q Belk was no exception. Q didn't have much technical experience, and thus moved tentatively on steeper pitches, such as the rock chimney below Camp 2. But everywhere else, he put his head down and roared. Climbing above Camp 2 the day after a blizzard, Q, Ev, and I started out taking turns leading. Climbing first is doubly exhausting after heavy snow. You have not only to break trail, but also to pull the fixed lines out from under the new blanket of snow. We traded off for a while, but our pace didn't suit Q at all. Taking the lead, he tore off ahead of us. Soon all we could see was the red splotch of his jacket, and the occasional cloud of snow as he reared back to tear out the lines.

I felt most comfortable climbing with Wes and Scott. They were gutsy, and both had high expectations. But as experienced instructors and guides, they also had an ingrained thoughtfulness. Wes was a particularly conscientious climber, always craning his neck, looking up and down the route to make sure his partners were proceeding as they should. I felt challenged with them, but always safe. I trusted their judgment. More than that, I trusted them with my life.

MOST of us carried full packs each day, lugging loads of food, climbing gear, oxygen bottles, and other essentials up the rock and ice faces. The climbing was hard and building our camps wasn't any easier. Because the mountainside was far too avalanche-prone for tents, we had to dig out snow caves, each large enough for four or five climbers and all their gear. The work was an endless grind, and some mornings were difficult to face. But still, each evening brought a warm sense of satisfaction. We were one day closer to the top of the mountain.

And each day brought us one day closer to one another. This wasn't always cause for celebration. At first everyone worked hard to be polite. But as the expedition wore on, the veneer of team spirit started flaking away. The first serious conflict came before Camp 2 had been officially established. The route to the camp was finished, and Scott and Wes had even put up a temporary supply tent. But we still hadn't dug the snow cave that would be the main residence, primarily because we decided it would be best to stock the camp without sleeping there. That way, we could build up our supplies above Camp 1 without sapping the food and fuel until necessary.

We all stuck to the plan for a week or so, until Michael and Mimi made a run to the second camp. Storm clouds had been brewing on the horizon since mid-morning, and when they called down to ABC at noon, Scott had specific instructions: Get down before the storm hits.

"No," Michael replied. "We want to acclimate up here for the night."

Scott stared at his walkie-talkie for a moment. "That's not exactly the plan," he said, frustration growing in his voice. "And you'll be up there a helluva lot longer than a night once the storm blows in."

"That's okay," Michael's voice crackled. "We'll take the chance."

Scott threw up his hands. *Fuck this.* He hadn't come all the way to Mount Everest to spend his time screaming into radios, so Michael and Mimi did as they pleased. In the end, they stayed up on the ridge for two solid days, eating the food and using the fuel as they worked to avoid the avalanches that threatened to sweep the tent down onto the lower Rongbuk Glacier. The avalanches got so bad that they had to dig the entire snow cave by themselves. But their skis, stored below on the edge of the avalanche cone, disappeared forever under several tons of new snow. Michael and Mimi came down looking chastened, but still the maneuvering for summit position had started in earnest.

Without a strong leader calling the shots, each climber had to decide for himself or herself when to climb higher and when duty required a descent. Fortunately, not everyone was competing in the summit sweepstakes. After a week of worsening intestinal cramps and congested lungs, respectively, Rick and Ev decided they were far too sick to risk climbing high on the route. Ben also took himself out of the running. He'd spent two years dreaming of trying for the summit, but one trip through that shaky avalanche cone above Camp 1 cured Ben's appetite for high-altitude climbing. From then on he was content to work as a support climber, and never traveled above Camp 1. The other support climbers never had summit aspirations, and that made them much more relaxed than the others. Base camp manager Bob was strong as a wildebeest and always eager to help the group in any way. Liz, who managed our food, also proved a solid climber, making carries all the way to Camp 3. Peter, the lawyer from Seattle, was warm, funny, and smart. He's as ambitious as anyone, but on Everest Peter's main goal was to have a good time. The rest of us had more specific agendas.

I still felt so vulnerable, still so wounded by what had happened in Springdale. Before, I thought that going to Everest would make all my other problems diminish. If only for a few months, I'd be able to live on my own terms, climbing and feeling strong, completely in my element. But even in the furthest reaches of the Himalayas the geography of my mind remained unchanged. I fixated on Michael and Mimi — why were we allowing them to be allied so closely, and at the expense of the entire team? Was the entire team going to dissolve into a loose federation of free-lancers, or was Scott ever going to wield his authority to bring us together? If he didn't create some sense of team responsibility, how could I be sure I could count on having a summit partner?

Insecurity bred defensiveness, and then I'd find it difficult to listen to my teammates without reacting to the insults I knew would be lurking behind their words. Resting at ABC one day, Bob approached me in the dining tent to ask if I could run a load of food up to Camp 1. I don't think I even looked up. "Fuck carrying loads," I snapped. I could be even more demanding and nasty when I *was* ferrying supplies. A week earlier I'd come down to Camp 1 expecting to find a fresh load ready to go up the mountain, but found an empty supply tent. Furious, I called down to Bob on the walkie-talkie.

"Where the hell is the gear?" I shouted.

"What gear?" Bob's puzzled voice crackled on the flinty radio speaker.

"The stuff *you're* supposed to carry up here, so *we* can carry it up the mountain."

Empty static bristled through the small speaker. Then Bob's voice came back. Tentative, but patient.

"What do you need right now?"

I sighed. "We need *stuff,* Bob. Stuff to carry."

"Well, what exactly?" Bob asked. "Food? Rope? Fuel? We've got it all down here. Just tell me what you need and I'll get it up to you —"

"*All* that stuff!" I shouted. "We're ready to make carries, but we need *stuff* to carry up the mountain!"

Bob came to Everest to be our base camp manager and a support climber. But only a few weeks into the trip, he was beginning to understand how it felt to be a servant. Every morning brought another round of radio conversations with climbers on the mountain who didn't quite feel up to hanging around to fix lines, or didn't see why they had to retreat for a day of humping fuel canisters from ABC to Camp 1. Dealing with all that required immense patience. But when Greg, our Chinese liaison officer, stuck his finger in Bob's chest . . . well, that snapped the wildebeest's back.

The call came from one of the members of the other American expedition on the Tibet side of the mountain. Picking up supplies down at their base camp tents, he happened to notice that Greg, a skinny, sulky college student sent to us from the Chinese government, had picked up a few lessons about American-style free enterprise from his summertime charges.

"Your guy is selling your tent space and food to trekkers," the climber said. Bob sent Geo, our expedition lawyer, down to check out the problem. Geo called Greg a thief and the conversation went downhill from there. Soon Greg came roaring up to ABC, shouting for Bob. He found him in the dining tent and dove toward him, caterwauling in thick English about the grievous injury Geo had done to his reputation.

"I demand apology!" Greg shrieked. "He called me a thief, and I demand retraction!"

Bob looked down and smiled. "But, Greg," he parried, "if you're selling our food and tent space, you *are* a thief."

The Allison family, 1965: Sidney, Stacy, Mom, Wendy, Dad, Leslie, Rodney

Curt Haire and Stacy hiking the Narrows trail along the Virgin River in Zion National Park

Scott Fischer

Stacy climbing the Mace in Arizona, 1978

Above: Stacy and Curt at Mount Robson, Canada, 1980

Above right: Mark and Stacy eating breakfast on Barry Sochat's property before work, 1982

Center right: Pik Kommunizma, Pamir Range, USSR, 1986

Bottom right: *The 1987 Everest climb*
Women on the climb: Stacy, Liz Nichol, Evelyn Lees, Mimi Stone, Melly Reuling

Loading yaks at base camp in Tibet (16,800 feet)

Peter Goldman standing at the edge of the glacier and the moraine

Looking up to Camp 2 and above (23,500 feet)

Q Belk and Stacy in the snow cave, Camp 3 (25,500 feet)

Advance Base Camp after a storm (18,500 feet)

The 1988 Everest climb
The team: Larry MacBean, John Petroske, Shirley (Jean's girlfriend), Don Goodman, Jean Ellis, Jim Frush, Stacy, Steve Ruoss, Diana Dailey, Bob Singer, Charlie Shertz, Geoff Tabin, Peggy Luce, Dave Hambly

A local bus in Kathmandu

Mount Everest

Jim packing boxes of gear for the expedition in a Seattle warehouse

At the end of Pujah, the blessing ceremony, with bits of sampa smeared on our faces and hair: back row, Charlie Shertz and three Sherpas; front row, Dawa, Geoff Tabin, Steve Ruoss, Stacy

Porters in Nepal en route to base camp

Terraced farms on the trek to base camp

Camp in a village on the way to base camp

Carrying loads under an overhanging serac in the ice fall

Base camp

The avalanche

Below: From Camp 2 at 21,500 feet, looking up Lhotse at our route, which goes just left of the jumbled ice in the center, crosses the ice face, and goes up to the left ridge at 26,200 feet

John walking across an eight-ladder-span crevasse

Camp 3 at 23,700 feet

Camp 4 at 26,200 feet

Sherpas on the corniced summit ridge

Stacy on the summit of Mount Everest

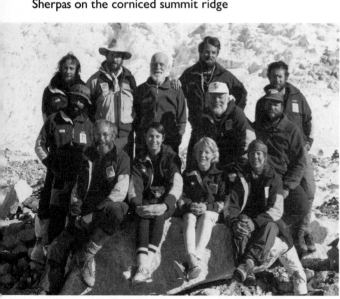

Here's the 1988 team again: top row, Charlie Shertz, Jim Frush, Bob Singer, John Petroske; middle row, Jean Ellis, Larry MacBean, Don Goodman; bottom row, Dave Hambly, Peggy Luce, Stacy, Diana Dailey. Missing is Steve Ruoss.

David and Stacy by Spirit Lake with Mount St. Helens in the background, June 1988

"I will inform the authorities!" Greg poked his finger into Bob's thick chest. "This will not be tolerated!"

Bob held out his hands to fend Greg's bony finger from his sternum. "All right, all right . . . just calm down."

It was just before five, and Bob had to walk up to the radio tent to make the round of evening check-in calls. He invited Greg to come with him, which was probably unnecessary, because the skinny Chinese man was glued to his heels like an angry badger, his litany of complaints and threats echoing off the rocky mountain hillside. Bob made his calls, checking in with the climbers in each of the high mountain camps. When he finished, he put down the walkie-talkie and stood up. He had barely taken a step when Greg was back at him, finger prodding his chest. Beneath his thick beard, the blood drained from Bob's ruddy face.

"There must be retraction immediately! I will lodge a formal complaint with the Chinese government and you must leave country immediately. I will not stand for such an insult to be delivered to the People's Republic of China, and you must understand that —"

The impact echoed against the rocks. Then the silence, as heavy as still water in a pond.

Bob knew he shouldn't have slugged the guy. Violence never solves anything, especially in the cozy confines of a wilderness expedition. And what about the political fallout! Greg was a government employee, for heaven's sake. Standing over our unconscious translator, watching the blood course from his rapidly swelling lower lip, Bob knew he'd made a mistake.

And once Bob woke him up, lent him a hankie for his lip, and escorted him back to the dining tent to have his lip stitched up, Greg was only too happy to tell Bob how dreadful his life was about to become.

"Your entire group will be deported," he said. "You will have to leave immediately, and none of you will ever be allowed on Chinese mountain again!"

A general uproar commenced, Greg yelling up at Bob and Bob shouting right back, and in the corner of the tent Renge, our cook, picked up a butcher knife. Bob saw him, out of the corner of his eye at first. Bob and Renge were buddies in camp, and when Renge saw trouble brewing for his friend, he decided to step in. Bob turned and watched Renge advance, step after step, walking toward Greg with the knife in his hand. Renge was still twelve feet away, but Bob recognized something in his face. An expression he hadn't seen since Vietnam, a cold kind of resolve. The knife glinted in the reflected light of the tent.

"Renge, NO!"

Renge looked into Bob's eyes and stepped back. Greg continued jabbering, unaware. Behind him, Renge put the knife back on the table.

That night Greg stormed back to base camp, where he sulked alone for another month. If he complained to the government, we never heard about it.

B Y mid-September we established our highest intermediate camps on the route — Camp 3 at 25,500 feet and Camp 4 at 26,500 feet — and then stocked them with loads of equipment, food, and supplies. I began to wonder about our schedule. Without a solid chronology to go by, it was hard to tell if we were spending too much time stocking our route. How long would our weather hold out? How long would we be able to keep our strength on the mountain?

On an expedition with a strong central authority, the leader is free to build up the summit teams like a pyramid. Two or three of the group's strongest climbers get tapped for the first trip, and the rest of the climbers work to support their journey. It works like a relay race. When the summit climbers return to base camp to rest, the other climbers stock the high camps, fixing the last portions of the route. Then, when the summiters head up for the final push, their load is lighter and they can move that much faster. It's inevitable that some climbers swallow their ambitions for the good of the expedition, but that's what expedition climbing is all about: you have to make a plan, and stick to it as closely as the weather and fate allow. If you fail to do this, you leave the door open for selfishness. As the pressure mounts, an uncentered team can veer quickly into chaos. A group not bound to a plan is always one person away from total collapse — the moment one team member abandons the interests of the group, the others will quickly follow. It didn't take long for our group to cross that line.

Given illnesses and changing priorities, our summit candidates boiled down to seven: Scott, Wes, Michael, Mimi, Q, Geo, and me.

Scott and Wes were already a team, as were Michael and Mimi. The rest of us were still free agents, and that fact made me nervous. It's best for summit teams to run small, usually no more than three climbers. Travel light and travel quickly, says the rule. The fewer climbers you take, the smaller the risk that someone will get sick or injured.

Settling on summit partners is an exacting procedure. Climbing at altitude is a dangerous business, and you need to feel confident that the climbers you're with are not only strong and conscientious, but also smart and honest. If you get into trouble, your partners' cool heads may be the only thing standing between life and death. And if they screw up — pushing themselves beyond their limitations, perhaps — then you may have to risk your own life to save theirs.

Once you're on the mountain, previous reputations mean nothing. The point is to keep a close watch on how everyone works on *this* climb, under *these* circumstances. And the assessments are unforgiving. Once you make a mistake, the others will have a hard time overlooking it. When you see someone else make a mistake, you can't help imagining how the next one could cost your life.

Geo was dead set on trying for the summit. He was sure he could make it, he said, and his background made a convincing argument. Besides being an assistant attorney general in Montana, Geo was also an accomplished climber and skier. He seemed balanced enough on the lower reaches of the mountain, despite his one main idiosyncrasy of carrying his razor in his pack. (Most men don't bother shaving above base camp, let alone at extreme altitudes.) But when he got to Camp 3 the altitude started to work on him. He had headaches, dizziness, even nausea. Geo had spent the night up there with Scott and Wes, planning to carry a load up to Camp 4 — our highest camp — in the morning. But when they woke up, Geo was obviously having a problem with the altitude, so Scott suggested he get back to Camp 1.

"Are you gonna need a hand getting down?"

"Naw." Geo waved Scott off. "I'm fine. I'll be back tomorrow."

So Scott and Wes started up toward Camp 4 and Geo headed down the mountain. It's a long haul from 25,500 to 19,300 feet, but if you start early enough, it's possible to make the descent before the sunlight fades. I was at Camp 1 that day, and when Scott radioed down that morning to tell us Geo was coming, we assumed he'd be with us by nightfall. When he still hadn't arrived two hours after dark, I went out with Mimi, Michael, and Dave Black on a search party. We found Geo just above Camp 1, stumbling down a hill. He seemed groggy, just this side of incoherent and about half a step from complete exhaustion. He'd been climbing down the mountain alone for more than ten hours.

"What happened to you?" We grabbed his arms and lugged him toward the tents at Camp 1.

"I had to shave," Geo replied incredibly. He tried to walk with us, but his legs were rubbery. His feet dragged across the snow.

"You had to *shave?*"

"Yeah," he muttered. "I wanted to shave at Camp 2, and I couldn't find my razor. I don't know how long I was looking. Christ, I don't even know where I put it."

I gaped at Geo in wonder. He'd descended the entire way, it seemed, while being almost completely out of it. Only someone with a serious detachment from reality stops a descent on the North Face of Everest to shave.

So, who could I climb with? I didn't trust Geo, and I barely knew Q. I liked what I knew about him, but even so I didn't feel secure enough to go to the summit with him as my sole partner. My only option, it seemed, was to convince Scott and Wes to take me as their third partner. But would they want to have me? They were already firming up their plans to climb as a duo.

After making their first carry to Camp 4, Scott and Wes decided they were ready to try for the summit. They retreated to ABC to rest for a few days, leaving the rest of us to finish stocking the higher camps. The next day Q, Ungel, and I made a run to Camp 4. I felt good up at the new altitude, and thought about popping the question to Scott and Wes when we called down on the radio that evening. But as we descended to Camp 3 I learned Q had already beaten me to the punch.

"I'm going to climb with Scott and Wes," Q said. "We talked about it yesterday."

Now I was stuck. I couldn't go to the summit with Michael and Mimi. They'd made it only too obvious that they weren't interested in climbing with me. And now Scott, Wes, and Q had filled up their dance cards and wouldn't have room for me. I was stunned. I could understand why Q would want to climb with Scott and Wes — they were the strongest climbers in the group — and he had no reason to suspect I was set against climbing with Geo. So he'd done the logical thing, and I was stuck. Now it looked like I wasn't even going to get a chance to go to the summit.

We spent the night at Camp 1, and when we called down to ABC at dinnertime, I learned that Ev and Rick were packing up. Rick's intestines weren't getting better, and now the racking cough Ev had had for the last week had been diagnosed definitely as pleurisy. They'd be gone by the end of the week, and I'd lose two of my closest friends on the trip. Every time I turned around, something else went wrong.

While I was making the familiar descent to ABC the next morning, my anxiety crescendoed. After months of dreaming about this trip, counting on making that summit attempt, praying that I could stand on top, I wasn't even going to get a shot. The expedition had turned into a microcosm of that last year with Mark. That last winter all alone, living in that half-finished house, perched alone on the hill without even any doors to protect me. Frightened in the dark; the howling winds and the creaky boards. And spending my days working toward a future alone, all the time thinking I was connected to someone, but being so wrong. Mark had it all — the business, the house, his girls. Everything except regrets. All I had was this expedition, this fractured group scrambling and tripping over themselves in their hurry to reach the summit first. In the end, the whole thing was a joke. I wanted so badly to be the first American woman — at least to have the chance to be the one. It was the one thing I could imagine being the antidote to Mark. The way I'd prove to myself that I wasn't worthless. That I could do something magnificent. Now it seemed I wouldn't be even *one* of the women up there.

I was in tears by the time I got down to ABC. I dumped my pack and then made a beeline for Ev. I told her my entire tale of woe, a bitter story of misfortune and deceit, but she just shrugged. She sympathized, like a good friend, but wouldn't let me feel sorry for myself. Like a good climbing partner, she recognized the obvious route upward.

"Why don't you ask Scott if you can go up with him and Wes and Q?"

"There's no way," I sniffled. "They've already got three people."

Evelyn shook her head. "Don't be an idiot. They know you're strong and healthy and you deserve your shot. He's not going to say no."

Later that afternoon Scott furrowed his brow and thought about it for a moment. I stood across from him, my face pointed down, feet shuffling the snow. "Four's a lot for a summit team," he said. "But okay. We're going the day after tomorrow."

I felt my face light up, and I reached out to hug Scott. "Thanks," I said.

"No problem," he said. "We're going to have a blast up there."

WHILE we were resting at ABC, Michael and Mimi headed for Camp 4, preparing to carry the last loads to the high camp before returning to ABC to recover for their own summit attempt. According to the scheme we'd hatched during our radio calls, they'd rest for a few days, waiting for Scott, Wes, Q, and me to reach the summit. Once we made it, or turned around, then they'd be rested enough to go up themselves. But as they settled into Camp 3, Michael and Mimi called down to announce that they had a better idea.

"We're feeling strong," Michael's voice crackled over the walkie-talkie. "The weather looks good, so we're going to make our attempt tomorrow."

Michael and Mimi had decided that our heavyweight expedition-style strategy was a loser's bet. On a route as complicated as the North Face, they figured it was smarter to take their opportunities where they found them. I had to admit there was a logic to it. Mount Everest weather is always a dicey thing, and if they did feel strong, and if the good weather held, then it would seem like a fine decision. Getting anyone up to the summit would make the expedition a success. Even so, Michael and Mimi's sudden departure from the team didn't do the rest of us any favors. If they were going up to the summit, they certainly couldn't carry their share of gear up to Camp 4. We'd have to pick up the slack when we headed up for our own summit attempts.

"So what the fuck," Scott said. "If they get up there, great. If they don't, we'll haul our own asses up there."

It was easy for him to say that. Lying in my sleeping bag that night, I couldn't help listening to darker voices. I knew that if Mimi succeeded — if she got to the summit — she'd get all the First American Woman glory, and I'd be just another also-ran. She'd gotten the jump on me, and I couldn't help feeling as though she had sneaked past me in order to get to the summit first. Dammit. I didn't want to get into this kind of competition. They were the worst feelings to have, the worst kind of bad karma to spread around. But I couldn't help it. *I needed it more.* Mimi already had all the self-esteem in the world. She was in medical school. She had a husband. Now she was going to be the First American Woman, too, and I could barely contain myself.

But why should I bother being any different from my teammates? By now we had all jettisoned whatever dedication we once had to the better interests of the expedition. We may have started our journey as a cohesive group of old friends, but as we positioned ourselves for the summit, we were little more than a group of mercenaries.

O N the mountain above us, Michael and Mimi launched their attempt on the summit. After spending the night at Camp 4, they woke up on the morning of October 15 and peered out of the snow cave. Above them the sky was clear, and the peak stood white against the blue sky. But the thin wisps of cirrus clouds scurrying above, along with the volcanolike plume of snow blowing off the summit, confirmed the problem. The winds were blowing up, gusting up to 100 miles an hour. Climbing would be next to impossible. But aware that they weren't strong enough to spend more than a few nights above 26,000 feet, Michael and Mimi knew they had only two choices: climb or descend. They decided to risk the climb. The winds might die, they reasoned. And they hadn't come this far to give up so easily. Bundling into down suits and strapping on oxygen tanks, Michael and Mimi ventured out into the killing wind.

They climbed through the morning and into the afternoon, up the Great Couloir, across the Yellow Band — the strip of crumbly rock that circles the top of the mountain. The wind continued, freezing their toes numb and knocking them off-balance. Finally, just above 28,000 feet, their momentum slowed and their resolve waning, Michael and Mimi knew they had to turn around. When they called down from Camp 4 that evening, I felt something reignite inside of me. *Now it's my turn.* After almost a week at ABC, Scott, Wes, Q, and I were rested and ready. Three days later, on the morning of my birthday, we started climbing for Camp 1.

W E spent the first night in Camp 1, then woke up before dawn to navigate the shifty avalanche cone and the vertical rock of Greg's Gully. We climbed up the ridge to Camp 2, following the footsteps from our earlier trips, then crawled into the snow cave early in the afternoon. To prepare for the rigors ahead of us, we spent the rest of the day eating and drinking high-calorie, high-carbohydrate food: mashed potatoes with butter, freeze-dried casseroles, packets of Excel, our chocolate-flavored energy drink, and hard candy. The next morning we woke before sunrise and prepared to climb the 2,000 feet to Camp 3.

We emerged from the cave at dawn, the eastern sky just rosy with the morning's first light. The wind came steadily out of the south, a searing blast cold and dry enough to burn the back of my throat. To protect my lips, nose, and cheeks I wore a neoprene face mask. Above my mouth and nose holes I layered a pile neck gaiter. The thick material didn't allow for much fresh air, but up here anything that preserved warmth and moisture seemed like a blessing.

To keep my body warm without overheating, I combined layers of polypropylene and down. I wore two layers of gloves — polypro and down — and also two layers of polypro socks under my plastic climbing boots. Still, once I crawled out of the cave, it took only moments for the cold to penetrate the layers and start gnawing at my skin. But I ignored the chill, focusing on my footsteps. As we moved up the steps already kicked into the ridge, my crampons squeaking in the cold, dry snow, I fell into the slow rhythm of the mountain.

Above Camp 2 the snowy ridge slopes gently for a while, then gradually tilts upward into a stiff 45-degree arc. After ascending straight up for about 300 feet, we veered to the right, clambering through a small band of snow-dusted rock just beneath the bottom of the White Limbo snowfield. The band is a small series of rock shelves, an amalgamation of boulders, really, frosted with a thin glaze of ice. We'd already fixed a line up the route, so I climbed easily, pulling myself up the rope with my jumar while my crampons scraped lightly against the stone. Only the last fifteen feet of the rock is vertical — a small cliff bridging the way onto the snowfield. Climbing up is a technical task, but nothing like climbing a rock cliff at Zion. Jumars remove most of the skill element in climbing. You look for footholds on the rock, but your real support comes from the rope and your harness. It's a little like rappelling in reverse.

At the top of the cliff we headed straight up White Limbo, following the team's shallow footprints across the smooth, hard surface of the snow. I always climbed gingerly on White Limbo. Despite the apparent ease of that section of the climb, you're actually quite exposed to the mountain's most dangerous elements. Avalanches can come roaring down from almost any direction. And without any nearby rocks or cliffs, the winds rip across the mountainside unobstructed, frequently gusting above 100 miles an hour.

Moving up the snowy face while the sun followed us into the sky, I had a spectacular view of Everest's summit, the vast white pyramid against the deep blue. Behind us a sea of white Himalayan peaks receded into the distance. Standing above the crowd was Changtse, directly behind us, then Pumori and then Cho Oyu, the huge flattop mountain off in the distance. On the north side of the mountains stretched the dusty brown Tibetan plain. And just beyond Cho Oyu, like a coffee stain on an Oriental rug, a dark, flat ridge of clouds. At that moment they seemed to be coming closer.

As we climbed higher, I'd throw a look over my shoulder, past Changtse and into Tibet. Each time I looked, the cloud line was closer and darker than it had been the time before. As the next hour passed, the clouds closed toward us like a curtain, covering Cho Oyu, then pulling closer. Above us, thin, white wisps of cirrus clouds scattered through the firmament, swept like dustballs by high-velocity jet-stream winds. Soon I could feel the wind pressing against my back. When Wes turned around to look, I shouted up to him.

"See the clouds?"

"Ugly!" he shouted back.

We continued up the snow face for another hundred feet, then slanted to the left. Scott climbed in the lead, about fifty feet ahead of me. Wes was between us, about twenty-five feet ahead, and I climbed twenty feet ahead of Q. We kept going for a while, following Scott's speedy ascent up the snowfield. But each time I turned around I couldn't help focusing on that ominous wall of clouds.

But was I the only one thinking that? I knew Wes had seen the clouds. There he was, turning around again. And continuing up after Scott. Maybe I was being too cautious. Too conservative for my own good. You've gotta push it, right?

So we kept going for a while — ten minutes, perhaps. I fixed my gaze on Wes's back, following his bright red parka up the line. He kept turning around, though, as if he was trying to convince himself of something. After everything, it's so hard to turn around. Then Wes stopped. He shouted something up to Scott, but I couldn't hear above the roar of the wind, the flapping of my jacket. They yelled back and forth for a minute, then Wes turned around to me.

"Up or down?"

"Down!"

Wes turned to Scott again. I couldn't hear, but I could read Scott's body language — he wanted to keep going. I knew his argument: if it hits us we can ride it out just as well up above. Then we wouldn't have to retrace our steps and even if it lasts a day or two we'll be in much better shape to reach for the summit. But going higher meant committing ourselves to living above 25,000 feet. And on Everest, there's never any telling how many days or weeks a heavy storm will hang around. If we did have to spend a few days and nights in a snow cave, we'd be much stronger in the lower cave. Scott looked off to the clouds for a moment, letting it sink in. Then he nodded.

Without another word we turned around and descended White Limbo, very conscious of the blackness ahead of us, looming that much closer now, and then found our way through the rocks and down the ridge to our snow cave at Camp 2.

The blizzard hit in mid-afternoon, though we hardly noticed. Tucked in our warm little L-shaped cave, we were completely insulated by the translucent snow. No matter how violent the tempest outside, we could barely hear the wind, let alone feel it. The temperature outside may have swooped to 30 or 40 degrees below zero, with the wind-chill factor, but our cave stayed a pleasant 32 degrees. As the wind screamed and the snow flew from the heavy black clouds, we sat up in our sleeping bags, drinking hot chocolate and chatting merrily. We fixed ourselves dinner, as the daylight faded, then snuggled in for the night. In the dark I lay back in my sleeping bag, daydreaming and waiting for the morning. By then, I hoped, the skies would be clear and we could return to our route, kicking steps to Camp 3, then to Camp 4, and then up and onto the summit.

When we woke up the next morning, Q and I found that our sleeping bags had been dusted with snow. During the night some spindrift had apparently floated in through the tunnel. While we brushed the snow off our bags, Wes peered up into the tunnel, trying to see how much snow had blown in during the night. His peering space was severely limited. The entire tunnel, Wes discovered, had been filled with snow. Which presented several problems, not the least of which was the fact that the tunnel opening was our only oxygen source: all our bottled oxygen had already been packed to Camp 4. Wes grabbed a shovel and started digging. After half an hour he managed to clear the passage, but when he came back he had snow stuck in his black beard. We learned we'd be staying put for at least another day. "It's snowing like a bastard out there," Wes announced.

Snowing so hard, in fact, that when Q bundled up to take a look for himself fifteen minutes later, the tunnel Wes had just cleared was already clogged. Q dug out the passage again, then used four ice screws to hang a tarp at the front entry, thus protecting our enclave from another onslaught of spindrift.

It'd been a hard morning, but during our ten A.M. radio call, we heard how easy we had it in our cave. During the night ABC had been buried under four feet of snow, Bob said. The end was nowhere in sight: "No sign of clearing," Bob said. "And the wind's howling down here. You guys may be up there for a while."

When Scott put away the walkie-talkie, we sat back and listened for the storm. Only we couldn't hear anything, just the muffled sound of the wind outside the walls. Wes cocked his head and wrinkled his brow. Outside in the tunnel our tarp wasn't even flapping.

"Awful quiet, don't you think?"

Wes put on his down suit, strapped on his gaiters and hat, and crawled into the tunnel to take a look. Pushing aside the corner of the tarp, he saw that another avalanche had filled in the entryway. Wes cleared the tunnel, but when Q decided to crawl out and stretch his legs an hour later, another spindrift avalanche had filled in Wes's hole. Now Q reached in for the shovel. Big, strong, and brave, Q is also claustrophobic. The snow cave had enough headroom to keep him happy, but lying in a clogged snow tunnel gnaws at him. After five or six minutes of work, he sank the shovel in the snow and ducked back inside to catch his breath. And he was just steeling himself to head back into the tunnel again when we heard a deep rumble outside the cave. A *whump,* from the direction of the entry, then a light cloud of powder filtering down. Q looked up at us, then poked his head into the tunnel.

"Shit!" he cried. His voice was muffled inside the tunnel, but then he leaned back into the cave. "Another fucking avalanche!"

This one had buried the shovel, so now Q had to dig with a pot lid. He managed about five minutes this time, then just as he started seeing light through the snow, Scott volunteered to relieve him. Q handed Scott the pot lid, but he threw it aside.

"Fuck digging," Scott said. "I'm gonna put on my suit and bust outta here like Superman."

In the tunnel, Scott hunkered down like a football lineman waiting for the snap. Counting down from three, he lunged forward, hands outstretched like a battering ram. Scott's first leap didn't work, and he bounced off the snow like a tennis ball. But he hunkered down again and launched himself into the snow one more time, finally bursting through the wall in a hail of fine white powder. From above, I expected to hear a chest-thumping roar of victory. Instead, he came drooping back into the cave, coughing and gasping. He'd forgotten to cover his mouth during his little leap and had breathed in some snow. Scott spent the next two hours coughing water out of his lungs.

Overloaded with fresh snow, the steep mountainside continued to slough the excess. And as the avalanches kept rolling down the steep ridge, it seemed there was little we could do to keep our tunnel's entryway clear. So we retreated back into the cave, hoping we'd have enough air to hold us until nightfall. By then the avalanches might have run their course, and we'd be able to clear the tunnel for the night. But by late afternoon Scott began to suspect something else. Trying to light the stove, he found that the flint of his lighter was only raising sparks.

"Oh-oh." Scott looked up, a stiff smile curling his lips. "You don't suppose it's just out of gas, do you?" The rest of us lunged for our own lighters. Lighters need gas to work, of course. They also need oxygen. When we each flicked at our own lighters and couldn't summon a flicker among us, we knew we had a problem.

"Right!" Scott clapped his hands. "Time to replenish the oxygen supply — *right now.*"

Q and Wes dove for the entryway. From where I sat, the walls of the cave seemed to draw inward, the womblike murkiness grew ominous. While the guys took turns tearing at the snow in the tunnel, I turned my attention to the side of the cave. One of our walls, I knew, would be close to the side of the ridge that looked over the couloir. The question was: how close? I took one of our three-foot aluminum ice pickets and started poking through the wall. The first picket knifed all the way into the wall without breaking through, so I picked up a second one and used it as a poker, pushing the first picket further into the snow. Then, with the first picket out about four and a half feet, I felt it fall out the other side. Pulling in the other picket, I peered through the small hole. A pinprick of gray sky was visible on the other side, and as the wind blew up outside a cold, dry shaft of air pushed against my eyeball and made me blink.

"Hey," I said, turning around to the others. "I struck air!"

"Great," Scott said, looking back over his shoulder. "But you also just sent one of our ice pickets down into Tibet."

WHEN you're riding out a storm in a snow cave, life boils down to a matter of time. Without books or cards or any intellectual diversion, the minutes and hours loom in their purest form. Sleep is the only shortcut, and after a day or two even that comes slowly. Depleted by the climb, squeezed by the pressures of altitude, and scrunched by the confines of limited space, an already abused body turns surly. At altitude the digestive system chokes, muscles atrophy, and any kind of movement presents a severe tax on your resolve. My back and shoulders were stiff from the endless hours of lying down. My hips ached from the hours of sitting up.

I wanted desperately to move, but we were stuck. Through two straight days, then three, then four, the black clouds hung low over the mountain. Just outside our little entryway, the arctic wind screamed like a jet engine, lashing the curtain of heavy snowflakes at a near-horizontal arc. Later we'd learn that we were sitting through the most violent snowstorm to hit Everest and the Tibetan plain in more than forty years. Until it was over we had no choice except to stay cavebound, waiting for the skies to clear.

The days passed slowly, but the nights were the hardest. Not wanting to waste the batteries on our headlamps, we bundled back into our sleeping bags and lay in darkness. At that time of year, nights last for twelve hours. I spent my time gazing off into the blackness and letting my mind wander. Up to the summit and then beyond. Back home, to whatever my life would become. Eventually I'd doze off, fading away in the blackness, only to find myself drifting back toward consciousness again. Lying there, reluctantly but fully awake, I could hear the deep, regular breathing around me. Time had passed, but how much? Before looking at my watch I'd try to recollect the hours. If I got into the sack at eight, and fell asleep sometime after ten, it could be anywhere from two A.M. to close to dawn — say, five or six o'clock. And if it were that late, I could start thinking about boiling water for breakfast. That would give me at least an hour of purposeful activity, then another half an hour of eating. Burning with hope, I'd focus on the luminous dial of my watch. It wasn't even midnight yet.

Food was our main diversion. Cooking and eating could take up hours of a day, and at altitude it's always good policy to take on calories. But it's a physical reality that the human digestive system never absorbs 100 percent of what you eat. Waste builds up in the bladder and the bowels, and eventually must be eliminated. In a crowded snow cave at 23,500 feet, in the midst of a violent snowstorm, this can present a problem.

It's easy to pee. We were all accustomed to carrying pee bottles to use in our tents at night. It's a simple system. Just use the bottle as you need to, then go outside in the morning and dump the contents into the snow. For most people, it's not very difficult to pee in semi-public circumstances. As long as you don't spill anything, it's not a traumatic experience. But try moving your bowels in public.

"I am NOT going to take a dump in this cave."

Scott made his intentions clear at the end of our first day of captivity. It might seem strange, given his overarching confidence and his years spent playing and working in the wilderness. Scott has no problem relieving himself in the out-of-doors, even in the harshest conditions. When you gotta go, you gotta go. And wandering off alone into the bushes or behind a tall ice tower can actually be sort of relaxing. But surrounded by people in an enclosed space was something else.

"There is no fucking way," Scott said.

His resolve lasted for two days. Then it became inevitable that

Scott had to join the rest of us in once a day exchanging his pride for the physical reality of being a human being. And even if you take to it more easily than Scott did, bowel movements in close company are still an unnerving, even painful process. Begging everyone's pardon, you reach for a Ziploc plastic bag and ask the others to turn their heads. But although their eyes are averted, the subtleties of the act in progress are usually painfully obvious to all. Odors tend to carry and linger. And the pressure of altitude seemed only to increase flatulence. We stored the plastic bags near the front entryway, where the contents would freeze.

ON the morning of the fifth day the clouds finally broke, and the sun rose into a clear sky. Stepping outside the tunnel for the first time in ninety-six hours, I could finally look out into the world below. The snow was everywhere now. Even the Tibetan plateau, once brown and gray, was covered by a thick blanket of pure white. The wind was still blowing, but it wasn't going to sweep us off the mountainside. Not down at this altitude, anyway. Up above, the summit was still trailing a long plume of spindrift. But for the time being we were okay. And most important, the horizon was crystal clear in all directions.

Still, before we continued up the mountain we had to consider how our bodies were responding to the altitude. We'd spent the last five days above 19,000 feet. Deprived of oxygen, there was no way our digestive systems could assimilate enough calories and nutrients to keep our muscles intact. Our bodies were slowly wearing down.

I could feel it once I climbed out of the cave and stood up. I struggled to draw a breath, my knees felt rubbery, as if I'd been going hungry for days. I knew the others felt the same way. But after all this time and all our work, this was our only shot. We went back inside to pack our stuff and get dressed, and Scott called down to Bob at ABC.

"Are you sure?" Bob's voice crackled.

"Absolutely," Scott said.

We retraced our steps up the ridge, through the rock shelf and then White Limbo. Everywhere the snow was hard and crusty, packed down by the wind. The gale-force gusts had faded, but without the cloud cover even the moderate winds were searing cold. My layers of polypro and down did little to warm my toes, and I had to stop regularly, swinging my legs back and forth to keep the blood flowing.

On White Limbo the days of gale-force wind had rendered the slope almost unrecognizable. The windpack had formed sastrugi — an eccentric pattern of uneven ridges and fins. Where the mountainside had once been smooth, the snow now swerved and undulated. We followed our ropes through the ridges for 300 feet. Then Scott turned around and shouted down to us.

"The ropes are gone!"

When I caught up with him, I saw it too. Our rope, once connected to the mountain by three-foot ice pickets, had been ripped completely out of the snow and ice. Now the lines were lying 150 feet away, strewn against the ridges in the snow. From where we were standing I could see the ropes were still intact, but the metal stakes had been torn out of the ice, one after the other, twisted like licorice whips.

Unroped, I walked more slowly despite the cold. Thinking about those metal pickets, twirled like string by the force of the wind. Feeling that much more respect for the mountain and the vast forces of nature. Now we were thinking the winds were light, but when I looked down, I could see the layer of powder constantly blowing across the mountainside. At my feet it blew up into a cloud.

We climbed the rest of the way to Camp 3 without our fixed ropes. As we got higher, the wind started to gust more strongly. When it blew up I'd have to brace myself on my ice ax, leaning down into the slope. The sastrugi made it difficult to find solid footing. I had to watch each step, leaning on my ice ax and planting my crampons with care. We veered left at the top of the slope, then traversed over to where Camp 3, another snow cave, was sunk beneath an ice tower, or serac. We arrived at about two P.M.

The storm had also plugged the entrance to this snow cave, so we spent the next three hours digging our way in. This entry presented a more complex dig than the cave at Camp 2. Because the serac hid a crevasse, we had to go a long way to find snow solid enough to support our cave. In the end the tunnel stretched fourteen feet, swerving left, curving right, then sinking down again into the cave itself. As the smallest in our party I had to do most of the digging, lying flat on my belly. When the tunnel sloped down, Q had to stretch out behind me, holding my ankles.

Once we managed to squeeze inside we fired up the stove to melt some snow for dinner. Beneath the pot the flame sputtered; like human bodies, stoves prefer to work where there's more oxygen. I was exhausted from the day's climb, but that night sleep came hard. The cave was frigid, since the long, diving tunnel worked as a cold sink. Whatever insulation the snow provided was negated as the heat flew up and out, and cold air from outside settled down on us like a blanket. And now that we were above 25,000 feet the altitude squeezed that much harder. Lying perfectly still, muscles relaxed, I could feel the weight pressing against my temples — the pressure of oxygen depletion. I slept fitfully, feeling the months of hard work and harder high-altitude conditions, bones poking through my skin, sore hips and shoulders. And every moment, the cold air biting at my face.

Still, we all woke up the next morning eager to climb higher. We knew we were getting closer. If our luck held we could get to Camp 4 by this afternoon. Then, when the sun rose tomorrow, we could climb out of our tent and head for the summit. We ate quickly that morning, shoveling in the oatmeal with a terse determination. No matter the weather, we had to keep making progress. If we found ourselves beaten back by the wind, we'd never be able to get back up again. We were already behind schedule, thanks to the snowstorm. The Himalayan autumn was eroding, our window of opportunity sliding closed.

I wriggled into my layers of down and then crawled through the tunnel, pushing my pack out ahead of me. I saw daylight ahead of me, and the instant I poked my head outside the cold air burned my eyes. The morning sky was clear and bright, and a cruel wind swept past us. Scott had gone out ahead, and I found him standing by the entrance, struggling with his crampons. I looked over at him.

"Brr!" My voice blew away in the gale. "Kinda cold out here."

Scott looked up. He'd stripped down to one layer of gloves to set his crampons, and the arctic cold was giving him fits.

"My fingers are freezing."

He slithered back into the tunnel to finish setting his crampons out of the cold. Meanwhile, Wes crawled out of the tunnel, slung on his pack, and adjusted the straps. He looked over at me. "Ready to roll?"

We went together, traversing around the front of the serac, then making the abrupt turn where the route continued upward. That's where the wind caught us full in the face. We both looked up at the same moment and saw the summit.

"Oh, shit."

A dense curtain of snow was blowing out into the sky. The cloud of spindrift was so thick it made Everest look like a volcano in full eruption.

"Oh, man, it's gotta be a hundred miles an hour up there," Wes said. When we ducked back behind the serac, Scott and Q were walking toward us. Scott flashed a smile.

"Let's do it!"

We shook our heads. Scott's smile faded.

"What's wrong?"

Wes pointed around the serac, up to the summit. Scott and Q went around to look. A few minutes later they came back.

"A little windy," Scott said. "You don't think we can make it to Camp Four?"

Wes shook his head. "Once we get a little higher I don't think we could even stand up."

I nodded. "We'll have to sit it out until tomorrow." When I caught Scott's eye, he screwed his face into a sour look.

"Shit!" Scott stepped back around the serac and looked up again, as if maybe this time the winds would have died, and the summit might look more inviting. Still, the deadly white banner flew from the top of the mountain. Scott pulled at the straps on his backpack, then walked back to the cave. "Tomorrow," he said, "we're going up this fucking mountain."

Another day in the cave. We sat in silence, each lost in our own thoughts. We'd worked so hard, for so long. We felt fine, even after our week in the snow caves. But here we were again, turned back for another day. After all this time no one had the energy to be angry. For a long time no one said a word. A gust of wind blew a small shower of spindrift through the tunnel, and it fell like hopelessness, into our hair, across our faces, and down our necks.

Drinking coffee a half hour later, we grasped a thin thread of hope. The weather could be better tomorrow. The winds couldn't last forever. "We're too close," Scott said. He set his jaw. His blue eyes turned hard and steely. "There's no way we can stop now."

BUT determination goes only so far. You have to recognize the true limits of survival, to know you can push yourself only so far without disaster. It's another part of that conscious decision I came to during the storm on Mount Robson, the choice between life and death. We had to stop. After the long day and one more freezing, endless night in the snow cave, we crawled outside only to find that, if anything, the winds above were blowing harder.

"Well, that's the ballgame," Scott said. The others came out, and then it took a few moments actually to start downhill. We just stood there. But then Wes took the first step, and Q followed, and then we were all moving, an army in retreat. I allowed myself a moment of mourning, then swallowed hard and boxed it away. I cleared my head and focused on the descent — taking a step, planting my ice ax, taking another step. I had a long way to go before the end of the day.

We started down from Camp 3 in mid-morning, heading across the top slope of White Limbo, then turning straight down the lumpy snowfield. I went slowly — minus the ropes that had flown off in the first storm — focusing on each footfall. We got to Camp 2 at two P.M., then spent the next two and a half hours breaking that camp, loading up the gear, separating out the pads, helmets, and the rest of the hard and soft gear, wrapping it in stuff sacks and tossing it off into the couloir. Down below I could see tiny specks scurrying around — our teammates, chasing after the gear. Heading off again at four-thirty we tried to pick up our pace, hoping to descend to the safety of Camp 1 with as much daylight as possible. It was easy going, at first, following our fixed line down a relatively shallow slope. But after rappelling down the vertical rock band, we turned down a brutal 50-degree snow-and-ice slope. And again, our ropes had vanished.

We went down the next 800 feet unroped, once again being careful to plant each step securely. When a section swooped close to vertical I turned around and faced the slope, walking backward, as if descending a ladder. Most of the way I down-climbed sideways, knees bent, careful each time to plant my crampons in the snow. The descent was murder on my leg muscles and knees; every so often I'd turn around and face the other way, to alternate downhill legs. But for two and a half hours, the constant pressure ripped at my thighs and tore at my knees. By the time we got to the bergschrund and the avalanche cone, my quadriceps felt like they'd been shredded by hot forks.

Scott, Wes, and I got to the bottom of the avalanche cone at eight-thirty. Q was somewhere behind us. Depleted by the altitude, Q had decided to climb down the steep sections with extra care, rather than try to keep up with us. A wise decision, probably, but now that it was past nightfall Wes and I didn't want to let Q get too far behind. Scott went off ahead — "I'll tell 'em we're coming" — while the two of us took off our packs and sat down, waiting for Q to emerge from the darkness.

It was warmer down below, and certainly more sheltered than the windswept faces above. But the night air was still frigid, and the winds still came gusting across the cliffs. Wes and I passed the time by jumping up and down, doing jumping jacks. When we got tired of that, we'd sit back down again, pulling our knees up tight against our chests to conserve body heat. An hour passed, then ninety minutes, but we still saw no sign of Q. We started shouting up toward the bergschrund, shining our headlamps up the avalanche cone, hoping to catch a glimpse. As ten P.M. approached we started feeling a little edgy. Where could Q be? Shouting up to him was a waste of time, with the strong winds. But why couldn't we see the glimmer from his headlamp?

Then we saw it, a twinkling about three-quarters of the way down the ice pitch. Q switched the light off, perhaps to save his batteries, and then we didn't see it for another fifteen minutes. Q finally made it down to us at ten-thirty, stumbling weakly through the uneven snow in the avalanche cone. From there the walk to Camp 1 took an hour. Seeing our lamps approach, they all came flying out of the tents — Scott and Dave, Michael, Mimi, and Geo. They'd already made hot drinks for us and had dinner waiting. I was so exhausted from the descent, and so happy to be back on solid ground and out of the cold, I could almost forget about what didn't happen on the mountain above.

THEN I was too busy to think about it. After breakfast the next morning we started dismantling Camp 1, loading up the gear and hauling loads back toward ABC. We worked at it all day for the next three days, ferrying piles of gear to the edge of the glacier, where our comrades from ABC would pick it up and carry it the rest of the way back. We were also buoyed by our miraculous recovery rate of the gear we'd thrown to the bottom of the couloir. Of all the sacks we'd tossed down from Camp 3 and Camp 2, we lost only one load to the wiles of the mountain.

Once we had everything in ABC, Ben and Peter went down to base camp to look for yaks. The yak herders are usually easy to find in late October. Most years they start coming up from their villages in the middle of the month, waiting for the Everest expeditions to finish packing and start moving out. This year we had no shortage of climbers eager to get back to civilization. We just didn't have many yak herders. Thanks to the snowstorm, most of them were still down in their villages, blocked by miles of impassable roads. The few herders who did somehow get up to base camp were in very high demand. Ben and Peter managed to isolate two or three, and even sit them down to negotiate their salaries. But it seemed that every deal they struck ended up getting broken. Whatever we could afford to offer, the Japanese team would immediately double and the yaksters had no trouble deciding which deal to accept.

After two fruitless days of trying to find a mode of transport to ferry the expedition back to Nepal, Ben sent a desperate note up to Bob at ABC. Scribbling in his terse hand, Ben wrote the bad news as a sort of Top Ten Reasons Why We'll Never Get Out of Here. The roads are still snowed in. The Japanese team keeps outbidding us for yaks. And the number one reason was the killer blow: probably no more yaks till spring. The early snowstorm had already blanketed the paths, and yaks don't do well in deep, soft snow. And thus with winter approaching, and with the rest of the team sitting on a huge pile of equipment at ABC — something like $50,000 worth of stuff, all boxed up and waiting for transportation — we knew we had to work out something quickly or leave it all behind. Luckily, some of the other expeditions took pity on us, and the other American group even sent over a few of their extra yaks to our cause. The other climbers were even kind enough to call Bob on the radio and let him know when someone else tried to stop the yaks en route between camps and outbid us for their services.

"You oughta know about this," the other base camp manager said on his radio call to Bob that afternoon. "I mean, it's your own guy that's trying to do you in down here."

Sure enough, it was Ben himself searching for a way to ship his own gear out of the mountains. Fortunately for us the yaksters decided against taking his counteroffer. Bob and Ungel went down to a nearby village later that afternoon and by the next day managed to rustle up enough yaksters to carry our group loads from ABC to the village of Peru, where we could rent trucks for the journey into Lhasa. Ben had to wait to ship out his stuff with the rest of us.

In the context of team spirit and even fair play, the thought that Ben would actively try to jeopardize the expedition's interests for his own shocked me. But it barely registered a shrug within the remains of our tattered group. By now almost all our pretenses had faded. Without a goal to hold us together, the remnants of the expedition flew apart as fast as legs and yaks and jerry-rigged sleds could carry them. It looked like those photos from the fall of Saigon — if there were helicopters, people would surely have been hanging onto the pontoons, kicking at each other in their rush to get the hell out.

To be fair, Ben wasn't the only one. Rick and Evelyn had left before we even went to the summit, both of them shattered by ill health. Q abandoned us right after we got back to ABC. Rather than waiting for the yaks to come and carry out his gear with the rest of ours, Q decided to become his own yak. He built himself a sled, using his skis as runners and a couple of duffel bags and a tarp as a framework. After he piled his mountain of gear on top, Q used some rope to improvise a harness, slinging it across his chest, and then set off, grunting and straining to pull the massive load across the snow.

The rest of us stayed until both base camps had been broken down. By then the official group responsibilities were finished: the yaks were coming, we had a truck waiting in Peru to carry the expedition gear to the Chinese government warehouse in Lhasa. And as those last days passed we worked together with false, merry faces, as if nothing had transpired among us during the previous three months. With those months behind us and only days ahead, it was easier to walk away in silence.

I could see the darkness in the friends around me. Wes kept his thoughts locked behind his new beard. Scott went sullen, drained by a chain of long days and sleepless nights. I got it the worst carrying the loads from ABC to base camp. After the blizzard made the higher ground impassable for yaks, we all had to ferry our own gear down to base camp. For most of the climbers that meant taking three trips with moderately sized packs. But when Rick and Evelyn pulled out, they'd left their gear behind, thinking the yaks would be able to bring it out. Then the storm changed everything, and since I'd promised to make sure it got out safely, I felt obligated to make sure their gear came home with the rest of our stuff. But when I went through the ranks to solicit some help, I ended up with only a series of shrugs and not-mes.

"They left," Bob said simply. "Their stuff isn't our responsibility."

But it was mine, so I carried all their belongings down myself, making six trips in six days. Each time I loaded on as much as I could possibly carry. Sometimes the contents of my pack would tower a foot and a half over my head, and tail down to the backs of my knees. The burdens were incredible — at least seventy pounds, sometimes more than eighty-five. I'd walk stooped over like an old woman, the pack digging against my hips. I steeled myself each morning by popping a few Percodans. The drugs deadened some of the physical pain, but as I walked alone, tripping under the weight, nothing could stem the dark tide rushing inside me.

Senses deadened by thick mountain glasses and the blare of Walkman earphones, I caromed between the rocks. Sometimes, when I was sure I was alone, I'd collapse in a dry spot and cry. I felt empty, abused by everything I'd ever been foolish enough to dream about. I'd had this feeling, this deep sense, that I was going to make it. That I was going to be the first American woman. I could almost touch it, turn it over in my hand. But then I didn't even come close.

Bending down to sling on that enormous pack, I'd stumble through the scree, through the tears and self-pity. Before we left, the mountain had lent me an identity. A purpose, something to talk about after I said hello. Yeah, I was living at my mother's house, but I had plans. I was DOING something. *You're going to climb Mount Everest? My God!* Now I was heading right back to Woodburn, and this time I had nothing.

8

BECAUSE I'M HERE

IT was raining when I got back to Seattle. I was traveling alone, sitting by myself through the twelve-hour flight from Bangkok. My sister Wendy and her husband, John, met me at the airport. I walked out of customs and found them in the international lounge, and Wendy gave me a cheery smile, the don't-let-it-get-you-down look. Waiting for an elevator in the parking garage, Wendy glanced from my hollow cheeks down to my bony hips and smiled again.

"Looks like you've got a little eating ahead of you."

Talking to John and Wendy at lunch, I tried to put a brave face on the climb. Demolishing a salad, then a cheeseburger and chocolate milkshake, I told them about the beauty of the Tibetan plain, the clear days on the mountain when the Himalayas stretched out beneath us in every direction. And we'd gotten so high on the mountain. Working a route that had been climbed only once, we'd managed to push ourselves a long way into the sky before the weather blew us back down.

Wendy nodded, eager to get the mountain behind us. "You did what you could," she said. "You got back alive. That's all you needed to do."

Was it really? I shrugged and looked away, out the window toward downtown Seattle. It was easier to say than to believe.

When we got back to their house, I sat in the living room, looking out of the window and watching the rain falling, gathering into thick drops and hanging from the telephone wires and the bare tree limbs. The entire world looked gray — the clouds, the buildings, the sidewalks, the raindrops. It all seemed so bleak. Even the trees were skeletons, dripping wet and shivering in the wind. Right then I felt just as bare, suddenly back in America and having to readjust to life at home.

I had a few short-term prospects. After Christmas I would come back to Seattle to help tidy up the final details for the expedition. The work would keep me busy for most of a month and, better still, would pay ten dollars an hour, so I wouldn't have to spend my first weeks in the States worrying about making money. I went over to see Scott the day after I got back, thinking we could put together a working schedule for January. He'd already been home for a few weeks, and when I found him in his scruffy Mountain Madness office in West Seattle, Scott had a fresh haircut and a new pair of Levi's. He was full of energy, and his eyes and cheeks had regained their usual glow. But it wasn't just the reunion with his wife and son that had reignited his jets. Scott jumped out of his chair when he saw me in the doorway, slapped his arms around my shoulders, and quickly dispensed with his how-are-yous. "Guess what?" Scott grinned at me. "I found another expedition to Everest. They're going up the South Col next summer."

"You're kidding."

"I already sent both of our résumés."

Another trip to Everest? I'd barely set foot back in the USA, hadn't even unpacked my boots and crampons. I wasn't ready to think about the climb I'd just finished, much less find the energy to plan for another one. But suddenly Scott had us headed right back to the airport, back up the muddy road to the rocky moraine at base camp. But with whom?

"Ahh." Scott waved his hand dismissively. "Local guys, all from Seattle. They're a bunch of jokers. Good old boys. I suppose they know what they're doing."

I could tell Scott wasn't wild about having to apply to someone else's expedition when he was so used to leading his own. I felt it, too. After three years of building our own expedition our own way, we were back to being supplicants. Someone else was going to look us over and decide if we were good enough to join them.

Seeing the distaste in my eyes, Scott smiled and wagged a finger. "Aw, it'll be fine. We can handle these guys. Worse comes to worst you and I'll stick together."

As 1987 ended I drove back to Woodburn for another Christmas. The familiar warmth of the family was comforting, and after a few days I felt myself lightening up. I wasn't exactly sure how I was going to get rolling again, but at least I had already started the process. If there's an upside to transition, it's having the freedom to reinvent yourself.

But in what form? If I decided to go back to Everest, I'd have to devote myself to that mountain for another year. Was I ready to keep the rest of my life on hold? There were, after all, two promising lights glimmering on the horizon. And only one of them led back to Mount Everest.

It had started a year earlier, a few months before I left for the first trip to Everest. I was spending one of my last days in Springdale, and went hiking with a few friends. One of them happened to bring along Nancy Shute, a writer who did a lot of pieces for *Outside,* and when she heard I was headed back to Oregon, Nancy's face lit up. "You ought to call my brother David," she said. "He's an excellent guy. He's just finishing his residency in Portland, but don't let that put you off. He's actually pretty normal. He climbs and he knows some great people."

Nancy gave me her brother's telephone number, and I scribbled it in my address book and brought it with me to my mom's house in Woodburn. When I got curious one night, I decided to call him. I found the number in my book and dialed, letting it ring ten or twelve times before hanging up. I tried again the next night, but when I couldn't raise an answer again, I slammed down the phone. Forget it, I thought. If I can't even get in touch with the guy to say hello, it's just not meant to be.

So I forgot about the number in my book. Then a week passed. I was reading after dinner, and the telephone rang. "Stacy? This is David Shute calling. Nancy gave me your number."

There was something in his voice — a pleasant, relaxed tone. He sounded friendly. Not too awkward, but not too smooth, either. We chatted for a few minutes — about Nancy, about where I'd lived in Utah. Conversation flowed so naturally it made me feel we already knew each other. After a while we started talking about going out. He was taking modern dance lessons, David said, and his teacher was giving a performance. Did I want to go? "Sure," I said. I started thinking aloud, planning my schedule. I knew I needed to work out, and when I mentioned it David picked up on it immediately.

"Why don't we go running that afternoon?"

"Great. Then we can get something to eat before the show."

"And maybe some dessert afterwards."

Then there was a silence. "Gee," I said. "That's about the whole day, isn't it?"

"Yeah." He laughed. "What if we don't like each other?"

But I did like him, even though I was surprised by how young he looked. David was twenty-eight then, but when he opened the door at his house I was sure I was looking at a roommate, or maybe someone's seventeen-year-old brother. This was a doctor? He had such a baby face, such twinkly blue eyes and neatly cropped blond hair. The guys I saw who looked this young were usually toting around skateboards. Sitting in the restaurant that night, I realized how much I liked looking into his eyes. They were so tranquil, but still gleaming with life. And he would look right at me when I talked, and listen to what I said without judging me. Just being with him made me feel more relaxed.

I enjoyed spending time with David, but I knew I wasn't ready to start a relationship. We dated casually for a while, sharing a few dinners and then some day trips as the spring brightened into summer. David was planning a trip to Asia that fall, so we hooked up after Everest and traveled through Asia for five weeks. Then David headed for Sumatra and I packed up for home, but the time together had deepened our bond. We left knowing that we'd pick up where we left off when he returned to Oregon in February.

So now there was David. He was so different from Mark, blond instead of brown-haired, fair-skinned instead of dark. David's eyes were smooth and waterlike, rather than flashing with sparks. David's voice was always gentle, and even when we had disagreements there was never any fierceness, only a measured jump in animation. I wasn't the easiest woman to get to know — it was still so soon after my divorce — but David made it easier. He moved slowly and waited for me to catch up. Sometimes it took a while for me to get up the courage to round the corner, but when I did I usually found him there, smiling gently with that look of perfect aplomb.

When we first started dating, back before the '87 expedition, sometimes it was hard for me to believe it was really happening again. Less than six months since my divorce, and here I was dating this guy. He seemed so gentle, so patient and good-natured . . . but once Mark had seemed like all those things, too. I'd pull David closer, then feel something jump inside me, and push him away again. Why did he want me? Why would anyone want me? One day, driving home from a day of rock climbing, I posed the question to his face.

"Why are you doing this?"

"Doing what?"

"Spending time with me."

David was silent, peering out at the road ahead. "I want to help you, I guess."

Help me? Now I could hear the condescension in his voice. "Why?" I snapped back at him. "Am I some kind of psychiatric project for you?"

David peered back at me, his face expressionless, but a set of question marks large in his eyes. "No," he said, gently. "I'm being selfish. I think you have great potential as a lover."

What a strange thing to say, I thought, and then I laughed happily.

So I had two roads to follow, but at least for the time being I could pursue them both in Portland. After the holidays I spent a few days driving through the city's neighborhoods with a real estate agent, looking to buy a small house. I had enough money for a fixer-upper, and once I had it in good shape I figured I could put it back on the market and make a profit. My family liked to think I was finally settling down again. They were less excited about my hazy plans to go back to Everest. One night during the holidays, when I mentioned Scott's idea to get us both on the new expedition, dinner conversation ground to a sudden halt. My sisters and brother looked at each other, silently.

"I don't see why you've got to go back," Wendy said sharply. "You were there once. Can't that be enough?"

I shrugged. "No."

A week after New Year's I packed my suitcase again and drove back up to Seattle to spend January working on the final details of the '87 expedition. Scott and I had about four weeks of work ahead of us. I had promised the equipment manufacturers that we'd keep close track of their products on the mountain, and now I had more than thirty items to evaluate and write up. Fortunately I had a lot of material to work with; before we started, Ev and I had given each climber a notebook of critique forms, one for each piece of gear and clothing we needed to grade. Back home I compiled the comments and then listed a few of the most striking comments and suggestions. Scott and I also went through our slides looking for the photographs that featured an individual product to good effect.

We were just wrapping up the last details of '87 AENFE when the deputy leader of the '88 expedition called. Don Goodman had climbed in the Northwest for years, and he already knew Scott's reputation. When he phoned us at the Mountain Madness office, Don was pleasant, even encouraging, but far from committed. They were going to interview applicants next week, he said. "Can you both come to our meeting next Thursday?"

Scott gave me a thumbs-up. "Absolutely. We'll be there."

Scott was grinning when he hung up, but I wasn't so sure. What could I tell them about myself to convince them to take me? I was still trying to resolve what had happened during the failed '87 climb. For the first time in my life, I'd come back from a climb feeling as if I'd lost something. For the first time, the time I spent actually climbing on the mountain didn't seem important to me. So what mattered? The summit? The First American Woman title? Was that the only reason I climbed mountains these days, to try to make a name by beating other women to the top of the world? I looked at Scott and shook my head.

"I don't want to go to any interview."

"Oh, come on."

"Really."

"Don't be such a baby. It'll be a breeze."

Scott waved his hand, and the issue was closed. I was going to be in Seattle only a few more days, and I let him pull me along. We were supposed to meet at Dave Hambly's house, an apartment in a modern building at the base of Queen Anne Hill near Puget Sound. Hambly, one of the older climbers in the group, was a British man in his late forties. His long face was shielded almost completely by a short beard and wire-frame glasses. Don Goodman was wide and chunky, Hemingwayesque. Johnny Petroske, the baby face in the group, stood in the back, smiling and looking like the representative from the senior class of Jesuit High. They all seemed nice enough, and Diana Dailey, the only woman on the team, made a particular effort to be friendly to me.

Now here was an athlete. Behind her smile Diana was all bone and sinew, weathered skin stretched taut over ridges of muscles, the veins popping out and stretching in all directions like a 3-D roadmap. For a woman in her mid-forties, Diana was a phenomenon. When she wasn't lecturing to her math classes or coaching the Ingraham High School track team, she kept up a fierce athletic regimen that would leave most high school jocks in the gutter. The seventy miles she ran each week helped keep Diana a top distance runner in her age class, but she was also a solid rock climber and mountaineer. Diana's obvious strength had not gone unnoticed by the climbing media. According to the murmurs of conventional wisdom, she was one of the odds-on favorites for bringing home the First American Woman title during the '88 Everest season. Diana seemed to enjoy the glory, but that didn't dim her big smile when I walked into her life. "I've heard so much about you," she said, gripping my one hand with her two. "It'll be great to get another woman on board."

I wasn't the only woman currently being considered to fill out the team. Peggy Luce, a twenty-eight-year-old bicycle deliverywoman in Seattle, had also applied for the expedition. Although far from an experienced climber — she had climbed only on Mount Rainier and Mount Baker, both in the North Cascades — Peggy was just as good an athlete as Diana. Spending her days pumping the pedals up and down the Seattle hills had done great things for her cardiovascular system.

The other male applicant, a wiry forty-two-year-old doctor named Jean (rhymes with Shawn) Ellis, also came with more athletic than Alpine experience. The only high-altitude climbing he'd done was on a guided climb on Annapurna IV, but Jean had been a top marathon runner in the early eighties, placing as an alternate on the 1980 Olympic team. Despite both Peggy's and Jean's excellent condition, it seemed a little strange to me that neither applicant had any significant high-altitude experience. Not that *everyone* on an expedition needs to have elite climbing credentials. And maybe this expedition already had its fill of top-flight climbers.

It was hard to get a handle on the team's depth because only a few members greeted us that night. Some of the climbers lived in other cities, Don explained, and even a few locals weren't in town, including team leader Jim Frush, who was off trying to write a novel in Nepal. Deputy leader Don called the meeting to order, and as he introduced himself to the newcomers Don waved his beefy hands in the air and cracked a few jokes at his own expense. "My role on the expedition," he explained, dark eyes twinkling, "is to make everyone else look good." We all laughed, and then the team members ran through their usual meeting agenda, discussing food and equipment and fund-raising. It took almost an hour for them to come around to interviewing their four candidates. Don focused on me first.

"So, Stacy," he began, absently clicking the ballpoint in his great paw. "Why should we invite you to join our team?"

I scrambled for an answer, then heard my own voice.

"Because I'm a nice person."

Don guffawed, craning his thick neck to look at the others as they tittered. I smiled weakly. I'd take the laugh, but I hadn't meant to make a joke. What a stupid answer. Grasping for something more articulate, I paused a moment, then started again. This time I focused on my climbing experience, a recap of the mountains and routes I'd been on, concluding with our recent bout with the North Face of Everest. "I'm a team player," I said. "I want to be part of the team, and I want to stand on the summit."

That seemed to make an okay impression. Goodman nodded, scribbled something onto his paper, then moved on to Scott, sitting just to my right.

"I wanna climb Everest," Scott began. He listed his achievements as a climber and as a leader. He knew how to give orders and how to take them, Scott said. He knew how to handle authority. When he was finished, Don nodded, said okay, and then moved down the line.

Peggy Luce, the bright-eyed, dark-haired bicycle messenger, started off by admitting her lack of mountain experience. "I don't mind being a support climber," she said. "I just want to go."

Jean Ellis spoke last, and also acknowledged his inexperience. But Jean emphasized his capabilities. He was strong and fit, an excellent candidate for high-altitude exertion. He also didn't mind working as a support climber, Jean said. And having another doctor on board would only make the trip safer. What's more, he had a unique angle. "I'll be the only black man climbing on Everest this year," he said. "It's a great angle for raising money."

So that was it, and when the interviews ended we all had a few beers and talked mountain talk for a while. After Scott and I left, I felt relieved. It wouldn't be like climbing with old friends, but at least Don and Dave had Everest experience. Dave had climbed in the Himalayas five times. And once Johnny opened up I learned that he had a decent résumé, too, a long history with the volcanoes in South America. We hadn't met everyone, and there were still a few mysteries in the group, but on the whole they seemed like decent people.

"They'll seem even better," Scott said, "once they invite us."

I smiled. "They will."

WE wrapped up the last details of '87 AENFE a few days later. I repacked my bag and drove back to my mother's house in Woodburn. Then the call came one evening after dinner. It was Don, and I could still hear the self-deprecating grin in his big, booming voice.

"I just wanted to officially invite you to join us," he said, and then I didn't hear much else. We talked for a few minutes, and by the end I had agreed to help Johnny Petroske procure the equipment. I didn't have the nerve to ask him the one question I was dying to have answered, though. *What about Scott? He's going too, right?* So the moment Don hung up I dialed Scott's number in Seattle. He picked up on the second ring.

"Did you talk to Don?"

"Yeah."

Something caught in Scott's voice, and for a moment I couldn't believe it.

"Don't tell me they didn't —"

"They didn't."

"You mean they took *Jean* and *Peggy*, and not you?"

"So it seems."

"You're kidding!"

Now I wasn't sure what to say. I never imagined they wouldn't invite Scott. Especially with two marginal climbers as competition, I figured they'd be more than happy to sign on a climber with Scott's résumé. "It's nuts," I said. "It's too weird." I thought for a moment, then blurted it out: "I don't think I'll go now."

Scott sighed. "Don't be stupid."

"No, really. If they don't take you, then —"

"— then they don't take me." He was being brave, a nice guy. "It's a drag, but you can't let that stop you. You've got a nice chance here. It's not a bad group, and they're organized. Go for it. I'll find another expedition."

So that was it. If I was going to go, it would have to be without Scott. I'd be on that huge mountain, with no one I knew to hold down the other end of the rope. How did this happen? Scott was going to be my anchor, the one person I knew I could trust, and Hambly and Goodman et al. decided he wasn't good enough. Something had tipped the scales in an odd direction, but what? Was it the money Jean said he could raise, or the prospect of having three women on board — and three chances to hoist the First American Woman to the top? Or was it something else, something about Scott that put them off? Maybe he was *too* experienced for them, unable to sit back and let someone else tell him what to do. Peggy was so gung-ho, she and Jean had both made it clear that they'd do *anything* to be part of the team . . . packing boxes, sweet-talking donors, spending weeks humping oxygen bottles out of base camp. And would a Golden Boy climber want to do that? So Scott didn't qualify.

I had so many reasons not to go. I wasn't sure I could trust my life to these people. I was still so burned from last year's disasters, still so shy about committing to anything. If I couldn't get along with friends on Everest, how was a group of strangers going to deal with one another? And what would it do to David? It's hard to pretend you're serious about building a relationship with someone if you spend four months of each year gallivanting in the Himalayas. And to top it off, I *still* wasn't sure if I was in touch with the real reasons why I might want to go.

Even so, I told Don to count me in. With or without Scott, with or without a clear sense of why I was doing this, or even if I *wanted* to do it, the pull of Everest was still too strong for me to shut the door. Don told me the date of their next meeting in Seattle and I promised to drive up to attend. And so I was on the team in body, if not totally in spirit.

I was back on the Everest path again, but at the same time I was with David in the Willamette Valley; we were spending all of our free time and most of our nights together. But I had to find a way to support myself. I knew I wanted to be a builder, and even though my blonde hair and slight body might at first seem out of place on a male-dominated job site, I figured my background as co-owner of Austin Enterprises in Utah would at least allow me to jam a toe in someone's door. But sexism died harder than I thought it might. Large men in wool shirts would grin into their coffee cups and wish me luck when I handed over my résumé. Developers in striped suits would grow quickly impassive, gazing past me even as I shook their hands.

Immediate rejection was bad enough. Then it got worse. One builder, a thick man named Tony, actually hired me to work on his construction crew. I happened to walk in the afternoon someone else had walked out, and after he glanced at my résumé, he decided to hire me. "We're starting a job on Monday," Tony said, writing down an address in a new subdivision in Gresham, a rapidly expanding suburb east of the city. "Be there at seven."

I came home ecstatic, but later that evening Tony called back. Discovering I wasn't home, Tony figured he'd break the bad news to my mother.

"Tell Stacy I can't hire her after all," Tony explained. "My crew won't stand for it."

Maybe Tony thought he was getting off easy, missing me and delivering the message secondhand. Unfortunately for Tony, my mother had no intention of letting him get off easy. She knew how hard it was for a woman to get a leg up in this world. She was furious! "What sort of a boss are you?" Mom snapped. For a moment there was a silence.

"What?"

"I can't believe you're letting your *employees* control you like that. That's how you do business? What sort of business do you run out there?"

"Well, it's not me, it's *them* —"

"You're the boss, aren't you?"

Tony muttered something — *sorry nothing personal it's business gotta go* — and then, click, slapped his phone back on the cradle. When I got home, Mom was still livid.

"What a weak-kneed man he is," she sputtered. "You're *lucky* he didn't hire you."

Perhaps. But I still needed to find a job.

I knew I wanted to start my own business eventually, but I wasn't ready yet. I wanted to get some local experience, not only to develop a professional reputation in Oregon, but also to prove to myself that I could work without Mark's guiding hand. I went back to my leaf-letting mode, making the rounds of builders and construction companies to distribute my résumé. Then I heard about an opening on a framing crew. The company was called T & R Construction, and according to their ad they needed to hire experienced framers immediately. Well, hey. *I* had some framing experience. A little bit, anyway. This wasn't something I had done a lot of with Mark, but framing a house is a crucial and fundamental part of building: the assembling of the structure's skeleton, pounding in the studs, the floor joists, gluing and nailing the plywood, the roof, the windows, sometimes the doors. It's the lowest possible position on a construction crew, a post that involves a lot of hammer-swinging, no brain-wave action, and a relatively small hourly wage. But it was building, and that's what I wanted to do. And when I called at the office — jaw set, shoulders tense, already anticipating the big brush-off — I was stunned. The co-owner was actually glad to see me.

"I'm glad you called." This was Wayne, the paperwork partner in the business. He found the jobs and worked the books while his partner, Dan, the less outgoing of the two, coordinated the work site. But Wayne had a lot of building experience, and he liked what I told him about my days in Utah. "I am *really* glad you came over," he said. "We've been looking for a woman."

"Really."

"Sure. Have you framed houses before?"

Barely. But I figured I'd be a fast learner. "Sure."

"Good. How about roofs? We do a lot of complex roofs, so we're looking to get more experience up there."

Roofs were another weak point of mine. But, again, I figured I'd be a fast study.

"Excellent." Wayne shifted some papers on his desk. "Can you start tomorrow morning?"

On my way home I drove over to a bookstore, bought four how-to books on framing and roofing, and spent the rest of the day locked in my room, reading. If I had to fake it, I figured, I might as well be well informed.

I tiptoed in to work the next morning, but I soon realized that everything would be fine. I swung my hammer and watched carefully. I made a study of Mike, the crew's most talented roofer. I read my books at night and learned as much as I could. The crew was young and friendly; they even seemed to like having a woman around. Once I proved that I could hold my own with a hammer and level, they even went out of their way to do some of the muscle work for me, carrying the big loads that were beyond my small frame. Wayne let me adjust my hours to make time for my afternoon workouts.

Working on the framing crew reminded me of why I had grown to love the business so much in Utah. Even when the work was boring, as it usually is when you're jumping from work site to work site doing one small series of basic tasks, there's a dignity to helping create a structure that will shelter people for generations. The work is fulfilling as a concept, and I loved it as a process, too: the logical progression of the work, the gradual realization, nail by nail, of a vision. No matter what happens, no matter how frustrating the events of the day, you can always step back at the end of the afternoon and see your work, see what the power of your mind and muscles has forged.

The one good thing I took away from my marriage, other than the cash settlement, was what Mark had taught me about building. We never built complex, multilayer roofs in Utah — that kind of house wouldn't fit into the aesthetics of the desert environment — but I learned quickly, and by the end of the winter I had a stronger grasp on that part of the building trade.

THE mountain gnawed on me that winter. I'd turn it around in my mind during the day, or it would turn me around in my bed at night. I'd lie there, staring blankly at the ceiling. Did I really want to go to Everest again? I still felt so drawn to that immense, crooked pyramid, still so driven to put myself on the top. I'd set out to do it — I mean *really* set out to do it — six years ago. Why was I still so compelled to climb that one mountain? I knew that the vision of Everest I had carried with me in 1987 had been perverse. I had started out with the right idea, I thought, but somewhere along the line something had flown off course. By the time I set foot on the mountain, the climbing itself, the actual step-by-step that had once been the great joy of my life, had become almost irrelevant. It struck me that I couldn't remember a single moment on Everest when I felt my spirit rise and merge with the mountain. It had always happened on other climbs — a flash of overwhelming delight, a sudden warmth. But it didn't happen this time, and when I got home I could understand why. From the moment I stepped out of base camp I was too preoccupied to see where I was and to feel what I was doing. Every step of the way, my thoughts were on the summit. The experience had left me bitter, which was something climbing had never done before.

But no matter how I felt then, maybe I'd feel different next time.

The annual Ski and Outdoor trade show came up again in March, and so I flew down to Las Vegas with a few of the team members to raise our expedition flag and chat up the manufacturers. Don Goodman was our point man during the long weekend, and our co-leader took on the throng of corporate reps like a presidential candidate. He did his own advance work, scoping out the booths on the floor ahead of time so he could impress each manufacturer with his good-natured charm and singular expertise on their product. For Johnny Petroske, just being at the trade show was a kick, and the sight of all that brand-new gear — tens of thousands of square feet of the latest, most advanced outdoor equipment — kept him happy all day. A boy-genius computer wonk for the Boeing Company, he'd already winnowed all our equipment needs down to definitive figures. Occasionally I'd take issue with one of his numbers — don't we need a few more pairs of long johns there? how about a few more carabiners for the route? — and Johnny would listen, always noting my opinion, but then patiently pointing out how his computations had brought him to his first number. "You see," he'd conclude, "I ran it through the computer."

Diana Dailey came to Vegas, too, and she and I shared a hotel room for the weekend. It was easy to like Diana, she was so friendly, so full of her own brand of high-octane energy. Diana talked and talked and talked, about her running, about training for the climb, about the other guys on the team, and weren't they all so *nice?* It was a happy surprise that the other experienced woman climber on the team would be so excited about having me on the expedition. Until I joined the team Diana had been the sole focus of the team's First American Woman hype. The attention delighted her, but even so, the thought of having another woman to climb with, and perhaps compete with, didn't put her off. At this point the race for the First American Woman crown was the last thing I wanted to talk about, but Diana had already reached a provision for how we women would settle the issue: we'd be on the same summit team and climb up together. Peggy was a support climber, so it was just the two of us heading for the summit. And going together was so fair and correct and so simple.

We didn't all get the same charge from Diana's nonstop electric current. Jim Frush was with us now, our leader, back from his sabbatical in Nepal, and from the moment I saw them together I could tell he didn't have much patience for Diana. When Jim figured Diana had gone on a bit too long, he never hesitated to interrupt her in midsyllable, changing the subject to some other topic or just cutting her off: "Diana. Be quiet."

Jim never said much, but I always had the sense something was churning beneath his surface. Jim was a handsome man in his mid-thirties, tall and muscular, dark-eyed, with shiny brown hair parted on the side and a dark mustache. He smiled down at me warmly. "It's so great to finally meet you!" He can be quite charming, but his years as a lawyer navigating the criminal code have left Jim with an instinctive caginess. He chooses his words carefully. When I finally had a chance to ask him why the group had decided not to invite Scott on the expedition, Jim got a serious look on his face and frowned. "Well, Stacy," he said. "I wasn't there. So I don't really know why. But the others just decided he might not really fit in." Now he smiled. "But I'm really glad *you* could join us!"

We had regular monthly meetings that spring, and as the out-of-town members gradually appeared I began to feel more comfortable with the team. There was talent here. Experience, people who had scaled some impressive peaks and then come back with the right ideas. Steve Ruoss, our thirty-four-year-old doctor from San Francisco, had sharp eyes, a pointed sense of humor, and a good dose of that Hippocratic air of supercompetence. Steve took a lot of responsibility, but never hesitated to speak up when a good critical word seemed necessary. And Steve shared his dry wise-guy wit with his doctor pal, Geoff Tabin, a short, bearded climber from Chicago. At thirty-two, Geoff had already climbed on Everest twice, and he was clearly determined to pull himself up to the top. His life's ambition, Geoff told everyone, was to be the first Jew to stand on top of Mount Everest. He delivered the line as though it was a joke, but I could tell Geoff was absolutely serious.

I had found a house in North Portland, a small postwar bungalow in a family neighborhood by the University of Portland. It was a cozy house, and in good enough shape to move into immediately. But even on my first walk-through I could count the changes I wanted to make. The place would need a new kitchen, for starters. A renovated bathroom would be next, then refinished oak floors and new paint everywhere. A lot of work to fill my free time, but I didn't mind. More than a year after my divorce I still had a lot of rebuilding to do.

I noticed it with David. We were still dating seriously, eating dinner together most evenings and spending our weekends rock climbing or biking or just going to the movies. We'd built a circle of friends we cared about, and who cared about us, but shadows from the past still lurked.

It would hit me at the oddest times. Play-wrestling and tickling each other around the living room, I'd feel a sudden bolt of terror. David was always gentle, but then I'd look through him and see Mark. I'd have to sit alone for a few minutes, breathing deeply, trying to calm myself. Other times, when David was out somewhere with his own friends, I'd track the passing minutes with a deepening dread. If he came over late, I'd confront him angrily to drill for explanations, searching for inconsistencies in his story.

"You said you'd be here at nine. It's almost ten-thirty."

"We had a few beers."

"For three hours?"

Hanging up his jacket, David would furrow his brow and peer down at me.

"Well, we had burgers, too, and then we played pool."

"Look, if you're having an affair, just tell me. Don't lie to me."

At this, blood would flow into his cheeks and his voice would rise a notch. "You know I don't deserve this."

Of course he didn't. I had no evidence, no real indication that anything was wrong. But I was sure it was going to happen. That even if he weren't having an affair now, he would someday. As much as I wanted to trust him, I just couldn't. Not after what happened before. So I kept something between us. A distance I could never quite surrender.

David understood. He knew about my marriage with Mark, and he knew enough about psychology, but understanding something doesn't necessarily make dealing with it any easier, and my fits of panic and perpetual distance frustrated him. David is a talker, he prefers to chew over his problems. I tend to swallow mine and keep them to myself. But as the months passed, it was obvious the shadows from my marriage were too dense to navigate alone. Even as I pushed him away David pushed back, insisting that I confront my past. "You don't have to do it alone," he said. "If you want to go to therapy, I'd like to go along."

So we started seeing a therapist together, and we worked to rebuild my reflexes to physical contact, to erase the ingrained fear that had grown out of Mark's flashes of violence. And again, we made advances, sometimes through discussions, sometimes through "nice touch" exercises, communicating through backrubs and other routine intimacies. Gradually I relaxed my guard with David, and then I tried to relax within myself.

I had always pushed myself. Growing up in my family, competing with my sisters and brother, I always worked to be better, to ski better than I had before, to get better grades, to swim faster. Part of that compulsion had been healthy: I wanted to see what I was capable of doing, to see if I could reach the horizon beyond the one ahead of me. When I was first with Mark, I felt we could do anything. I thought we had a synergy — *together we could have everything!* But then something changed. I grew to depend on him. Eventually my dependence dwarfed my own strength, and then I felt strong *only* when I was with Mark. But I was blind to his weakness, and when he spun me into his orbit I was too weak to hold on to my own sense of reality. When the violence started, our pattern was set. We were locked together, beyond reason. By the time Mark slapped the divorce papers in my hand my entire sense of self had been whittled away.

The day Mark left me, I ran over to Randy Aton's house and collapsed on his shoulder. "I'll never find anyone again," I wailed. Randy tried to comfort me, telling me how screwed up Mark was, how screwed up he'd always been, but I knew better. I careened through those weeks, even sinking so low, one gloomy night, that I found myself contemplating suicide. It never went further than a thought, but the moment was chilling. I had been emptied — seeking strength, I'd ended up losing my own — and now I felt so worthless, I could actually imagine, even briefly, that I'd be better off dead. At that moment I knew I wasn't contributing anything to life. And life, in turn, held nothing for me.

Except the summit of Everest. The First American Woman. By the time I got to Tibet that title represented everything I thought I needed: a new identity, a new sense of self. The fact I didn't take those last few steps onto the summit overwhelmed all the other steps I'd taken on that journey. When I looked ahead, I could see only the top of Everest.

Before, I climbed for purer reasons — for the challenge and excitement, the beauty of the wilderness and the friendships that grew there. Curt and I didn't climb the Cassin Ridge to impress people or earn a place in some record book. We chose the harder route on Mount McKinley because it posed a physical and mental challenge.

That's how I saw it then, but then things got tangled. When I let the First American Woman race capture my spirit, when I let myself believe that one title would change my life, I lost sight of my true reasons for climbing. That's why I found it so hard to commit myself to the '88 expedition: I couldn't bear to push myself for the wrong reasons. *It's not enough for me to believe in what I'm doing. I have to believe in the reasons I'm doing it.* Now I had to come to terms with the truth: that a personal triumph does not come from winning a race. No, it comes only after you can take a good, honest look at yourself. The real triumph comes when you can accept yourself in any weather and in any state, and still be able to say: That's me, and I'm okay.

FOR me that meant more than coming to terms with my own sense of climbing. I also had to make sure I understood how my climbing affected the other people in my life. Mountain climbing is an exceptionally selfish sport, after all. Going after a big peak means making a stiff investment in both money and time. You're gone for months on end, off in the most remote, dangerous corners of the globe, in the subzero temperatures, the freight-train gales, the murderous snowstorms, the tomblike crevasses spiraling here and there beneath your boots . . . perhaps only just beneath the thin crust of powder snow that your left foot is about to burst through. . . . Imagine how it feels to be left alone at home. Waking up in the middle of the night, reaching over and feeling the cold half of the bed where your mate should be — but that mate is in Nepal right now. When the telephone rings, late at night, you swallow hard before answering. You never know what you might hear. The other side of the bed may never be warm again.

I always heard the rumblings from my own family. *It's so selfish of her, going off to climb and God only knows when or if she's coming home. . . .* Couldn't I see what I was doing to them? Hadn't the family had enough of people just disappearing? It's hard to keep caring about someone, after all, if she seems bent on self-destruction. Resentment comes easier. A certain detachment. It's a defense mechanism, the way your arms shoot out to break your fall when you trip. It's less painful to fend it off than to take it head-on.

David thought about it seriously when we first started dating. I was preparing for the '87 expedition then, gradually putting everything else on hold. He saw me getting excited, conceivably preparing to walk off the face of the earth, and he had to ask himself: *Do I really want to fall in love with a woman who has this dangerous avocation?* The man was a doctor, he knew about probability, and he knew what violent death looked like. In the end, however, he figured he could take the risk. Later he told me I spurred him along by promising that Everest '87 would be my last peak. "This'll be it for me," I said. "The last big mountain."

Then I started to change my mind. Once I had a clearer vision of what climbing meant to me I remembered why I had been so drawn to Everest in the first place. And the more time I spent with the other climbers the more I came to appreciate them. I liked them. I could trust them. I could imagine climbing with them. So I was in tune with myself, with my climbing partners. The people on the mountain, I concluded, were not going to be a problem. But what about the people at home? I understood the selfishness involved, I could see how hard it would be to watch me walk back into the unforgiving realm of steep ice and rock. But I needed their support. Before I left I needed to know that they understood why the mountain was so important to me. And as the spring waned and the expedition drew close, I knew I had to make my case.

Even before I made up my mind to go back to Everest I knew one thing for certain: if David ever told me *not* to go — *it's me or Everest, take your pick* — I would have immediately chosen Mount Everest. As much as I loved David, I just wasn't about to change my life to suit the purposes of any man. Fortunately I never had to make that decision. David understood me better than that.

He could see it from the first time we ever went rock climbing together. It's an intense focus, he says. A clarity in my eyes that I get only when I'm climbing. My voice gets higher, the words become more animated and flow faster. It's almost like I'm in a trance, I seem so completely connected to what I'm doing. There was something deeper going on. Something he wasn't going to try to unwire. "I know it's important to you," he'd say. "If you want to go, I'll be here when you get back." And he left it at that.

But what about my family? I had already sensed my sister's disapproval — *why do you need to go back?* — and I had long since assumed my mother felt the same way. When I first started rock climbing, and then venturing off on my first mountain expeditions, she never held back her opinions. Why did I have to center my life around something so dangerous? At first she made a point of telling me why she didn't like my climbing. I ignored her, but even when she stopped I always assumed she felt the same way, but had just gotten tired of talking to a fence post. I underestimated her.

I always underestimated my mother. She was devastated when my father left, and that image stayed burned in my mind. I remembered how she cried at night for months, how she seemed resigned to living a smaller life in his absence, rather than starting a new one. When Mark left, I was terrified that my life was doomed to be an echo of hers, a sad life of limitations and disappointments.

But I was wrong about my life, because I was wrong about her life. What limitations? My mother is the personification of strength. Maybe she was crushed when my father left, but then she pulled herself together and went on as a single woman. She raised five kids by herself. She worked full-time — the same tough job, counseling delinquent adolescents — for twenty-five years. She had grown to understand why I climb. She knew exactly why I had to climb Mount Everest.

"Of course you should go," she said. "Climbing is how you express yourself."

And that's exactly what climbing is to me. That's why I was drawn to the sport, and why I continue devoting myself to it. *Expression.* What a painter does on a canvas, what a writer can do with the twenty-six letters in the alphabet. It's the key that unlocks my spirit, the clearest representation of who I am. When I'm focused, climbing is almost an unconscious act for me. I don't have to drive myself, I'm already driven. Always higher, never bothering to look down, never worrying about what I might find above me. There may be difficulties ahead — of course, there *will* be difficulties. Life is a constant maze of problems and puzzles. But now that you're alive the key question is, how do you respond? And what does your solution say about your life?

BEFORE British mountaineer George Leigh Mallory died on Everest in 1924, someone asked him a question: Why do you want to climb Mount Everest? He came up with an answer that was simple and almost Zen-like in its clarity: *Because it is there.* It sounded so brave, so daring. You could see the shrug in his shoulders, the steely glint in his eye. *Because it is there.* It had the ring of manifest destiny, of a struggle and a hard-won victory. *Because it is there,* Mallory said, and his words have defined all those who climbed after him. You could taste the conquest. The battle was joined, and once again Man would emerge victorious. He had seen, gone, and, of course, conquered.

But that's not why I climb.

I climb because *I'm* here.

I don't battle the mountains. I don't conquer anything, even when I do pull myself onto a summit. For me the triumph comes in every step, in every breath and heartbeat. It's the sheer pleasure of being on the planet, of seeing the mountains around me and, for a brief moment, being a part of them. My spirit leaps, my voice joins the heavenly chorus of the living. I climb for a simple reason: because I'm alive. And that's why I went back to Mount Everest.

9

BUILDING THE ROUTE

AT the airport on the day of departure there was a palpable electricity in the air — electricity, lights and cameras, boom microphones, hands armed with pens and notepads. We were surrounded by reporters.

Almost by accident, our expedition had grown into something of a civic event. It had started a year earlier, when Jim called on the *Seattle Times* in hopes of landing a cash donation from the state's biggest newspaper. The publisher passed on the sponsorship deal Jim had in mind, but when he called back he offered something just as valuable: *Why not let us turn your climb into a series of stories?*

The story was a natural for the *Times*. Seattle had a bond to Everest that stretched back twenty-five years, back when hometown boy Jim Whittaker set his American foot on the summit. The Northwest climbing population had exploded since then. Taking a step-by-step look at a modern expedition vying to put the first American woman on top would be a great way to update Whittaker, while at the same time saying something to all the outdoorsy Northwesterners.

The *Times* assigned the series to Sherry Stripling, a one-time sports writer who had recently carved out a position as the feature section's recreation editor. Sherry was a trim, athletic woman who pedaled her bike to work and had even tried out an ice ax and crampons on a local peak. She had a natural affinity for climbers and their compulsions, and so she sat in on a few meetings in the winter of '88, and soon after cranked out her first article, a piece focusing on our drive to collect equipment. Sure enough, the story touched a chord, particularly the part about our need to find clothes for free. "Underwear for forty people adds up," read Jim's quote. "And we like to change it occasionally." As we hoped, the readers of the *Times* flew to our aid. Maybe not quite as we hoped. Several readers sent in individual pairs of boxer shorts.

Sherry wrote a dozen other articles before we left, most describing the chores and trials we faced just trying to get to the foot of the mountain. The attention fed on itself, and by the time Sherry came to see us off at the airport (she would follow us to base camp a few weeks later) she was tailed by an entire gang: TV cameras, other newspaper reporters, radio reporters, a few wire-service folks. We had promised to make some farewell statements, so when we finished checking our luggage we all gathered for a short press conference in an airport meeting room.

We sat behind a long table at the front of the room while Jim went down the line introducing each of the climbers, spelling out our names and hometowns. Jim thanked a few of our larger sponsors by name, then read a short statement explaining the group's objectives. Coming back alive, he said, was everyone's first priority. Then Jim folded up his little notecard and smiled. "Right. Any questions?"

It took about ten seconds for someone to shout it up: "Will you put the first American woman on top of Everest?"

What do you say to these guys? I looked over at Diana, saw a small smile flicker across her lips. Jim answered coolly.

"We want to put the whole team on top."

Unsatisfied, another reporter tried his own spin: "Will the men on the climb work harder to put a woman on the summit?"

This time Diana answered. "Let's turn it around," she said. "I think it's time we say the *women* are going to help put the *men* on top!"

Good one! The reporters scribbled it down. Then it was time for us to leave. A camera or two followed us to the gate, along with a few friends and family members, all waving and shouting for good luck as we boarded the plane and flew off into the deep blue sky.

WE spent two nights in Hong Kong, then arrived in Kathmandu. Once settled, we spent a few days shopping for fresh fruit and vegetables and the last few items of gear we needed on the mountain. Jim and Don, meanwhile, spent most of the next eleven days locked into the Nepalese Ministry of Tourism, negotiating the tariffs and import charges for our gear.

None of us had come to Kathmandu burning to spend eleven days hanging around, but while we were stuck we tried to enjoy ourselves. We started each day with a communal breakfast, meeting at a small teahouse down the street from the Kathmandu Guest House.

Diana and I shopped for food together, and we spent a couple of afternoons looking for trinkets and clothes in the open markets at Durbar Mar, a crowded public square. Diana was full of energy — always moving and talking and noticing the world around her. But if she seemed nervous at times, Diana kept her wits about her.

I spent only one afternoon with Steve Ruoss. Tall and laconic, he did his share of the chores, then spent the rest of the day exercising or exploring the city with Geoff Tabin. Geoff Tabin also had a sense of humor, but his was more boyish. Crude, sometimes, particularly when it came to his physical appetites. At dinner he'd put his hand on Steve's shoulder and grin up at him. "Wanna go out and grab a beer tonight?" Steve knew what this meant, so like a good married man he'd smile and shake his head. "No thanks, Geoff. I already got myself a woman." At breakfast next morning Geoff would regale us with tales of his romantic adventures. A part-time writer, he never let the facts stand in the way of a good story.

I also had a chance to spend time with our East Coast–based teammates. Larry MacBean, a middle-aged businessman from Maine, brought a well-honed sense of order to his role as base camp manager. Charlie Shertz, a thirty-four-year-old anesthesiologist from Pittsburgh, was a sporty guy. His black hair was shoulder-length, his beard long and wispy. Back home Charlie drove a sleek Porsche and stocked an impressive wine cellar. When we left town, Charlie would start each day by bellowing a standard morning greeting: "Sixty-three [or whatever the current count was] days until sex with humans!" Bob Singer, on the other hand, was accustomed to a more staid existence. Everything that we were doing was new to Bob. A sixty-year-old neurosurgeon from Richmond, Virginia, Bob had never worked too hard at being physically fit. But getting involved in our trip changed his life. To prepare he started lifting weights and hiking, even walking the entire Appalachian Trail. Perpetually clean-shaved and practically bald on top, when Bob hit Kathmandu he announced that he was not going to shave again until he got back to the States.

All climbing expeditions in the Himalayas employ a sirdar, a Sherpa manager to coordinate the Sherpa climbers and porters. Most sirdars (and most Sherpa climbers, for that matter) work for established trekking agencies, but when Jim set out to hire the sirdar for our group, he had a better idea. A few years earlier he'd climbed in the Himalayas with an independent sirdar named Karma. He charged less than the trekking agency sirdars, and Jim figured the savings would multiply when Karma hired independent Sherpas to accompany us on the mountain. So it would be a great deal: in the end, Jim thought, we could save thousands of dollars.

In Kathmandu it seemed like a fabulous idea. Karma was well connected; when we needed to store our 460 boxes of gear, he'd found us an empty house to use as a warehouse, at a fraction of the usual warehouse cost. He combed the city for available Sherpa climbers, and did a good job rounding up a crew of twenty-six, plus four cooks and kitchen helpers and three mail runners, to deliver packages and messages from Kathmandu to base camp. But there was something about him that seemed curious to me. He was a chubby middle-aged man, partial to baggy LaCoste shirts, loose-fitting golf wear that stretched to cover his prominent belly. How, I wondered, could this couch potato even make it up to base camp? The first person Karma hired for us was Kirken, a cousin he brought on board to fill the crucial position of climbing sirdar — the coordinator of all the climbing Sherpas. But Kirken was a more enthusiastic drinker than he was a climber, as it turned out, and on our expedition his thirst for Nepalese beer was rivaled only by Karma's.

But none of this was evident in the city, and we finally left Kathmandu on the morning of August 5. After loading our 460 boxes into a truck, we piled into a small bus and set out to Jiri, the small hillside village at the end of the road. The morning was warm and wet, the heavy breeze full of flowers and mud and the odor of rot — half-eaten vegetables scattered on the road, the garbage piled on the sidewalk, the human waste in the ditch. The bus rumbled up the road, lurching across each rut and bump, gradually climbing higher into the emerald mountains.

Unlike the Tibet side of Everest, the west side has no road for vehicles beyond Jiri. The path is steep and rough, a stiff up-and-down climb, gaining 30,000 feet and losing 15,000 feet in the space of 125 miles. It usually takes more than two weeks to trek into base camp.

Tucked into a dingy guest house in Jiri, we went to bed early, planning to rise before dawn and get a fast start on the path to Everest. Most of our gear was still packed up in boxes and duffels, so I borrowed a sleeping bag from Charlie and settled in for the night, stretching out on a wooden bed. But I was too tired to complain — exhausted, actually — and so I rolled up a sweatshirt for a pillow and shut my eyes, floating off immediately.

Then I was awake. Not quite conscious, but not asleep, either. Squirming, trying to get comfortable. But freezing cold! My muscles were tense, close to shivering. I hunched deeper into the sleeping bag, searching for the warm spot . . . but there was no warm spot because it was so damp. Damp? The bag was damp, my T-shirt was soaked with sweat. My eyes were open now, burning into the blackness, my head reeling, the twisties so real I could almost feel a breeze on my forehead.

My fever dropped by morning, but when I sat up in bed, still dizzy, so clammy and weak, I felt like bursting into tears. What a hellish time to catch the flu. The others were putting on their shoes, stowing their gear, ready to fly up the trail. I wondered if I had the strength to lace up my own Nikes.

But lace up I did, tried to eat a little breakfast, drank some purified water. One of our doctors gave me some antibiotics, and then I was ready to walk. I had no choice. Once Karma finished parceling out the loads of gear to our throng of porters, it was time to go. *Forget about being sick, just move.* I hit the road at a conservative pace, keeping my head down, concentrating on my footsteps in the mud. The air was heavy and dank, T-shirt weather, despite the morning rain. I looked up, after a while, and noticed that it was beautiful. The thick gray clouds brushing against the hillside, the lush green vegetation across the terraced brown farmyards. You had to watch the path, though. The rains made mud and where the mud wasn't sticky it was terribly slick. Like ice, I discovered. It reminded you to stay aware of your center of gravity.

I soon recovered from my bout with the flu, and took to hiking with Steve, who kept a jackrabbit pace. I always preferred walking quickly on the trek, especially when there were leeches around. In Nepal, leeches are the state nuisance. During the monsoon season they're everywhere on the damp, jungly hillside; small, brownish, slimy creatures hanging on to the vegetation, waiting for the next warm-blooded creature to come brushing past. Once on board, they go to work, scuttling to a likely place and then attaching themselves with their pronglike fangs. Then they inject their special anticoagulant and start sucking up blood, engorging themselves and dropping off without raising a tickle. The bites aren't dangerous; they don't hurt or itch, and they rarely get infected. *But it's so gross!* If you happen to notice some on you, in the act, you can snatch them with your fingers and try to pull them off. This is complicated, though, by their stretchy bodies, which can go on forever, like rubber bands, and their sticky skin. Once you've succeeded in pulling them off your leg or arm, it's a whole other trick to get them off your fingers.

And if you don't happen to notice the leech in the process of leeching, you probably won't feel anything until long after it's dropped off. Because even though the leech is gone, the leech's anticoagulant is still working.

Or someone else will notice it. Steve and I were walking briskly one afternoon when something on my leg caught his eye. He looked down for a moment, then glanced up again, smiling.

"Gee, Stacy," he said, evenly. Doctors are used to everything. "Either you've just started your period or you've had a leech on your thigh."

Sure enough, a thick line of bright red blood was dripping down my leg. That was a stunner, but not quite as traumatic as the leech that tormented Geoff Tabin a day or two later. We had just finished breakfast, getting ready to set out for another day. It was a warm morning, and Geoff was wearing his especially short pants, a tight pair of shorts that weren't much longer than a Speedo bathing suit. I thought I noticed a mole on Geoff's inner thigh when he stood up, but it didn't make much of an impression until a few minutes later when someone else noticed it and pointed toward his crotch.

"Hey, Geoff, is that a birthmark or a leech?"

Geoff looked down. Then he seemed to explode in about five different directions.

"Fuck!" He leaped into the air and started slapping at his thigh, jumping up and down like a colt under his first saddle. "Get a knife," Geoff shrieked. "Cut it off! Cut it off!"

But most everyone was too busy laughing, so Geoff had to calm himself enough to pluck off the leech with his own fingers. Even Geoff thought it was funny, after a while. By the end of the afternoon he wrote a poem, "Leech on My Dingus," to commemorate the event.

We hiked through the lower hills for the first week, through the rains in the morning, the heavy afternoons with the thick clouds swirling beneath us in the valley. Enormous, treelike rhododendron bushes covered the hillsides, their leaves and branches bearded with hanging lichen. Wildflowers burst up all around the trail, and the hillsides draped spectacular waterfalls, the thin crystal spray streaming hundreds, sometimes thousands of feet.

We woke up with the light each morning, ate a quick breakfast, then set off up the path, following our huge band of porters up the muddy way to Everest. As we climbed higher into the mountain country the air cooled and the vegetation lightened, thinning in the drier air. We slipped the leeches, finally, and as the terrain grew more mountainous prepared to exchange our troop of porters for a herd of yaks. We'd make the change in Namche Bazar, taking two days in the village to acclimate to the higher elevation.

Namche Bazar. I knew this town. Six years after I had married Mark in that smoky house, I was going back to Namche Bazar. I knew I couldn't avoid it. In Nepal, the road to Everest leads right through the place. I'd already spent so much time trying to untangle myself from the past, and now here I was walking into town, wondering how it would make me feel. As we came closer, I bore down and prepared for the worst . . .

. . . And then nothing happened. I could see the old Namche Bazar everywhere around me. The pitch of the roads, the profile of the mountains on the horizon, the whitewashed buildings with the bright stripes of colored trim. I'd certainly spent some important days here — but these were important days, too. I was headed for Everest! The horizon! I had friends to talk with, books to read, a letter to write to David. I had more important things ahead of me.

IN the highlands the lavish tropical hills gave way to stark, rocky terrain. Even the villages became smaller and dingier, absent the gleaming white and gay colors brightening the buildings in the lowlands. Life is harder in the upper reaches, an existence scarred by gritty winds, burning sun, and harsh winter storms. The sparse grasses that bristle between the rocks are closer to gray than green.

We moved like an army, trooping up to the mountain with our endless line of equipment boxes and food parcels. Before Namche Bazar our porters stretched for nearly a mile. When we switched to yaks we loaded down an entire herd. They left Namche Bazar a few days before we did, and when they did it looked like a Himalayan cattle drive. Up above we'd be accompanied by twenty-six Sherpas, helping us set our route and lug the gear up to our camps.

Once all mountain-climbing expeditions looked like armies. In the days when Sir Edmund Hillary and Jim Whittaker were making the first ascents on Everest, the traditional "expedition-style" climb was the only option. In order to make the uncharted terrain as safe as possible, the climbers and their armies of paid helpers humped everything but beds and sofas up into the mountainside camps. They spent weeks setting the route and building the camps, then returned to base camp to rest for days at a time. And as a matter of course, they strapped on oxygen bottles to make breathing easier in the thin environment. At the time it seemed the only way a man could survive at altitude.

As the years passed, however, more climbers opted for smaller, stripped-down expeditions, like bands of revolutionary guerrillas. For one thing, climbing without legions of porters and Sherpas is much more affordable. What once required hundreds of thousands of dollars and dozens of men shrank to a few grand, counting airfare, and two or three buddies. And to some climbers it also seemed a more honest style of climbing. "Alpine-style," as the new philosophy came to be known, emphasized self-reliance. The smaller teams carried their own gear up the mountain. Sometimes they didn't establish permanent camps, preferring instead to move their tents en route to the summit. And no matter how high the mountain, Alpine-style climbers avoided using bottled oxygen.

The 1987 North Face expedition landed somewhere in between the two models. We didn't hire Sherpas to help us on the mountain, but we did build up our camps and brought oxygen to use above Camp 4. Most expeditions still use some of the old-style principles. But when word of our $250,000 expedition got out in '88, some climbers decided our full-blown expedition-style party was distressingly anachronistic. After all, Reinhold Messner had climbed all the way to the top of Everest by himself, and without oxygen. So why did *we* have to spend a fortune to buy up half the climbing gear in Seattle and then call out the Sherpa cavalry to drag us up the mountain? And if we did make it to the summit, could we then call it that much of an achievement?

I understood the controversy, but I really didn't pay it that much mind. The first guiding principle behind our expedition was for every member to come home alive and with all standard parts present and operable. We wanted to give ourselves the best possible chance of summiting. What's more, we wanted the climb to be fun.

I've climbed in big groups and small groups, with lots of support and with no support whatsoever. Ultimately, I don't believe either style is superior to the other. Every climber needs to decide for herself how much she's willing to risk. For me it was simple. As one friend of mine reminded me, I couldn't go kayaking or play the piano without fingers. I wouldn't have much fun walking barefoot on mossy rocks if I didn't have toes. No matter what help we had from Sherpas or oxygen, all of us would climb the mountain on the strength of our own abilities. No one from outside the group was going to guide any of us up the mountain. And no matter what happened, we were going to remain true to ourselves, and true to our own sense of mountaineering. And that's the whole point to me — mountaineering should be a personal statement.

WE walked into base camp early in the afternoon of August 19, a full day ahead of schedule. We were at 17,600 feet now, at the base of the mountain on the Khumbu Glacier. We were one of eight groups that would be camping on the glacier, so we set up our tents close to a team from Korea. The glacier was both crowded and bleak. Garbage from previous years dotted the terrain. The ice was lumpy and uneven, and littered with boulders and small shards of rock. Peggy, Diana, and I shared a dome tent, and when we located a flat spot we cleared away as many rocks as we could, then spread out a layer of cardboard to absorb the remaining lumps. We all set up our tents in close formation on a small ridge, then put up two larger rock-and-tarp structures, one to serve as a kitchen, the other as our dining room and meeting area. This last was dubbed the Club Flamingo, its entry marked by a shocking pink plastic yard ornament. For reasons that predated my entry to the expedition, the faux-birds had become an icon for the group. We were each issued a flamingo to carry with us in our packs, and there were a few extras tucked into the equipment boxes. Flamingos marked our path and our camps on the mountain. They may look tacky in your neighbor's front yard, but at base camp on the Khumbu Glacier the little explosions of pink were actually quite cheery.

The flamingos didn't have much competition in the cheery department. Beyond the monochromatic backdrop, base camp offered little in the way of comfort. From below we could hear the glacier creak and moan, straining against itself as it shifted steadily downhill. I knew we were relatively safe down there, and that a huge crevasse wouldn't yawn open and swallow my tent. I knew this intellectually, but emotionally I wasn't convinced. In my sleeping bag at night those eerie moans and squeals cut like an icicle in my chest. And from above us came the constant sound of avalanches. An explosive crack as a load cut loose from the mountain, then a deep, troubling rumble as it plummeted down through the darkness.

And just off to the northeast, beyond the far end of the glacier, loomed the bottom lip of the Khumbu Ice Fall. Just before dinner one day, Steve and I walked over to take a closer look. The valley floor rose steeply a few hundred yards away from base camp, and the spot where the glacier hit bottom crested upward with a line of ice mounds and towers. Steve and I walked between the ridges, where the blues and whites of the ice mixed with a dirty brown dusting of moraine crud. Most of the towers crested twenty or thirty feet above us, and we walked around them as if in a maze. It was beautiful and spooky. Scattered along the ice we found all manner of climbing debris: twisted aluminum ladders; the odd boot; a tent pole; a tangle of rope, all of it coughed up by the glacier after a slow, cold trip down the middle of the mountain.

Steve paused to gather up some rope to bring back to camp, and when I turned past the next ridge I saw something lying on top of the ice. A yak carcass, it seemed to me, but when Steve caught up he knew better. Yaks don't wear wool clothing.

We walked up to take a closer look. He was mostly bones, and his right arm was missing, but this was a human skeleton. Steve bent down for a closer inspection.

"A Sherpa, I'll bet," Steve said. He reached down, a long finger just brushing the tuft of dark hair that still bristled from the skull. There was no telling when the Sherpa died, what killed him, or how long he'd spent entombed in the glacier. But like the boot, the tent poles, and the tangle of rope, the mountain that had consumed him ultimately spit him out at the bottom.

"Should we tell someone?"

Steve shook his head.

"Nope. The guy will become a tourist attraction."

I looked back to Steve. "Maybe we should cover him up."

Steve nodded, put down his coil of rope, and reached for some rocks. We worked for ten minutes or so, gently piling up rocks to hide him from the sun and wind, return him to the landscape. When we were done we stood back for a moment, then picked up our things again and headed back to base camp.

THE South Col is the easiest route up Everest, but as the dead Sherpa proved, it's not risk-free. Far from it. True enough, our route wouldn't confront us with the vertical ice walls I'd encountered on the North Face. We wouldn't struggle with the thousands of feet of rock you find on the East Face route. The West Ridge is long and technical, and most of the other routes are so hard or risky they're rarely challenged. But if the mountain's other faces are more steep, the South Col's mortality rate is just as high.

One major reason was right above us. Unlike the more technical faces on Everest, the most hazardous section of the south side looms right above base camp: the Khumbu Ice Fall, 2,000 vertical feet of ice. Raked with seracs, riddled with deep crevasses, the ice fall tumbles slowly down the thin throat between Everest's West Shoulder and Nuptse, the mountain immediately to the east, like frozen river rapids, through its thin bed. Moving downhill at about three inches a day, the ice changes constantly, building into huge towers in some places, splitting into gaping chasms in others. As the ice moves and breaks apart, the balance in the ice fall shifts. Crevasses can widen or close by several feet in the space of a few days. Towers the size of small buildings can capsize without warning.

Ultimately, the ice fall serves as a kind of one-stop Alpine danger center. Along with the tumbling ice towers, climbers must beware the yawning (and frequently hidden) crevasses, plus the sporadic avalanches that plunge into the narrow funnel from the cliffs on Everest's West Shoulder. It's one of the most infamous statistics connected to Everest — for every ten climbers who enter the ice fall, one does not emerge. Climbers have their own nickname for it: the Mouth of Death.

The first chore of any South Col expedition is to find the easiest, safest route through the ice fall and make it as secure as possible. But before we began poking our way up the mountain we took some time to present our case to the gods. A few of the Sherpas spent an afternoon building a six-foot stone altar on the edge of our camp, standing a pole in the center to serve as a central stringing point for our lines of prayer flags.

A few mornings before we planned to take our first steps on the mountain, we climbed out of bed early and gathered at the altar for the Pujah, a Buddhist blessing ceremony. The Sherpas were already there, chanting and burning juniper branches for good luck. We each made offerings to Buddha, arranging them on a shelf on the altar. The Sherpas laid out sampas, balls of barley flour. The climbers offered up the things nearest to our own hearts: M&Ms, Fig Newtons, a bottle of whiskey. The chanting went on for close to two hours, rising in wild crescendos, then falling to a murmur. Occasionally they'd call us to throw handfuls of rice into the air, as another offering to Buddha. We didn't comprehend the religious significance the Sherpas did from the ceremony, but it gave us all a chance to feel joined in a team effort, to reflect on the mountain and challenges ahead of us. When it was over we all threw barley flour in the air, smearing it on everyone's face and hair. The white streaks represented a long, happy life. And with the ice fall just ahead of us, we were especially eager to wish for long lives.

THIS was a strange year on the south side of Everest. Through 1987 the Nepalese government had allowed only one expedition per climbing season on their side of the mountain. This changed, however, when someone in the Nepalese government noticed how much money their friends in the Chinese government were reaping from the Tibet side of the mountain.

The Chinese may be Communists, but they knew a thing or two about supply and demand. And because the demand for climbing permits on Everest was practically infinite, the Chinese sold permits for each *route* on the Tibet side. That way they managed to squeeze four or five times as many teams on the mountain, and thus make four or five times as much money during each climbing season. Now the Nepalese wanted to jump onto that gravy train. So starting in 1988 each individual route on the south side had its own team building camps and stringing line toward the summit.

The suddenly heavy traffic on Everest in '88 led to new complexities. Many of these stemmed from the long-term impact four or five times as many humans would wreak on the fragile mountain environment. But the most immediate problem was getting along with seven other expeditions. Even when we walked into base camp and found only one other group waiting for us, we knew that in the space of two weeks, Nepal's Everest base camp would swell into a small international village. It didn't take long for the relations among the eight teams to develop UN–style convolutions.

The biggest conflict involved the path through the ice fall. In previous years, the one team allowed on the Nepalese side knew it had no choice but to build the entire path through the treacherous terrain. But this year there would be eight unrelated teams following the same route through the ice fall. Obviously, no one team should have to provide all the raw material and effort to build the path. Jim and Don had anticipated this while planning our expedition and, trusting at least one of the other teams to do the same, brought only about two-thirds the number of ropes and ladders required for the route. The team of South Koreans had made the same bet, and so once we met up at base camp we soon struck a deal to pool our gear. Things didn't get complicated until the other teams pulled into town.

Once we cut a deal with the Koreans, Jim divided our team into three rotations, each group going up to work on every third day. The climbing began officially on August 29. The alarms went off at two A.M., so that the bulk of the day's work could take place well before the midday sun heated and loosened the ice. After a quick breakfast the first group donned their boots and headlamps, met the Koreans on the edge of camp, and then set out through the darkness. This time I got to sleep through this wake-up call. But my day would come soon enough.

Setting the route through the ice fall can take anywhere between six days and two weeks, an eternity spent zigzagging around impassable towers and seeking out natural ice bridges to cross the crevasses. What can't be avoided must be bridged, and so we brought along seventy-five aluminum ladders, each of which had to be carried into the ice fall and then hoisted over or across the obstacle. Each ladder could span an eight-foot barrier, but when we encountered something larger or wider we had to rig the ladders together, connecting the spans with rope and custom-built metal clamps.

Each day in the ice fall meant playing an obscure, dangerous game of trial and error. We'd meet the Koreans at three A.M., then walk across the glacier to our equipment depot at the foot of the ice fall. There we'd pause to strap on our crampons, then clip on to the rope and start up past the ridge of ice that marked the entry to the ice fall. From there we'd follow the rope through its tangled path, up to where the previous day's work ended. By now the sky would be paling with the dawn, and the texture of the ice would begin to throw shadows in the dim light. We preferred moving as quickly as possible. We wanted to be safe in the ice fall — not make any impulsive judgments, always take time to do the right thing — but the only problem with that was what we all knew: that no matter where you were *inside* the ice fall, you'd be about a thousand times safer if you were anywhere else *outside* the ice fall. The sooner we set the route through to the top, the better.

The ice fall made me feel like a deer during hunting season. Very alert and skittish, always ready to bolt. And it was so beautiful in there — the jagged towers scraping the air, frozen clear in the dawn, the rising beams of morning sun playing on the sparkling ice. But I was always aware, ears open, eyes wide, toes feeling for the slightest vibration, the rumble in the distance. I saw everything and ignored nothing.

We made group decisions, and tried to be as logical as possible. Which was the bigger threat: avalanches or crevasses? One morning we took a moment to consider this. We were about a third of the way up the ice fall, poking around for a route beneath the West Shoulder of Everest. If we set the path closer to the mountain, we could avoid a long line of crevasses. But being closer to the hill also meant being closer to the avalanches that would, on occasion, come roaring down the 1,500 vertical feet from the overhanging glaciers. So what to do? We stood for a moment in the pink light of early morning, our breaths coming out in white puffs. We searched one another's faces, then headed toward the shoulder.

We got so used to the sound of avalanches. The crack of release, the dull rumble as the snow and ice spills down the slope. Some avalanches are larger — and louder — than others, and you look up when you hear a big one start to go. But even in the ice fall that morning, below the overhanging, snow-covered cliffs, that one sharp snap didn't faze anyone. I'm sure I heard it, somewhere in the back of my mind. *Crack!* Then the low rumble, but we just kept working, pounding in the ice pickets, threading the rope and moving up . . . all of this while the avalanche came rolling down, a dull growl at first, then louder. Then it built into a solid rumble, then a roar. At this, I looked up. A cloud of white billowed up as the avalanche tore down the slope, steadily gaining size and force. It was coming closer to the ice fall. And it was headed straight for us.

Straight for us!

Now we all saw it. A blue bolt of fear shot down my spine. When I looked at the others, one of the Koreans was unhitching himself from the line. Running for cover? No. He snatched a small video camera from his pack and darted up onto a small serac to point his lens at the roiling cloud.

And it was still headed in our direction!

I turned to look at Jim, who was standing next to me. "Is it going to hit us?"

He gazed up the hill, stone-faced, his mustache dark against pale cheeks. "I don't know."

Now it was louder, the white plume growing wider and closer. In one movement, Jim and I unhitched from the line. The two Sherpas working alongside us did the same, and we all scrambled away, searching for a safe spot.

"Cover your mouths!" I shouted at the Sherpas. When it hit us, even if it just dusted us, the ice particles could damage our lungs. *Don't breathe the ice!* It's easy to suffocate in a thick cloud. I pulled my neck gaiter over my mouth and nose, and watched Jim cover himself with his scarf, pink and soft . . . a gift from his girlfriend. As the roar grew even louder, I could feel the ice beneath me tremble. I wanted to run, but where? I'd fall into a crevasse . . . but I had to get out of the path! So I followed Jim, scuttling about ten feet behind a chest-high seam in the ice. We huddled with the Sherpas, hunkering down, waiting for the snow and ice to hit us.

I pressed my chin against my chest and braced myself, anticipating the impact, the wave of snow sweeping me off my feet, spinning and pummeling me, burying me. I could feel the impact, the cold wash of the snow, the blank white as it consumed me . . .

. . . And then it didn't come. Instead, the rumbling lightened, then stopped. I felt a cold wind rush over my head, the air displaced by the wave of snow and ice. Then silence. I kept my head down for a few moments. When I looked up, a thin cloud of ice particles danced in the air, sparkling white against the blue morning sky. The snow had slapped against a small wall of ice almost a hundred feet away — and stopped.

We all stood then, tentatively, for a moment. Standing up, then dusting off. Looking around, resetting the eyes and ears, glancing at each other, and taking small steps back to the line.

"That's it," Jim said, to no one in particular. A thin smile tugged on the corner of his mouth and he clapped his gloves together. Now his cheeks were pink again. "No big deal! Let's get back at 'em."

IT seemed like a slightly bigger deal when we got back to base camp. Our teammates had heard it and seen it all from down there, so when they saw us two hours later walking back to the glacier, the others came running out of their tents. How was it? Did it come close?

Not yet, anyway.

The next morning at base camp felt wonderful. I slept until five-thirty, then woke up on my own. I could feel my muscles — the burn from yesterday's labor still smoldering — and work my shoulders, the blood moving now. So few luxuries on a glacier at 17,600 feet, but this was mine, lying in bed, waiting for Jetta, our nice cook, to bring around the mug of hot tea he brought to help ease our way into the day. I lingered even longer, feeling the hot tea settling into my stomach, radiating heat all the way into my fingers and toes, feeling so warm and relaxed . . . then I heard the explosion.

It was a bomb. An explosion that registered in my sternum. I vaulted out of my sleeping bag, pulled a jacket over my long johns, and stepped into my boots. I didn't pause to lace them. I scrambled out of my tent and bolted upright, searching the mountainside. A huge one . . . but where? In the tent next to mine, Charlie was leaning out, his long black hair still tangled with sleep, steam still rising from the tea mug in his hand.

"Avalanche!" I shouted at him.

I didn't have to shout. Now we could see it clearly, even from a distance. A huge white cloud billowing from the West Shoulder, the biggest I'd ever seen, sliding down toward the ice fall. Two tents away from me, Dave Hambly leaned out in his underwear, camera pressed against his face, shutter whirring. We watched it together, faces slack with helplessness. Don, Peggy, Diana, Geoff, three Sherpas, and at least that many Koreans were up there setting the route. But where? All we could do was watch the snow and ice tumbling down the slope, hitting bottom and rolling into the throat of the ice fall. Across the route! And then it was quiet again. I held my breath.

Jim, standing in his long johns and a down jacket, stared up toward the ice fall. When he broke his trance, his eyes flickered, then hardened.

"Let's get a rescue going."

He turned and walked quickly toward the Sherpa tents, shouting for Karma. Charlie, in unlaced boots, dove back for the tent he shared with Jim, pulling out the base camp walkie-talkie. After an avalanche that size Don would certainly call down. I could practically hear his voice — *Hol-ee shit! Didja get a loada that one?* — but just in case: I hunkered in my tent, pulling on socks and pile pants, stepping into my climbing gear. Maybe we'd have to help someone down. A turned ankle. Or something. Outside, I could hear Charlie, his voice high-pitched, yearning.

"Base camp to Don. Come in, over."

Nothing. A click, as he pushed down the button and tried again.

"Base camp to Don. Looked like a big one up there . . . let us know what's happening, over."

Charlie stared at the radio in his hand, then gazed up to the ice fall again. Could he see someone waving? Of course not. He didn't see anything.

"Base camp to Don. Give us a shout, okay? Looked pretty big."

All we could hear on the walkie-talkie was the caustic scrape of radio static.

Up in the ice fall the first warning had come half an hour before. A sharp crack from above, then a small white cloud rolling down from the ice cliff on the West Shoulder. Working on the route, Don glanced up at the avalanche, then quickly back to the line he was setting into the ice. *Another small roller? No big deal.* The snap twenty minutes later was even smaller. Don was deep into his work by then and he didn't even look up to trace the path of the ice down the slope. The climbers were spread up and down the line, Don working most closely with a young Sherpa named Kami, pounding in ice pickets, feeding the line through the carabiners. Moving up another ten, twelve feet then, doing it again, whacking away at the picket, planting it good and solid in the ice, clicking on a carabiner, then snapping it around the line. And that's what they were doing, standing in the middle of the most exposed stretch of the route, when they heard the noise above them. *Kaboom!* This time it sounded like a cannon, only louder. It got everyone's attention.

To Don it looked like the entire ice wall had broken away. He watched it fall for a moment, saw it hit the slope and blow apart. The force of impact took out a chunk of the slope, and the slide gained momentum as it rocketed down the steep hill. From below it looked as big as a tornado, and it was blowing right toward them. Don craned his neck. He knew he had about six seconds, maybe eight. An eternity to think in, but too little time to move. And where would he go? There was nothing, not even a lip of snow, to lie behind. All he had protecting him, Don realized, was the slim rope and the skinny pickets they'd just spent the last two hours pounding into the ice. Don motioned to Kami and clipped both of them back on to the line; then they huddled together. The ice beneath their feet shook. The thick white cloud of ice particles loomed above, swallowing the pale morning light. Don and Kami turned sideways to the onslaught and hunched over, making themselves as small as possible.

Don could feel Kami trembling. "Cover your mouth!" Don shouted over the roar. Kami nodded, and then he could hear Kami praying. Don cupped his hands in front of his mouth.

Then it hit.

The cold wind ahead of the avalanche tore Don's hands from his mouth. His hands flew away, and then he jerked sideways, feeling the fixed line strain behind him. The first wave of ice came in the cloud, a hail of sharp fragments that sliced skin like razor wire. The next wave of debris consumed them both, pitching Don and Kami backward with enough force to tear the fixed line away from its three-foot pickets. Uncovered, Don's mouth sucked in the thick cloud of ice particles. He couldn't breathe. He was somersaulting, pitched like a rag down a thirty-foot ice cliff.

So this is what it's like to die in the Khumbu Ice Fall.

But then it stopped. Don's eyes were closed. He wasn't sure where he was now. Wasn't sure *if* he was now. All he knew was the hollow silence, the cold, something dripping off his chin. He was dazed, but alive. Don opened his eyes, slowly, and saw only white. Gradually the world came back into focus. The place where he had been standing seconds earlier was now thirty feet uphill. Glancing down, Don saw red, the droplets of blood starting to flow from his shredded face. Now Don tried to move. His arms seemed to work — his left hand was kind of numb — but his legs were stuck, buried beneath him in the snow and ice. Now Don was sitting on his knees. He was alive! He was okay! A little banged up, but still — he heard moaning.

Kami.

Next to Don, only Kami's face emerged from the snow. The brown skin was battered and torn by the ice. Mixed with melting snow and hot tears, the blood dripped pink. Kami tried to move, struggling against the weight of the snow. He groaned again, and Don reached for him, cradling his head in his arms.

Then he heard a voice echoing from above. Don looked up and waved. The others made their way down, carefully, crunching in the rough ice, and reached for Don's arms to pull him out of the snow. Don motioned to Kami.

"I'm okay. He's worse."

THE silence was eternal. But ten minutes after Charlie first tried to rouse him, Don finally answered.

"Everyone's alive."

There was something in Don's voice. A catch. Something wasn't quite right.

"Yeah. Looks like . . . maybe we're gonna need some help getting down."

Everyone was alive. Thank God, everyone escaped. But both Don's and Kami's faces had been sliced, diced, and battered by the fragments in the ice cloud. Don broke a finger and netted a black eye during the fall. Kami suffered the same cuts and bruises, and the impact against the ice had torn ligaments in his knee. The others in their party had barely been knocked over by the tumbling debris. But Don and Kami . . . the moment I saw Don, walking slowly across the glacier, I took a breath. It looked like he'd been on the wrong end of a pool cue in a bar fight. Kami looked even worse. They'd had to carry him down, and his bruised face was distorted with pain.

We were relieved to see them all, to have everyone back safe and relatively sound. After everything we'd heard, all the horror stories and tales of sudden death, we'd finally been touched by the ice fall's brutal power. It left most of us a little terrified. And the only one who wasn't frightened, it seemed, had been there to take a tumble in the avalanche.

Peggy got knocked over and then swept about ten feet by the rushing snow. But she stayed on the surface for the whole trip and when she got back to base camp she shrugged off the experience, apparently unperturbed by her close call. When Johnny gave her a hug and asked her how she was, Peggy beamed happily.

"It was great," she said, eyes fairly glistening with excitement. "Better than a ride at Disneyland. I'm so glad to be alive."

No one said anything then, but I saw a stunned look pass between Steve and Johnny. Steve shook his head, slowly, his face frozen into a cold smile. *Oh, sure,* it said. *What could be more fun than being buried alive?*

We recovered from the avalanches, and then managed to punch our route through the ice fall in six days. That was barely half the time we had planned on, but working alongside the Koreans gave us a larger, faster-working group of climbers. We established Camp 1 at 19,500 feet, on a flat spot between the gaping crevasses just above the ice fall, then went back to base camp for the night.

It felt good to make progress, and as the first week went by, the team built a nice working camaraderie. Don had packed an inspirational desk calendar in one of the boxes, so we started each day with a new slogan posted at the Club Flamingo. We also had a birthday party one night. Don, Jim, and Larry all had birthdays in early September, so we planned a big dinner party to celebrate. Diana, Peggy, and I decorated the Club Flamingo, then baked a cheesecake and brought out one of Charlie's bottles of scotch.

Now that most of the seven other expeditions had found their way up to base camp, the International Village had taken form. Tents were scattered across the lumpy glacier, and we had everything from expedition-style armies to Alpine-style klatches to daredevil soloists.

A large group of French climbers arrived in base camp a few days after we did. The French throng actually consisted of three parties traveling together, and not very happily. Each faction was centered around its own daredevil and though they weren't competing directly, each knew the others' success might compromise their own publicity they'd receive at home. And publicity could turn into commercial endorsements, and those could mean big money, so imagine the potential for conflict. Indeed, there had been some ugliness during the trek — an argument flared up, someone threw someone else's gear into a river.

The first stuntman, Jean-Marc Boivin, planned to jump off the summit of Mount Everest. He came armed with a parapente, a gadget of French devising that crossed a parachute with a hang-glider. Boivin was a man of many achievements, but he had earned his greatest renown by leaping, *avec* parapente, from dangerous or unlikely places. Now he had set his sights on being the first man to fly off Everest.

Another daredevil, Marc Batard, was hoping to fly *up* the mountain. He planned to break the world's record for speed climbing by dashing to the summit by himself in twenty-four hours or less, all the while broadcasting his progress home live via a microphone to a French radio audience. The third crew, led by Serge Koenig, hoped to lug a video camera and signal transmitter to the summit and broadcast the first live pictures from the top of Everest.

Batard had little time to lose. While he was busying himself on the south side of the mountain, fellow French adventurers Michel Parmentier and Benoit Chamoux were gearing up to mount similar dashes up Everest's North Face.

Daredevils, yes. Parapentes, yes. Radio transmitters, yes. Camera crews, yes. Equipment to get any of them through the ice fall . . . well, not exactly. With so many other teams climbing the same route, the French *knew* the ice fall path would be set up before they even arrived at base camp. There seemed little point, then, in lugging all that rope and gear up from Kathmandu.

We were appalled. Working with the Koreans, we'd invested thousands of dollars in the route, as well as gear, time, almost our lives! Why should we let another team benefit from our labors without ponying up even a *token* consideration? Of course, we were going to let the other teams use our route — that was the plan all along. Just not for free. Working with Larry MacBean, who earned his living in Maine as an international business executive, Jim and Don set up a share program, wherein each team who hadn't helped build the route would pay our team and the Koreans a fee — about $2,000 for each additional team — to help maintain the ropes and ladders in the ice fall. The French were not thrilled with the prospect of having to pay for using the route, but they knew they didn't have time to fight about it. After a brief, occasionally bitter argument, the French threw up their hands, signed an IOU, then became proud part-owners of the ice fall route.

Then the joint New Zealand/Czech team pulled in to base camp, and Jim set out to explain the situation to them immediately. But the initial conversation between Jim and Rob Hall, the Kiwis' co-leader, revealed a fundamental disagreement. The New Zealanders, Hall explained, were not excited about spending money to buy in to the ice fall route; mostly because they didn't have any money to spend. And yet they were here and, as far as they were concerned, were going to climb through the ice fall on the established route.

Rob Hall, Gary Ball, Lydia Bradey, and the small team of Czechs with whom they shared a permit were a bit underfunded, but experienced, respected, and ready to climb. Certainly, they thought, one of the other wealthier teams, maybe all of them, would see their plight and be more than happy to help them along. Weren't climbers supposed to help each other out, particularly in extreme danger zones? One exchange with Jim disabused them of this notion. Then things started to get ugly.

Perhaps Jim and Rob Hall are too much alike. Rob's a big man, too, a craggy, Lincolnesque figure with a sly sense of humor. But Rob's personal warmth is no match for his goatlike will, not to mention his strong opinions about climbing etiquette. When Rob first approached Jim to ask about the ice fall route, I'm sure he saw it as a courtesy, plain and simple. No one would ever deliberately try to stop someone else from climbing a safe route, no matter what. Holding the right-of-way at some extreme capitalist ransom was, to their minds, mountainside usury.

But Jim also had his own take on mountain etiquette. To his mind, climbers arrived not only with rights, but also with responsibilities. They're supposed to come to a mountain *prepared*. And if charging climbers to help maintain a route they were planning to use without having helped build it in the first place violated some doctrine of the International Climbers Code, then showing up totally unequipped to get past the ice fall surely violated another, equally crucial mandate. Rob was furious. Jim was adamant.

"Only co-owners get to use the route," Jim said.

"Fine, then," Rob replied between clenched teeth. "We'll send you a check." When Jim got home he spent a long time waiting for that check to arrive from New Zealand. It still hasn't.

I T was time for bigger things. Now that the route through the ice fall was set we were heading up the mountain. Assuming the weather didn't turn vicious, this was the last night we'd all spend together on the glacier. From now on, most of our healthy climbers would live on the mountain, helping to set the route and establish the camps, then ferry gear up to stock the higher points.

Shouldering loads, we set out the next morning for Camp 1. Almost everyone turned back for base camp that afternoon, but Charlie and Geoff spent the night to acclimate, and the next morning started fixing the route up the gently sloped Western Cwm (a Welsh word, pronounced "coom," meaning valley) to Camp 2 at 21,500 feet. Once established, that camp would become our mountainside headquarters, while Camp 1 served as an equipment depot.

Work on the route started before dawn and finished by midday. Down at base camp Larry and Bob would parcel out the food and gear that needed to go up the mountain, then the Sherpas would carry the loads up through the ice fall, leaving the gear at Camp 1 for the Americans to take higher. This arrangement worked for two reasons: fewer Sherpas were needed up high on the mountain, and the Sherpa crew down below was large enough to keep any one member from taking daily trips through the shifty seracs and crevasses. Once the loads were at Camp 1, we'd climb down from Camp 2 to pick up the gear and take it to the camps above. As always, the acclimatization strategy was one-step-up, two-steps-back: climb higher during the day, drop off a load, and then retreat to a lower camp to rest for the night. It was a conservative approach, but it lowered the risk of altitude sickness and helped us stay strong.

When the assignments came out in the morning, I strapped on my crampons and went where I was told. Some days I got to venture high on the route, other days I hung low, humping loads up from Camp 1. The cwm was riddled with crevasses at the bottom, but after a few hundred feet of switchbacks and traverses to avoid the schisms, the glacier became solid again and the climb more direct. From there it was a long, flat walk up to Camp 2. Above that camp the glacier sloped gradually for another quarter mile. Then our route slanted right, heading straight up the Lhotse Face to Camp 3, four small tents dug into the steep mountainside at 23,700 feet.

It was all uneventful climbing, despite the swift elevation gain between Camps 2 and 3. Yet for some reason the stretch between Camp 2 and the bottom of the Lhotse Face was my least favorite on the mountain. When I started climbing higher, I found I always felt sluggish outside Camp 2, walking in the dark and the cold, my toes frozen and brittle. In that one stretch it seemed to take more energy to keep up with Steve or Geoff, or whomever I ended up climbing with for the day. But I always regained my rhythm once we got to the steep ice and snow. It was always colder up higher, even in the sunshine. My toes stayed numb, and I stopped regularly to swing my legs, trying to keep the blood moving. But I preferred the steeper pitches. Even with my jumar hooked solidly to the line, the slope gave me something to think about.

Once we got onto the mountain, the climbing teams changed almost daily. I climbed with Steve and Geoff some days, and on others with Jim or Johnny. Still, there were a few climbers with whom I rarely worked. I climbed with Don only once, and never climbed with Jean, Peggy, Dave, or Diana. I barely even *saw* Dave and Diana. The two of them seemed to be on an entirely different circuit — when I was at one camp, they were at the one just above me, or just below. But none of the separations were deliberate. Personal preferences aside, the team never allowed itself to grow cliquish or factionalized. If anyone had reservations about anyone else, they were kept private.

As the days passed, we continued poking our route higher on the mountain. Up to Camp 3, then higher, up toward Camp 4, way up on the shoulder between Everest and Lhotse, that ridge of snow called the South Col. The weather was sweet and clear, and the team went higher, working together in even-tempered concert. *Getting higher, getting closer!* Unlike last year's expedition, we had a rock-solid understanding we had agreed to in Seattle, back before we even hopped on the airplane and left U.S. airspace. There would be no spontaneous summit bids for us. Jim and Don, our leaders, wouldn't even choose the first summit team until the group had set the entire route and established Camp 4, the peak camp on top of the South Col. Once that happened, the three climbers who had climbed the highest on the mountain while staying strong and healthy would be offered the first shot at the summit. Then, while the other climbers put the finishing touches on the route, the first team would retreat to base camp for a few days of rest, gathering strength at the lower reaches before setting out for the final sprint to the summit.

I'm sure everyone felt a few rumbles. It's inevitable, when personal goals compete with group needs. But the infrastructure stayed together. We had a team and a plan, and the teammates were committed to furthering the prospects of both, even when opportunity or misfortune tempted otherwise.

For instance, at one point late in the route-setting process, Johnny was carrying an early-morning load up near the top of the South Col, just 3,000 feet from the summit. It was a beautifully calm morning, but our first summit team was still resting at base camp, and so Johnny and the others were playing support climbers, just stocking the camps. Seeing Johnny carrying a load within striking distance of the mountaintop, a summit-bound Frenchman was perplexed. "You better get to the summit while you have the chance," he said.

Johnny shook his head. "Nah. Not my turn."

The Frenchman rolled his eyes and gestured heavenward. "It is insane," he said, "to have these skies and just sit beneath them." Johnny shrugged and continued up with his load. He'd take his shot when it came to him.

Charlie Shertz wasn't even going to *get* a shot — this much was made clear during his first journey above Camp 1. Despite Charlie's years of high-altitude climbing, this time his body didn't feel like working in the thin atmosphere. (It's one of the flukes of high altitude — sometimes your body floats to the summit without protest, other times altitude sickness can strike at base camp.) Noticeably weakened at Camp 1, Charlie pushed himself up to Camp 2 the next morning, but at 21,500 feet and only two days above the ice fall, Charlie knew his climb on Everest was over. He retreated for base camp that afternoon, and could have easily continued back to Kathmandu, back to the world of hot showers and fresh food, and then back home. But Charlie was dedicated to our expedition. He stayed at base camp, helping Bob Singer and Larry MacBean work the logistics until the entire group finished climbing, dismantled the route, and left for Kathmandu.

Even when the bonds were holding tight, I could hear the scrape of personal ambition. Who was the highest on the route? When am I going to catch up? In the end the daily assignments were Jim's decision. He was the leader, the final authority. Alone or in consultation with co-leader Don, Jim seemed to make fair decisions, then stuck by them. And for a while that was just fine.

But sometimes I had to wonder about Jim.

Soon after we started carrying gear to the lower camps on the mountain, Jim asked Geoff to examine each team member's eyes. Sometimes the strain of altitude can cause retinal hemorrhaging, which is usually a symptom of even greater problems. It's not a foolproof way to diagnose an oncoming cerebral edema, but some doctors think a good look into a climber's eyes can tell a lot about how he or she is adjusting to the pressures of high altitude. So Jim asked Geoff to make the rounds, then pressed one additional instruction.

"Don't tell anyone the results," Jim said. "Just tell me."

Geoff nodded, sure, right, whatever. But then he thought about it some more. What was *that* supposed to mean? Geoff wasn't exactly sure. And the more he thought about it, the more he lost his enthusiasm. Maybe Jim wanted to use medical information to help him decide who might be a stronger summit candidate. But why the secrecy? And how could Geoff peer into someone's eyes — into the eyes of one of his *teammates* — and then announce that all information on the condition of his or her retinas, and perhaps cerebellum, was being withheld for Jim's perusal? It didn't sound right at all, so when Geoff performed his first two or three examinations he made a point of explaining to each climber exactly what he had found. This enraged Jim, and when he confronted Geoff they traded *fuck yous* for a while, then stormed off to their own tents. Word of Jim's supposedly private eye examinations spread through camp, and a day or two later someone drilled him about it at the morning meeting.

Are you keeping secrets from us? Jim blanched.

"Geoff misunderstood me," he said, backpedaling furiously. We never heard another word about eye examinations, secret or otherwise.

I didn't exactly *distrust* Jim. He was doing a good job, and he was doing right by me, as far as I could tell. I liked climbing with him — when we were on the same rope I knew I could trust him with my life. But the pressure of leadership separated Jim from the rest of the team. And as the expedition went on and the tension on the team increased, the pressure would force him to make some decisions he would later come to regret.

THERE were so many advantages to getting tapped for the first summit team. It's the peak of the expedition; everyone is still focused on the climb; there's virtually no risk of running out of supplies. When you're on Everest in the fall, climbing earlier means having a better shot at avoiding a winter storm. And if something goes wrong in mid-attempt — a storm, an accident, or illness — there's more time to retreat, let the others go, and then try again.

We all wanted to go first. It wasn't exactly a head-to-head competition, but I kept track. And as each day passed I knew exactly how I stood in relation to the others. Don was as strong as a bear, even with his broken finger. Johnny had been close to the front of the pack all the way to Camp 2, then felt a little loopy and retreated to Camp 1 for another night of acclimatization. Dave and Diana tended to lag behind, starting late in the morning and then climbing slowly, but both had incredible endurance, and both had climbed as high as anyone. Jim was right up there too, along with Geoff and Steve. Even Jean and Peggy, both support climbers, were doing well.

I felt strong, and kept up the pace. It felt good to move on the mountain, to feel my body working against the thin air and brittle cold. As I moved between base camp and Camp 2, the altitude hadn't troubled me. And climbing straight up the Lhotse Face to Camp 3 didn't throw me back either. I was nervous when I set out from Camp 2 that first morning, but when I got up there, trudging up the line, the thin rope draped down the steep white slope, I felt fine. So I dropped my load at camp, stopped for a snack, then set out again, climbing with a couple of Sherpas now, heading up to fix a few hundred feet of rope on the route to Camp 4. We managed to get in about 1,000 feet by early afternoon, then turned back to descend to Camp 2 for the night. I felt great! I made another carry to Camp 3 a day later, then went back again the next day, climbing with Jim and Steve. This time we planned to spend the night at the higher camp, then set out early the next morning to fix the rest of the line up to the South Col at 26,000 feet, where we'd establish Camp 4 on the ridge. But then, just as the three of us crawled into our sleeping bags at Camp 3 that afternoon, the horizon turned dark. Through the door of the tent we could see the black line of clouds sweeping across the pale blue sky, closing straight for us.

"I hate to be the voice of doom," Steve said, peering out toward the oncoming storm, "but this looks fucked." I nodded, reached for my boots.

"I think we better get out of here."

Jim didn't argue. An exposed camp on the Lhotse Face was the last place you wanted to ride out a heavy blizzard, what with all that snow weighing down the snowpack. We rolled out of bed, threw on our down suits and boots, and plodded down the steep, icy slope back to Camp 2. The snowstorm hit at dusk, and by the next morning a thick layer of clouds had glommed on to the entire mountain. We couldn't move in either direction. We spent the next day huddled with the other climbers at Camp 2, hiding in our sleeping bags while the winds tore across the mountainside. But even when the climb itself cannot proceed, the business of the climb goes on. So as the storm raged that afternoon, and as the murky light faded to dusk, Jim and Don sat down to talk strategy.

So far the weather had been good to us. We had been moving quickly, and now, after two weeks, we were close to finishing the route. If the winter winds and snow kept their distance, we were in excellent position to send everyone who wanted to go up to the summit. But counting on another ten days of perfect weather — well, that was one monumental *if*. And if this snowstorm blew into a week-long extravaganza (a more likely-sounding *if*) like the one that had planted Scott, Q, Wes, and me in the snow cave last year, maybe none of us would end up on the summit.

Time was the bottom line. No matter how smoothly things had gone, we were moving into the end of September now. The days were sliding away, and already we were pinned down by a massive storm. If we kept to our original plan — the one we'd all agreed on in Seattle, the one that held us all together — and didn't choose the first summit team until we had finished the route, we'd keep everyone on the mountain for at least another four or five days. Counting the three days of rest a summit team would require at base camp after that, following the original plan would push all the summit attempts into October. And on Everest October is frequently a wild, wintry month, a month of snowstorms and windstorms — the average wind speed on the summit is 150 miles an hour. Not the sort of conditions a person would want to walk into.

Suddenly, it seemed we were getting behind the game. The other teams on the west side were sending their summit climbers down to rest at base camp. The French and Korean climbers were already getting ready to head for the summit. And here we were all up at Camp 2. So Jim and Don made a decision: forget the plan. We could no longer afford to wait until the entire route was set. Once it was calm enough to move, the first summit team would descend to base camp to fatten up for a few days. The rest of the climbers would go up the mountain to finish off the route to the South Col and then build up Camp 4.

Now all they needed to do was decide who was going to be on that first summit team.

No one knew it, except Jim and Don, but the one guiding principle that we had agreed on — the objective system that would give us our first summit team — had just been scrapped. Now politics could enter the equation. Which of us could claim the *right* to make the first attempt? Was it Jim, because he was the team's leader? Or Jean Ellis, who came aboard as a support climber, but who had also brought with him a major financial contribution? And which woman should get first shot at the summit? I knew I was a leading candidate. The First American Woman title itself had receded in my eyes, but the summit, by contrast, had not. I wanted my shot, the sooner the better. In terms of strength, climbing ability, hauling capacity, and altitude reached, I matched anyone in the group, man or woman.

But there were rumblings.

Until we left Kathmandu Diana had seemed relaxed around me. She was so welcoming when I joined the team, so eager to include me in her pursuit of the summit. Before we left home we'd even talked briefly about climbing to the summit together.

I didn't walk with Diana much during the trek, and when we got to the mountain we climbed in different groups. When we did meet, I thought I could feel a tension emanating from her. What I didn't know, as the wind whipped my tent that afternoon at Camp 2, was that the issue had already been decided.

I was lying in my tent, writing a letter to David and listening to the wind, when Jim crunched over in the snow and squatted down outside the doorway. He pulled back the flap and peered in, a few snowflakes hanging on his wool hat.

"How you doin'?" he said.

"Okay."

"Good. Do you want to be on the first summit team with me and Steve?"

"Sure!"

"Good. We'll head down to base camp to rest once we can make it down."

Jim left, and I went back to my letter. For a moment. Then it hit me. *I was going back to the summit.* I dropped my pen and pulled back the tent flap. There wasn't much to see. The mountain was shrouded in the clouds now, just a small slope of glacier above, disappearing into the mist. But I could see it in my mind. The summit was up there, and now I was going to have another shot at it, another chance to fulfill my truest ambition. It was thrilling and frightening. Thrilling to have a wish granted, frightening to know that wishes often bring curses with them.

JIM and Don had decided to stick with most of the original precepts of their plan, only with a slight variation. The three climbers who had climbed the highest on the route got to go first. Working on the route to Camp 4 had qualified Jim and me. Steve's afternoon at Camp 3 ushered him in. But Steve wasn't the only climber to have reached that high, and judging strength is always so subjective. When word filtered through camp, the rumbling gathered force. Jim and Don had laid out four summit teams: Jim, Steve, and me on the first team; Don, Diana, and Dave on the second; Geoff and Johnny on the third team, and Peggy and Jean on the fourth. The news didn't bring unanimous joy. Geoff — working on his third attempt on the mountain — was frustrated to find himself so far down the list. Diana was furious that she was behind me, and Dave wasn't happy either.

Any leader who puts himself on the first summit team, no matter the circumstances, is bound to face criticism. And as the rumbling became public on our team, Jim was no longer above reproach. *Jim put himself on the first summit team!*

Not everyone was angry, however. Don agreed with Jim — he'd helped him make the decision — and not even the angry climbers extended their rage to Don. He was as eager for the summit as anyone on the team. Johnny didn't complain, neither did Peggy or Jean. If the fix was in, as the rumblers had it, wouldn't Don have put the kibosh on the dirty deal? You'd think so — but according to Don, it was a fair decision. *We chose the people who climbed the highest.*

Suddenly it was just like the '87 expedition, except now *I* felt like the villain, cutting in line and dashing for the summit. And I wasn't the only one with a touch of guilt. Even as we prepared to return to base camp, Steve grumbled. "I don't know why we're doing this," he said darkly. "We should have finished the route first." But then again, Steve didn't feel bad enough to turn down his slot on the summit team. Neither did I.

But I had to do something. The next morning I looked for Diana. I wanted to say something, anything, before we left. I poked my head into her tent, and found her finishing off breakfast.

"I don't know how you feel about this," I said. "I just want you to know I didn't have anything to do with this decision."

"I know you didn't," she said. Diana peered up at me, sitting up in her sleeping bag. Her voice was flat and she looked pale. I could see the weight of the expedition suddenly pushing down on her shoulders. "I'm not mad at you. I'm mad at Jim. He should have chosen both of us, you know."

10

NOWHERE ELSE
TO CLIMB

WAITING was the hardest part. Before, there had been action — climbing, carrying loads — now there was thought. Sitting around base camp all day with little to do except ponder. We talked about relaxing, Steve, Jim, and I, but talking about it was as close as I ever got. Who could relax when there was so much time to think?

I traversed the hours with meals and naps and empty time spent gazing upward, contemplating the mountain. Contemplating, and cutting away. It takes so much energy to climb, so much concentration to propel yourself up through the ice and rock. You really can't be bothered with anything else. No extraneous fears, no anxieties, no regrets.

Climbing requires coolness and reason. Efficiency of thought, just as the physical act requires an efficiency of motion. You don't wave your arms when you climb. You don't load down your pack with gear. (Some climbers saw off their toothbrushes to save the unnecessary "gram-age.") So I sorted out the thoughts I didn't need to take with me. Anything that didn't affect the climb, anything I couldn't control, I took out of my head and put it away.

I spent the morning of the third day by myself. After breakfast I walked across the glacier and sat on some boulders, looking out toward Everest. The sun reflected against the rocks, and as the air grew warmer I took off my sweater and folded it up for a pillow. Closing my eyes, I ran through tomorrow's regimen. Waking up before dawn. Leaving camp and climbing through the ice fall. Through the heat of the Western Cwm, then up to Camp 2. That was the first leg, and we'd be on our way. I could feel a wave of adrenaline.

After lunch, Jim, Steve, and I made the final checks on our equipment. Pasang was packed and ready. He sat with the other Sherpas, playing cards and smoking cigarettes. Pasang was a great smoker. He did it constantly, which prompted all us nonsmokers to nickname him "Little Chimney." But he was also a great climber and spoke fluent English. Appa and Pemba, the other two climbing Sherpas, weren't due back in camp until mid-afternoon. Steve and I spent the rest of the afternoon outside our tents on our lawn chairs, reading and dozing in the strong mountain sun. Eventually the shadows lengthened, a cooler breeze came across the glacier, and we could smell the first signs of dinner from the kitchen tent. Steve looked up from his book and glanced at his watch. "So when are Pemba and Appa coming back?"

"Anytime, I guess."

"Mid-afternoon, right?"

"That's what they said."

Steve went back to his book.

It was four o'clock, then five. And still no Appa and no Pemba. I felt uneasy. I walked over to the edge of camp and looked down the glacier. Nothing moved. *Where the hell are they?* I walked back to my tent.

Then the sun set, and they still hadn't arrived. At dinner we sat with the base camp regulars, expedition managers Bob, Larry, and Charlie, the *Times* reporter Sherry Stripling, photographer Denise Eberhard, all of us spooning up chicken soup in silence and keeping one ear tuned to the empty glacier. But as darkness fell, the black shroud descending over the glacier for the night, I could see the others giving up.

"So," Jim said, leaning his chin in his hands. "Where the fuck are those guys?"

"Kind of lousy for them to stand us up," I said.

"Let's go without them." Steve said. "For Chrissakes. We're all ready. We're big kids. Why do we need them?"

"Who's gonna carry the oxygen?" That was Jim, his voice rising, though it was hardly a question.

Steve shrugged. "We can't carry our own oxygen?"

"Pasang's here, he's ready to go," I said. "Can't we take him and two of the other Sherpas?"

Jim shook his head. "None of those guys are rested. Not the ones who've already been high on the mountain, anyway. And none of the others have gone above Camp Two."

"So we sit on our asses for another day?" Steve's voice was smooth but tight. Jim nodded.

"We sit on our asses. But if they're not here tomorrow we'll go without them."

Steve shrugged. I nodded.

"Fine."

One more day on the lawn chairs, staring up into the clear blue sky, traversing another set of hours with my books and my reels of thoughts. Finally, just before dinner, Appa and Pemba walked into camp, calling their hellos. Jim came out of his tent to meet them, and Steve and I followed. Jim was leaning forward, hands on his hips. His prosecuting attorney stance. "So where were you?"

Appa smiled. "Roof on house fall down," he said. Jim made a noise, something between a sigh and a cluck. Appa kept smiling, Pemba looked at his feet. "Long time to fix," he added.

Jim shook his head in resignation. "We leave in the morning."

Appa nodded, then turned to walk to his tent. Pemba followed. When they were gone, Steve laughed his dry guffaw and walked back to his lawn chair. "Roof fall down," he said. "Right."

Later, I lay in my sleeping bag, waiting for sleep. Awake in the dark, with an unruly crowd of night thoughts jostling for attention. Would I be strong enough to keep up with Jim and Steve? And assuming we made it past Camp 3, beyond the highest spot I'd climbed so far, would my body continue to adjust to the altitude?

The glacier creaked again. At least I was focused on climbing this time. I knew the title was still out there, though. Maybe this time I would get it. Would that make a difference? I knew it could open doors. Despite — or perhaps because of — the relatively obscure stature of mountaineering, the American media would certainly throw their arms around the first American woman to climb the world's tallest mountain. And I wouldn't reject their attention if it happened to me. But by now I knew a few cameras and microphones wouldn't change me. Even if I got to the summit, I wouldn't be anything more than what I was right now. Right now it was all about climbing, about taking a run at my own limitations. Could I do it? Did I have the physical and mental stamina? After more than a decade, I had to know how it felt to go all the way. To burst through the boundaries and stand on top of the world. This was the last time I'd even think about it. We'd leave in the morning, and from there I'd worry only about climbing.

WHEN my wristwatch beeped at three-thirty I sat up and waited for my eyes to clear. Outside, I could hear the clanks and bangs of breakfast in the kitchen tent. Jetta was scrambling eggs. A soft wind flapped through the tent door, and I slipped out of my sleeping bag and concentrated on dressing for the climb. First my one-piece polypropylene climbing skin — sort of like long underwear, with a zipper through the crotch. Then a polypropylene turtleneck, a pair of polypro pile pants, water-resistant overalls, and an Entrant pullover. Down below, I slipped on two pairs of polypro socks — a thin pair for a lining and a thick pair for warmth. Finally, I laced up my plastic climbing boots and tiptoed out for breakfast.

The meal was quiet and swift, the sound of spoons against tin, scrambled eggs and chapaties being eaten very quickly. Then it was done and Jim, Steve, Pasang, Appa, Pemba, and I slung on our packs. We moved quietly, in deference to the second team, still sleeping in their tents, but Charlie and Bob followed us out to the edge of camp. "Go for it, you guys," Bob whispered, waving us on. "Have fun," Charlie hissed. "But be careful up there."

It was four-thirty, still more than an hour before dawn. Shadows from our headlamps danced across the glacier as we moved. Stiff and tense in the darkness, I took short, choppy steps. My pack settled against my back and rubbed the sore spot it had burned into my hips during the first few weeks on the mountain. We hiked in silence, hearing only our own breathing and the rhythmic chafing of our pants.

At the bottom of the ice fall we paused for a few moments to strap our crampons onto our boots. With the sun already coloring the eastern horizon, we needed to move quickly. Crampons set, we walked to the start of the fixed safety rope and clicked on our jumars. The early morning air was still and cold. As the sky paled, our steps were punctuated only with the sound of our effort — the crampons chunking into the ice, then clanking on the ladder rungs. We moved steadily, with few words. My pack dug into my lower back, I grew thirsty, then hungry, but we kept moving. Lhotse loomed ahead of us, Everest hid beyond the ridge on our left. We climbed onward, barely stopping to catch our breath.

After three and a half hours of steady climbing, we emerged into the daylight on the low edge of the Western Cwm, near the tents of Camp 1. The Mouth of Death was behind us, and with the sun just starting to heat the snow and ice, we could afford to take a rest. We doffed our packs and sat down for some water and chocolate.

Hoping to avoid the intense heat of the day in the cwm, we set out for Camp 2 after ten minutes, traversing the valley to cross the wide crevasses, then moving straight up the blank valley floor. As the sun grew stronger, we stopped to take off our crampons and lose a few layers of clothes. I stripped down to my first layer of polypropylene, and then we set out again for Camp 2, now a group of colored specks in the distance.

We got to Camp 2 by late morning, and settled into our tents to avoid the heat of the day. I stayed inside my tent for most of the afternoon, napping, reading one of Johnny's spy novels, drinking water, and eating. It felt good to be back on the mountain, after all that time in base camp, traveling light with blue skies and slack breezes ahead. It was a perfect day for climbing, which, when I thought about it, made it frustrating to be as low as Camp 2. There was no telling if the weather was going to get worse immediately, but I knew there was no telling it wasn't, either. We should have been higher. Everyone else certainly was. While we were cooling our boots that day, two of our Korean friends went up the South Buttress, the route just to the left of the South Col. The two French daredevils clambered up from the South Col, along with three other French climbers, four Sherpas, and a Swiss climber.

With a dozen climbers elbowing for room on the summit, it was the busiest day up there in Everest history. Down at Camp 2 the teams got the news from their climbers in staticky bulletins, breathless accounts radioed down from walkie-talkies on the summit, or later from the radios in their high camps. Whenever the reports came through the camp, an electric buzz radiated from tent to tent.

The biggest news came from the French. After three failed attempts earlier in the month, Marc Batard finally completed his oxygenless, twenty-four-hour dash from base camp. And fast on *his* winged heels came Jean-Marc Boivin, lugging his parapente. After taking a few moments to catch his breath, Boivin peered around to check the conditions. Calling down on his radio, Boivin gave the all-clear. Departure time: approximately ten minutes. I went out to watch, standing with a crowd of climbers from all the teams, and saw Boivin soar off the summit. His rainbow parapente was first a pinprick, then grew larger as he swooped down toward the floor of the cwm. Boivin made a smooth landing, glasses off and endorsement-friendly smile on full blast, about ten feet in front of his bank of cameras.

I went to bed early that night and when my watch beeped before dawn I jolted awake. Outside, the night sky was clear and the temperature was cold, somewhere just above zero. Perfect climbing weather, so I scooped up some snow and then fired up my stove to melt some drinking water. I was still finishing a quick breakfast of tea and hot cereal when I heard Jim, Steve, and the Sherpas outside. They were making their last equipment adjustments for the day's climb, all ready to go, and I wasn't even finished dressing. Dammit. They weren't going to wait for me — no reason to, on this part of the mountain. But even when I know the route, I don't like being left behind. I didn't want to let them get out of my sight. I dove for my crampons, strapping them to my boots as quickly as I could. I took one last look around the tent, then stepped outside. The others were walking now, just a few feet away, but gaining speed. In one movement I swung on my pack, tightened the straps, and moved after them. I caught them easily and fell into line.

The flat part of the cwm passed quickly enough this time, and once we crossed the bergschrund, the last major crevasse before the face arcs skyward, we clipped on to the fixed line and I fell into my usual climbing rhythm. It got colder as we climbed higher. Most of my body stayed warm, heated by the effort and spared the leeching effect of a strong wind. But my extremities had a harder time. The chill seeped in through my thick mittens, crawling into my fingertips, then toward my palms. My toes, in the meantime, were beyond pain, so used to the cold they just gave up the ghost and went numb. Whenever I stopped moving I swung my legs like pendulums, trying to keep the blood moving.

For the next four hours we climbed at a measured distance from one another, each climber separated from the next by one of the aluminum stakes holding the rope to the ice. The sun rose, a pink ball bouncing up from beyond the jagged horizon. By the time we approached Camp 3 the sun was high and white, bright enough to be little but a blur in my eyes.

Now we were getting up there. Down at Camp 2 the altitude made life harder, but it was still almost normal. During the day you could tarry outside, if it wasn't too hot, and enjoy the warmth of the sun on your shoulders. But in tents perched on tiny platforms dug into the mountainside at 23,700 feet, there was no heat — only a blistering cold, the thin air rushing past in a biting, miserable gust. When we got to the tents we didn't pause to catch our breath. With toes and fingers stiff and bonelike, far too long past sensation, we shoved our packs inside the tents and dove for the thick high-altitude sleeping bags. I shared a tent with Steve, and we spent the rest of the afternoon wrapped up tight, eating and drinking all the freeze-dried shrimp, candy bars, and powdered energy drinks we could hold. When that got boring, we played the Symptom Game.

"Are you eating enough?" Steve offered me some candy. I listened to his breathing to check for gurgling, the first sign of a pulmonary edema.

"Any headaches?" No.

"Nausea?" No.

"Poo problems?" No.

Toward nightfall, we ate dinner and tried to go to sleep. Steve dozed off almost immediately. I listened to him breathe, hearing the wind flapping the tent. The breeze was stronger up here, blowing unfettered across the face. From above, small ice chunks came skittering down the slope, scraping past and sometimes thwacking against the zippered nylon door of the tent.

I stayed awake. In the morning we'd head toward the unknown. Up to Camp 4, to climb higher than I'd climbed this year. Then, the next day, moving even higher, beyond where I'd ever climbed. The thought made me electric with anxiety — the climb, the expedition, the year, eleven years of mountain climbing, were about to come to a climax. My heart thudded against my ribs. The wind blew, the tent flapped, I examined the darkness. I don't know how long I was awake. Eventually tension gave way to exhaustion, and I sank into sleep.

We woke up before dawn again and set immediately to melting snow and fixing breakfast. I drank a few cups of hot chocolate and ate a granola bar, then concentrated on getting dressed, loading my gear into my pack and preparing my oxygen tank. The tanks had been stashed in the tents the week before, when we first set up the camp.

Leaving the camp, we traversed a shallow slope for a few hundred yards, then started up again, climbing straight up a 50-degree ice face. Jim led the way, and soon gained distance from Steve and me. Behind us, the Sherpas brought up the rear. Born and bred in the Himalayas, the Sherpas have lungs like leather. Even at 24,000 feet they can squeeze enough oxygen out of the air to power themselves through the thin environment. I wished I could, too. As I climbed, the large, eighteen-pound aluminum cylinder of oxygen sat in the middle of my pack, balanced just like scuba gear on a diver. The rubber mask fit over my mouth and nose, secured with a strap. I knew the richer air would keep my head clear and my extremities warmer, but lugging it around was incredibly uncomfortable. Condensation was forever building up in my mask and dripping down, accumulating in a cold pool that sloshed around my chin.

Above us the sky was clear, a vivid powder blue in the morning sunlight. The clouds beneath us — hovering around 20,000 feet — were soft and billowy. The breeze blew gently, and as the day wore on, it grew warm enough to trade my wool hat for a pink baseball cap. We were heading for the summit and our horizon was clear in all directions.

Jim, Steve, and I climbed into Camp 4 just before two P.M. We were at 26,000 feet now, well into the empty edge of the atmosphere. In the piercing light of the afternoon the only signs of life on the mountainside were two small red tents, set up a few days earlier by the other expedition members. One tent was full of equipment, so we set up another, working quickly, our backs to the cutting breeze. We squatted down to chip the anchors into the ice, exaggerating the movements to keep our bodies working against the cold.

That task finished, we stowed our gear and dove for our sleeping bags. The Sherpas shared one tent, Jim took the equipment one for his tall, broad self, while I shared the third with Steve. The next day — our summit day — would be the longest of the climb. We ate a quick dinner at four P.M., then set our alarms for nine that night. To have daylight at the summit and during the descent back to camp, we'd need to make an early start. We would start climbing at midnight.

This time we wore oxygen masks to bed. Steve dozed off almost immediately, but again sleep was far from me. The mask was my first problem. Condensation kept dripping on my face. And I was cold. Even in my down sleeping bag, with two layers of polypropylene, the thin, frigid air sucked the heat from my body. The minutes crawled by, the hours stretched and sagged. My breath was dripping on my nose and down my chin, and my toes and fingers felt cold and stiff. Eventually the sun set and darkness came. The wind blew softly, the night stayed clear. No storms in sight.

Time seemed to hang suspended. I could barely lie still, and Steve was unconscious. His chest moved with deep, uncluttered breaths. I checked my own breathing. Also okay. And no headaches, no nausea. I was fine. But how would I be tomorrow? The summit day. I'd kept up with Jim and Steve so far, but tomorrow was the crucial moment. New territory. More steep faces, more cliffs, gullies filled with deep, soft snow. Knee-high for Jim and Steve was a long way up my thigh, and here I was, hoping to keep up with their powerful footsteps. And for a small woman, that's no small feat, even in good conditions. Jim was a rugged six feet two, broad-shouldered with powerful tree-trunk thighs. Steve was a shade under six feet and skinny, but taut as wire and as fast as a jackrabbit. On a 50-degree glacier or a vertical face, he climbed like a spider going up a wall.

I remembered those stories Jim Whittaker used to tell about his climbs on Everest's higher reaches. He was so exhausted by the climb, so sapped by the altitude, his pace slowed until he was a slow-motion movie of himself. He'd take a step, Whittaker said, then count to ten. Then he'd take another step, count to ten, then take another step. That was life at 28,000 feet, he said, and I wasn't sure I could climb like that.

Outside, ice chunks skittered past the tent. We were 3,000 feet from the summit. How could Steve sleep now? I wanted to move. Feel the weight of my pack and just go now.

W E were close to Mrs. Schmatz now. This was one of those real-life Everest horror stories climbers love to tell. In the early eighties two German climbers, Mr. and Mrs. Schmatz, were climbing for the summit together. They got to the top and I imagined them up there together on a clear, cold morning, enjoying the view. The descent should have gone without a hitch. But Mrs. Schmatz soon grew tired. The climb had taken more out of her than she thought — maybe she was too focused on keeping up with her husband. It's hard to know, because soon after they started down together, Mrs. Schmatz sat down to rest, and never got up again. She died of exhaustion where she sat. She's still up there, somewhere around 28,000 feet. When the snow recedes off her in the springtime, descending climbers leave empty oxygen tanks or pat her head for good luck. According to the legend, you can still see her hair — blonde like mine — flowing out from her wool hat. Apparently she's well preserved. But good luck or not, she was the last thing I wanted to bump into. The long blonde hair, the pale, white skin, captured in the ice, a life-sized warning to every climber who ventures that high . . . you don't belong here. But I knew I was stronger than that. I had the will and the drive. I felt good. I was healthy. I'd made it to Camp 4, and now the summit was just a few steps away. I knew I could make it. I couldn't forget the other mountains I'd climbed. The years and the experience, last year's Everest expedition. I could do this.

My mask dripped. My toes, my feet, my ankles were cold. I was wide awake. The hours dragged. I rolled around, searching for the warm spot in my sleeping bag. But it wasn't there, and I huddled alone in the cold, keeping still, waiting to move.

Finally, my watch alarm cut the stillness. It was nine P.M. I reached over to shake Steve, and sat up, reaching for my headlamp. "Time to move!" I unzipped the tent and reached out to scoop some snow into a pot while Steve, still groggy, fired up the stove. In the extreme cold and thin atmosphere, it took two and a half hours to melt the few quarts we needed. Meanwhile, we sat in our sleeping bags, working through some beef jerky, nuts, chocolate, cups of our high-carbo, high-cal drink. Nothing seemed appealing, but I jammed in everything I could hold, and then a little more for good measure. Finishing breakfast, I poked my head outside to gauge the weather, trying to figure out how much to wear.

Outside, the night was about 20 below, with only soft winds. I kept on my polypro underlayers. Without stiff winds, we wouldn't face much of a chill factor, so I left off my thick pile pants. For body warmth I zipped on my bright red down climbing suit. Two layers of polypropylene socks fit beneath the plastic climbing boots, and heavy neoprene overboots snapped above.

It was past midnight now, and Steve had finished dressing. For a moment he sat by the door, watching me adjust my socks, pull on my boots. I'd heard the Sherpas gathering outside our tent a few minutes earlier, crunching in the ice and chattering to themselves. And Jim was already outside, adjusting his crampons, slinging on his backpack. They wouldn't wait long, standing in the cold and wind. We were still a team . . . but today was different. You look after each other on summit day, but you think about yourself more. I fumbled to strap on my crampons, and Steve glanced out the tent door. He shifted impatiently. "I'm going out," he said, and ducked through the flap. Panic shot through my stomach. I didn't want him to leave without me. *Why am I always so slow in the morning?* I finished attaching my crampons and dashed out after him. By the time I managed to get my pack on, Steve, Jim, and the Sherpas had already started away from camp. Oh, don't leave me, I thought. Not on this desolate, alien plain. I hurried to adjust my oxygen mask, checking the regulator, setting the gauge. The empty tents rattled in the breeze, and I started up across the snowfield, racing to catch my partners before they vanished into the darkness.

THE snow was smooth and bone white, reflecting the light of a huge full moon. Stars scattered across the rest of the sky, and we walked without headlamps, our path lit by the pale glow from outer space. Wearing our billowy climbing suits, faces covered with heavy oxygen masks, we scuttled through a surreal landscape. Balancing between the sheer white light and deep black shadows, we were tiny and insignificant. Astronauts in empty space.

We moved as quickly as we could, kicking steps into the frozen crust on the snow. Climbing a few feet apart, we kept our heads down, concentrating on our own breathing and the rhythm of our steps. Even in a team of climbers, climbing becomes a solitary pursuit. Especially in the outer fringe of the atmosphere, where communicating means shouting above your oxygen mask. It's hard enough to draw the breath to keep moving. Conversations are cut to the quick, thoughts and directions boiled down to hand signals and two-word fragments.

We climbed through the night, muscles gradually loosening as we moved up the face of a 40-degree glacier. Jim led at first, punching in his ice ax, leaning forward and kicking steps with the toe of his big boot. Then we'd rotate the lead, Pasang, Steve, me, then Jim again. Appa and Pemba climbed behind us, following our tracks. It seemed easy at first. The ankle-deep snow was crusty with ice, the outcroppings of rock we used to mark our progress came and went at a steady clip.

Up there, the altitude weighed heavily on every step. My heart hammered against my ribs, and the entire core of my body burned with the effort to breathe. Even with the hissing stream of whole oxygen my lungs ached and my toes were numb with cold. It hurt to move, but I ignored the pain. I focused on the task and kept moving, step after step. The rustle of my body suit, the squeak of the crampons in the dry snow. No dark thoughts, just effort. Occasionally I'd stop for a breather: a few deep pulls of oxygen and a bit of leg-swinging. Then we'd start up again, and I'd return my attention to my feet, counting my steps. At 100 I'd take ten seconds to catch my breath. At 200 I'd reach a hand up to crack my oxygen mask, breaking the film of ice formed by my moist exhalations.

Pasang was out in front, but after an hour Appa and Pemba had dropped back, trailing by a hundred yards. We stopped to rest for a moment, and Jim looked down at them, two shadows moving slowly in the dim light. He motioned toward me and shouted through his mask. "Wait for 'em." His chest heaved for a moment, then he shouted again. "Back too far. Find out what's wrong."

"Okay," I shouted, but felt something else. *Why me?* Sure, someone should wait for them — if they were feeling sick, or if their equipment was troubling them, we had to help them out. But me? It didn't seem fair . . . but no time to argue. Jim took a big step forward, and Steve followed, Pasang on his heels. I watched them go. If I had to wait too long, I might never make it to the top. But they continued upward. I turned around and headed down for Appa and Pemba.

I reached them after a few minutes. "What's the problem?" I shouted. Appa pointed to Pemba's oxygen tank. "No air!"

I motioned for Pemba to turn around, took another step so I could reach him, and then checked the connections for leaks. The hoses seemed secure enough . . . nothing was broken . . . so I reached for the gauge. Here was the problem.

"It's not turned on!" I shouted. I unscrewed the valve and re-checked the connections. Pemba panted in the thick air. Now he seemed to relax. Meanwhile, Appa took off his heavy outer glove, propped it in his armpit, and reached into his pocket to take out a candy bar. He unwrapped it and took a bite. Now everything seemed to be back in order. Good. We could start after the others. Appa took another bite of candy, then stowed the rest in his coat pocket and zipped up. I dug in my ice ax, stepped to the side, and took a step forward. We were ready to go, swinging our eyes forward, leaning into the hill. Appa let go of his zipper, then reached up into his armpit for the mitten he'd left there. He reached for it and had it in his hand for a second. Maybe the cold was already piercing his thin liner glove. The frigid air is so shocking, one layer of polypropylene affords little protection. As the blood stops flowing, the growing numbness brings on thoughts of frostbite. So Appa was reaching for his mitten . . . and he had the mitten in his fingers . . . but then he dropped it. Without it, his hand would freeze.

For an awful moment we all watched the mitten go. It hit the ice, skipped, and cascaded down the slope. *No!* Appa lurched after it, stiff and clumsy in the layers of heavy clothes. His hand brushed against it, but the mitten slithered out of his grasp and continued on its way, bouncing and skipping down the slope.

I gasped into my oxygen mask. We watched it go, helpless as it cascaded down the glacier, spinning on the lumps and grooves in the ice. Then, miraculously, it stopped. Thirty feet below us, pinned against a shallow, windblown ridge. Slowly and carefully, Appa climbed down after it. Blocking it with one boot, he reached down gently and picked it up, sliding it back on his hand. He rested a moment, then started back up the face. I stood there with Pemba, impatiently swinging my legs back and forth. Glancing up ahead, I watched the dim outlines ascending above us. Finally Appa drew alongside us. We started up after Jim, Steve, and Pasang — now almost 300 feet ahead. It took half an hour to catch them.

W E climbed up a long, steep face through hard-packed snow, aiming for a group of gullies at the top of the snowfield. According to our maps in base camp, the gullies, a line of thin snow-filled grooves, would lead up to the long ridge that stretched across the mountain to the summit. After a hundred steps I stopped for some breaths. A hundred steps later I had some water. I cracked my oxygen mask at a shallow ridge.

Appa and Pemba had dropped back again, but Pasang was keeping up with us. My feet were still cold, my lungs still ached, but we were cruising. We didn't have to take long rests, we weren't getting hammered with winds or heavy clouds. And so far, we were a long way from Jim Whittaker's "Take a step, count to ten, take a step" plan. I checked my oxygen flow, making sure it was still at 1.5 liters a minute. I monitored my own condition: my head was clear, my lungs were clear. My toes were still back at Camp 4, as far as I knew, but I was easily in step with Jim and Steve, even after having climbed down to find the Sherpas. It was still well before dawn and we had already gained significant altitude.

At five A.M. we reached the bottom of the gullies. We rested for a moment, while Jim craned his neck to look down for Appa and Pemba. Steve and I shared some water with Pasang while Jim squinted, searching for them in the faint morning light. He watched for a moment, his heavy breaths clouding his mask. Then: "*Fuck!*"

We all looked at Jim, still gazing down the mountainside. "Shit!" he shouted. His voice was small and muffled in his mask. "They turned around!"

My jaw dropped. Steve looked over at me, lowering the water bottle from his mouth. "Well, goddamn," he said. I followed Jim's gaze and started down numbly, at the figures retreating in the distance.

We were hundreds of feet away, and our Sherpas — *along with two of our oxygen tanks* — were retreating. Sherpas we'd counted on. Oxygen we needed to get to the summit and back. Thought we needed, anyway. For a moment we stood there, mute, helpless, watching them vanish into the blackness.

"What the hell . . . what happened?" Jim murmured. Peering down, he squinted to focus. Sick or injured men would move slowly, but even at a distance we could see them making good time. Plodding down the path, retracing the steps we'd made a half hour earlier. So what was it: Fatigue? Fear? A collapse of the will?

All Sherpas are well paid, relatively, but Sherpas who summit Everest are in an entirely different bracket. It's like earning a doctorate. When you've got the Ph.D. after your name, you can charge the premium rates. Maybe we should have realized earlier that Appa and Pemba weren't sure they wanted to finish their dissertations. Like when they stayed home for an extra day instead of returning to base camp. "Roof fall down," Appa had said, and maybe it was true. And maybe it wasn't. *Maybe they just didn't want to go.*

Now they had made that certain. And one more thing, too: the roof had just fallen down on us.

I pictured the mountain, trying to figure how long we'd been climbing and how close we were to the summit. Maybe six hours, possibly more. Could we make it there and back to camp with one bottle of oxygen apiece? I looked at Jim.

"Think we can make it?"

Steve fumbled for his gauge, hanging down close to his chest. "Check how much you've got. What flow are you on?"

Jim and I looked at our own gauges. When they're full, the tanks hold 4,000 pounds per square inch of oxygen. When we left camp, we'd all set our regulators at 1.5 liters of oxygen a minute, so we each had about 3,000 psi's left. Back at base camp, we'd figured on using something close to 8,000 psi's to get from Camp 4 to the summit and back again. So far we'd made faster progress than we had planned. Even so, the math didn't compute: our oxygen supply had just been cut in half. No way could we get up and back on 3,000 psi's — not if we wanted to breathe oxygen all the way. But no one mentioned turning back. We turned down our gauges to one liter a minute and prepared to climb up into the gully.

"So besides the oxygen, how are we doing?" Steve said.

"Great, except I can't feel my feet," Jim said.

"Cold feet, but feeling strong," I said.

Pasang nodded. "Fine."

"Me too," Steve said.

I put the bota bag inside my down suit and started up into the gully. The entire stop had taken about three minutes.

THE four of us made our way up the gully. I led at first, breaking through soft, calf-deep snow. The trench was narrow, about twenty-five feet across, and quite steep, sloping up at about 45 de-

grees. In the dim early morning light, we could see what seemed to
be the top of the gully ahead of us — it sloped up for a few hundred
feet, then crested on a ridge. According to our calculations, that ridge
would lead across the mountain to another ridge that sloped up to
the summit.

We'd been switching off the lead all morning, but when the snow
in the gully grew deeper, and I sank almost to my knees, I asked Jim
to go ahead. We slogged through the deep, soft snow for more than
an hour, without seeming to make much progress. Gradually the
morning grew light enough for us to see our surroundings more
clearly. But even after ninety minutes in the gully, the ridge we were
aiming for, the one that seemed to mark the top of the gully, still
appeared to be as far away as it had when we started.

Somewhere beyond our side of the mountain, the sun was breaking through the edge of the night, sending the first waves of light up
through the darkness. We were still walking in the shadows, but we
could feel the texture of the snow change. The icy crust turned soft,
and now we sank even deeper, past our knees in the heavy snow.

At the bottom none of us was sure which gully to take, so we had
deferred to Pasang. He was the only one of us who had been that
high on this route, and when we got to the top of the snow face, he
told Jim that the lowest gully was the fastest way to the summit. So
we followed Pasang's lead, but after two hours of struggling upward,
step by miserable step in the soft, hip-deep snow, we started wondering if we'd made a mistake. That ridge in the distance just wasn't
getting any closer. We kept moving, gasping, straining, panting into
our sodden masks, but we weren't *going* anywhere.

Growing desperate, Jim started weaving back and forth, looking
for an easy route up to the side of the gully. Meanwhile, Steve and I
stopped to dig some test pits in the soft snow — if the snow was
unstable, this would be perfect weather for an avalanche. Especially
here, in the dead center of a natural avalanche corridor.

The snowpack seemed firm enough and we continued climbing,
but as the morning light grew stronger, my thoughts darkened. The
visible skyline was still miles away. *It's too late for us,* I thought.
Almost seven A.M. now. Somehow we'd become bogged down. If we
were still as far away as we thought, we'd never make the summit. I
looked at the walls around us, then up to the distant ridge, and my

spirits sank. The snow was too deep. It had taken us too long to climb through it. I gripped my ice ax and took another step.

Then the sides of the gully flattened a bit, and Jim — still traversing, still looking for the way out of this endless gully, maybe to another gully where we could find a way onto that distant ridge — headed up the right side, then disappeared past the edge of the thin valley. Steve, Pasang, and I followed. When we got to Jim, he beamed down at us.

"Hey," he called down. "We're here!"

Jim didn't figure it out until he climbed up the side of the gully. He was hoping to see if the next gully provided quicker access to the ridge we were aiming for, but then Jim discovered there was no next gully — just the other side of the mountain. Apparently, the groove we were climbing in had swerved to the left, curving gently until it ran parallel to the ridge. The shadowy skyline we'd been gazing at since dawn — that distant, unreachable target we thought we were aiming for — was actually the summit of Everest, still a thousand feet in the distance.

We stopped for a moment, standing in the full morning light for the first time that day. It was just after seven. Time to make a decision. We figured our tanks had about six hours left on them. Since Appa and Pemba had vanished, we had only one replacement for the four of us. Pasang's stronger lungs could work on a lighter oxygen flow, but we were still nervous about heading up to the summit without at least enough to guarantee a 1.5-liter flow until we got back to Camp 4. Which meant, as of now, we had to get up and back to camp in six hours.

Jim turned to Pasang. "How long to the summit from here?"

Pasang looked up the ridge, then back to Jim. He hadn't gone to the summit, but he'd been this high before, and knew the terrain better than any of us. Pasang glanced around, then looked back at Jim. "Five hours," he said.

A gust of wind rushed past. I leaned on my ice ax, Steve shifted his weight. Budgeting at least three hours to cruise back down to camp, that made the entire trip something like two hours beyond our oxygen supply. And maybe we could squeak by — maybe we could survive the trip without *any* oxygen. It had been done before . . . two days ago by Batard! But maybe we couldn't.

I looked over at Jim, silently, and he shrugged.

"That's it, then." His voice was thin in his mask. "We go back and try again tomorrow."

I gazed up toward the summit, then back down the ridge, where we'd just struggled for the last two hours. There had to be another way. After all this time, all this effort, I wasn't going to turn around. The weather was perfect, and there was no way to guarantee that it could hold on for another twenty-four hours. I was not going to just turn around and go home, no way. After years of planning, hundreds of thousands of dollars, incredible commitment from people some of us had never even met . . . we *had* to get at least one person up there. No matter what you say, it does come down to a black-and-white concept: the expedition either touches the summit or comes home ready to explain what went wrong. We had to try. There had to be a way. But what were the options?

Options . . . my head spun. We could keep going, and when we got close to the summit, we could turn off the oxygen, then use it only when we absolutely needed it! Or maybe not all of us could go. . . .

"Look," I said. "One of us should go. Let's draw straws."

Steve nodded. "Right." Jim rolled it over, looked up at the ridge, then back at us. He shrugged. "Fine." Jim looked over at Pasang. "Choose a number between one and ten."

Now my heart was racing. I felt myself starting to float out of my boots and off the ridge. We were going to draw for it . . . and I was going to win! I knew it. I was going to the summit. Alone. I dug in my crampons. I wanted to go. So much of my life was focused on this, so many years had led to this moment. But just now the thought of being alone up there, without Jim and Steve to lean on, the thought of climbing that ridge with only Pasang . . . I was terrified.

Pasang peered back at Jim. *Choose a number?* What sort of wacko Sahib game was this? But he did what he was told. Pasang nodded back at Jim, who turned to Steve.

"Eight," Steve said.

They both looked at me.

"Four."

"I'll take six," Jim said. We all looked over at Pasang.

"Three," he said. "It's three."

Now the three of them looked at me.

"Congratulations," Jim said.

"And good luck," Steve added. We'd already been standing for a few minutes. The cold was seeping through my boots, crawling up my toes and into my ankles. My fingers were numb. I could see the others shifting in their boots. We had to start moving. Jim looked over to Pasang.

"You can come down with us, if you want to."

"No," he said. "I go up."

"You'll run out of oxygen," Jim said.

"I go up," Pasang repeated.

Steve and Jim looked at each other. They knew they could keep going. The conditions were perfect, this could be the day. They could turn the flow of oxygen down to a trickle, and as long as they felt strong they could keep going higher. But what do you risk for a summit? Steve had a wife, his career; Jim had his girlfriend, his place on Bainbridge Island — how much are you willing to risk? They turned around to start back down the gully.

They were leaving me, and now I was floating off the ridge. I'd have to get to the summit without them. Just with Pasang, and I'd never really climbed with him before. I knew he'd climbed well with us so far. But I didn't really know this guy. It was all up to me. And I would make it. I knew I would, not just for me, but for Steve and Jim. And the entire expedition. *Oh, my God!* Was I cold? I couldn't feel anything. For a second, I couldn't even move. Then they started to go, and I shouted after them.

"I . . . I . . . need some help with my oxygen tank."

Steve walked back and took the second oxygen bottle from Pasang's pack. I disconnected my regulator from my first tank, then Steve helped me place the new tank in my pack and connect the hoses. He fiddled with the flow gauge, then patted my shoulder. "Have fun. See you back at camp." Then he left.

I watched them disappear into the gully. Now they were gone. *I've got to depend on myself.* I sucked in a deep breath and reclaimed my courage. I could feel the cold now, could feel it eating into my hands and feet. I turned quickly and walked back to where Pasang stood.

"Okay, Pasang, you ready to go?"

"Yes."

I took the lead and we started up the ridge toward the summit.

Up the ridge, step after step. It curves to the left for a while, then takes a sharp jog to the right. The ridge makes relatively easy climbing, a hard-packed surface sloping up at perhaps a 35-degree angle. And it's not even a knifeblade. The path is a good ten feet wide, a nice buffer between yourself and the 500-foot drop looming on either side. So I concentrated on climbing, my heart banging away, my body trying to squeeze oxygen from my lungs. I focused on the effort. No anxiety, no problems. Just keep moving, no matter what. And I would have, except for my sunglasses, which kept fogging up.

It was my oxygen mask, my hot breath leaking out of the top, from the base of my nose right into my glasses! Moisture would start to build in the low center of the lenses, then as the heat rose so would the haze, like a fog bank rising out of a swamp. Then I was blind again, and I'd have to stop, pull them off, reach into my parka, and wipe the lenses on my polypro shirt. My view restored, I'd start up again . . . but then so would the fog. Higher and higher, minute by minute, creeping up until I was blind again, and the process repeated itself.

We continued up the ridge as best we could, gradually pulling closer to the steep, rocky slope leading up to the south summit, the sharp rise and false peak that stands on the south edge of the final ridge. Looking behind me, during my sunglass-maintenance stops, I could see a few of the Korean climbers approaching. Our old friends from the ice fall had come up from the South Buttress, and now, on the final approach, were moving as fast as they could. The first one caught up to me about a hundred yards from the south summit. I could hear him behind me, and stopped as he drew close. From behind his oxygen mask he flashed a big smile.

"Hello!" It came out like a gasp, too tired to even have an accent.

"Go on by," I panted. He nodded and continued past me. I set my sights on his pack, and starting moving again.

I waited for Pasang at the base of the south summit. There are two major obstacles on the final stretch to the true summit, and the south summit is the easier of them — a brief, steep stretch of rock, ice, and snow, leading up to a twelve-foot-wide summitlike mound. A thin cord — not even a rope — snaked up through the rocks, but when Pasang caught up I warned him away from it.

We clambered up through the rocks, walked across the top of the mound, then climbed down the far side. A short saddle ridge came next, about fifteen feet, leading to the vertical thirty-five-foot cliff called the Hillary Step. Ahead of us, the Korean had stopped for a snack, waiting for his compatriots to catch up. We joined him there, protected from the wind by the lee side of the south summit, and I took out my bota bag of water hanging around my neck, inside my down suit. I took a bite of a Snickers bar and contemplated the ice wall in front of me. The Hillary Step is the highest technical climb in the world. Ten thousand feet below, this particular cliff would be a breeze. The surface of the ice is mottled with natural ridges, gaps, and pockmarks. But at a hair below 29,000 feet, things look different. Especially with an 8,000-foot drop just below. So while I stood there, breathlessly chewing a mouthful of peanuts and nougat and chocolate, I felt anxious. A lot of big mistakes had been made by people climbing easy walls. And right then, in the middle of all this uneasy rumination, I understood something that made me even less easy. I realized, with a grim certainty, that I really had to go to the bathroom.

I could feel the tension in my bladder and bowels. A heavy, gravitational pull, and if I ignored it, in this environment, the consequences could be brutal. Something had to happen.

Just then the two other Koreans came down from the south summit, and walked over toward us, still resting in the shadow of the Hillary Step. They came waving and smiling, but when they saw me there, a wisp of blonde hair trapped outside my oxygen mask, they stopped and gaped. *We know her! From the Americans!*

"*Stacy?*" The older one looked at me as if I were Mrs. Schmatz, come back to life.

"Stacy? Stacy! Is that you?"

I shrugged. "Hello!"

He shook his head in wonder, and patted me on the shoulder. The Koreans rested for a moment, then started up again, one after the other scaling the ice-covered Hillary Step. I was glad they went ahead, relieved to see them all scaling the cliff with so little difficulty. I could do it, then. But I had to do something else first. When the last Korean disappeared over the top, I turned to Pasang.

"I have to go," I said. He nodded and gestured to the ice in front of us.

"Okay," he said.

"No. I have to *go*." I gestured toward myself. At this, Pasang's expression changed.

"Ohhhh," he said. "To go." He looked around, took a step back. The small section of ridge we were standing on didn't offer any convenient hiding places. No seracs or ridges, just bare, hard snow. Pasang took another step. "Where?" he said.

"Right here," I said. "Turn around."

He did, and I unzipped my down climbing suit, then reached in to unzip the other layers. Thank God, all high-altitude climbing gear is designed for this. Each piece zips up through the crotch, making mountainside body functions a relative snap. No pulling things over your head, no exposing large tracts of flesh to the skin-cracking chill. Just zip, zip, zip, and you're in business.

Squatting a little on the snow, I looked out into the empty morning sky and functioned with a great feeling of relief. It took only a few seconds, and then I zipped up my layers. Feeling the warmth building against my skin, I covered the evidence, digging a small hole in the snow with the blade of my ice ax. When I was done, I called out for Pasang.

"Okay!" He turned back around. "*Now* let's go."

I approached the wall first. Looking up to the lip of the cliff, I could see the bright sunlight reflecting off the loose snow. When the wind gusted, the dry snow took flight, a white cloud shooting sideways into the golden sunlit air. The wind had blown gently all morning, but now it seemed to be kicking up again. Another gust sent a new cloud of white powder spiraling into the air, and this time I could feel the push of the wind at the bottom of the cliff. It was coming from the side now, so we were no longer protected by the south summit. Inside, I started to churn. Would the wind be strong enough to blow me off the ice wall? The thought was just playing through my mind when another burst of wind swept across the ridge. Stronger this time, and then my head was cold. My face snapped up, reflexively, and saw it soaring off, a bright pink dot against the cloudless sky. The wind had swept my pile hat right off my head, and now it had taken flight, out into the air and down, 8,000 feet, into Tibet.

"Shit," I thought, and I reached up to take my first handhold.

I swung my ice ax, dipping in the tip, and hoisted myself up. I focused on the wall and shrugged off the fear. *Just another wall. Nothing special, just be aware. Know what you're doing.* It took about three minutes to climb the ice wall, and when I pulled myself onto the top I turned around and beckoned for Pasang. He looked up at me, hesitating. I waved again and he nodded, but didn't move. He could feel the wind, too. The wind and the emptiness falling away beneath us. One slip on the ice, and everything was over.

"It's okay!" I shouted down. Pasang looked up and nodded. He steeled himself, almost visibly, then reached for a hold and started up the ice. Moving slowly, carefully, planting his ice ax, then taking another step up. I watched him climb for a few minutes, then turned around and started walking again, up the final ridge toward the summit.

I could see it now, off in the distance. That last glint of white against a powder blue morning sky. Two hundred yards away. A slow uphill walk in the thin air, perhaps fifteen minutes. Each step a physical strain against the altitude, the desolate air, the sudden bursts of high-velocity wind. But there it was, almost close enough to touch. A few more steps, and I would.

But first, the ridge. It slopes up from the left at about 35 degrees, then peaks to the right as a series of cornices — ridges of overhanging ice and snow, poised above a sheer 8,000-foot drop. A stress fracture in the snow, crawling up the ridge a few feet to the left of the drop-off, marked the fault line. I kept to the left of the crack in the snow, trying to avoid riding a broken cornice down into Tibet, but still keeping a buffer between my path and where the slope turned steep and fell away on the left.

The worst was behind me, but I was so high now, so exposed. A sudden gust of wind, I thought, could lift me right out of my boots and sail me all the way back to base camp. Or one of these icy overhangs could snap. Or I could catch a crampon on my pants and tumble down the other side of the ridge. Death was everywhere. I forced it down and drilled myself onward. I went as fast as I could, one foot down, then the other. Walking with my ice ax, chunking the tip into the snow. Keeping an eye on the stress fracture, on the bottomless slope to my left. Glancing up, seeing the end of the ridge in the distance. The end of the ridge, and the end of the world. I could make it. As long as I kept moving, I was going to make it.

Pasang was on the ridge now, following my steps about seventy yards behind me. In the distance I could see the Koreans, small specks of color sitting in the snow. They were on the summit. I was so close. But I couldn't think about it yet, not with these cornices, the drop-off, the stress fracture swerving between. I had to follow that line, and keep moving. I was still digging for breath, feeling the thunder in my chest, still keeping tabs on my numb toes. And still climbing.

The air looked like crystal. The sky was so blue, the sun gleaming yellow and powerful. Even in the cold the rays felt palpable, as if they carried a physical weight. I could see everything. Up above, a few wispy clouds skimmed by the sun, riding the highest winds in the firmament. Behind me I could look down into Nepal. All but a few of the tallest peaks were covered by thick, billowing clouds. The sky was clearer above the brown plains of Tibet, spread out ahead of me. I could see the plains, rolling away, and closer in I could see the Rongbuk Glacier, where I'd been standing exactly a year earlier.

Now I was seventy-five feet away. Walking carefully, minding the crack in the ridge and the tip of my ice ax, my crampons squeaking in and out of the snow. *One foot in front of the other.* Fifty feet. Closer to the Koreans now, close enough to see them snapping pictures of each other. So close, but I wouldn't let myself feel it yet. Not until I was there. Something was swelling inside me, but I pushed it down. I had to keep moving, stay focused on the crack, the steps, reaching out with my ice ax, pulling in another two feet. Taking another step, then another, and reaching out again. Walking faster, feeling the adrenaline starting to flow, surging through my veins and running hot into my fingers and even my dulled toes.

Twenty-five feet. It was unbelievable. Now I knew I was going to make it. I could see the Koreans talking on their walkie-talkie. Just beyond where they stood I could see blue sky.

Ten feet. This was it. I checked my watch — just past ten-thirty. September 29, 1988. The Koreans were watching me now, the leader reaching out to shake my hand. "Good, very good!" he called, and beneath my oxygen mask I smiled. But I barely heard him, and kept going, those last few feet to where it ended. It was so strange. After everything, I was walking onto the summit of Mount Everest. It was right there, I could see it clearly just ahead of me. The last few steps, just a little higher, and then there was nothing. The end of the ridge, and then nothing but that clear, empty air.

I stopped climbing.

There was nowhere else to climb.

I was standing on the top of the world.

I felt it now, everything I'd kept bottled up as I came up the ridge. It billowed up from my core, a blinding wave of emotion. I could finally let it all go, the months of controlling my thoughts, of channeling all my energy toward this one purpose. Behind my glasses my eyes blurred. I was wide open now, and I was aware of everything. The wind in my hair, the sweat on my back, the blood washing through my wrists and ankles. I made it. For myself, for Steve and Jim, for everyone. I was standing on the top, looking down on the world. It was real — that fragile dream I'd first had so many years ago. The vision I'd nurtured so carefully over the years, the one I almost lost touch with last year. I had taken it back and it had all come true. I was strong enough. I was good enough and lucky enough . . . and I had come out the other end. After everything, I finally had.

Pasang was still ten minutes away. So it was just me. A small patch of snow, a lot of sky, and me. The cloud of emotion thinned, then vanished. My eyes were dry again. I took little steps and turned around on the snowy crest of the summit, this way to look over Nepal, then that way to see into Tibet. Behind me the Koreans hung together in a tight circle, laughing and chattering to their base camp on the walkie-talkie. Now I felt strange. *I was on top of the world, but I was alone.* This wasn't how I wanted it to happen. During all those years of wishing, dreaming about it, working for it, I never once imagined I'd be alone when I got to the summit. I wanted to hug someone, to make this dream explode into life by seeing it reflected in someone else's eyes. But I was on top of Mount Everest by myself.

Then Pasang came up. He pumped his ice ax in the air, hooting and yipping with everything he had left in his lungs. The Koreans looked up from their radio and greeted him, slapping his back, pumping his hand. The sight popped the lid off my emotions again, and I walked over to him, reaching out to Pasang and wrapping him in a bear hug. "We did it," I said, my eyes going hot and cloudy again. "We really did it."

The Koreans were putting their packs on now, taking their first steps down the ridge. Then they were gone. Pasang and I had a minute or two to stand alone on the summit, then it was time to get to work.

Back home we'd engaged donors by promising to entwine their own names with the summit. Now that we were really on top of Everest, we had to provide the payoff. Opening my backpack, I dug in for the Honor Roll, the small roll of microfilm listing the names of all the people who had donated money to our expedition. I scraped a shallow pit in the snow, laid the roll of film inside, and covered it over. But our corporate sponsors expected a more tangible kind of testament. I gave Pasang the camera, then reached into my pack for the corporate banners.

There were twenty-five of them wrapped in a stuff sack, some as small as a handkerchief, a few as large as a tablecloth. I planted my pink flamingo in the snow, then sat down and unrolled the first banner. Pasang snapped a few photos, and then we moved on to the next one, then the next. The task soon grew tedious. My smile started to hurt, and I began to get cold. To make things even more difficult, the wind was blowing up again. The gusts kept blowing my parka hood off my head. That made me worry about holding up the larger banners — what if one blew out of my fingers?

After a while I pulled off my oxygen mask and took a stab at breathing the thin, cold air of the jet stream. My body felt it immediately — my core temperature plunged — but my head stayed clear. It seemed livable, and it made me think of Jim and Steve. I wished they had come up with me.

During the half hour it took to shoot the corporate photos, Pasang and I were all business. Once we were done, however, we had a few minutes to ourselves. We snapped a few pictures of each other, and I shot a series of panoramas. Then I reached into my pocket for my own artifacts. Climbing the mountain gave me something to take away. It felt only appropriate to leave a small part of me behind. I had a little piece of turquoise a Tibetan yak herder had given me in 1987. He'd lived in the shadow of the mountain for his entire life, but never dreamed of climbing it, so I promised to take something of his to the top. I had a baggie of blessed rice I took from our altar at base camp the day we set out for the summit. I had a prayer scarf, a snapshot of me with David, and, finally, a Susan B. Anthony silver dollar.

I looked at my watch. It was getting late now, after eleven. We didn't have that much time, but I still felt I had to ground myself. I thought about the mountain's spirit. The Mother Goddess of the Earth. I thanked her for being kind enough to let me climb her. I prayed she'd let me get down in one piece, too. I looked at my watch again, and saw I'd already been on top for close to forty-five minutes. I caught Pasang's eye and gestured down. He looked surprised.

"Now?"

"Soon. In a minute," I said.

We stood together, looking out over the world beneath us. I wanted to remember everything. The cold, dry air between my lips, the wind pushing against my back, the way the silvery wisps of cloud jetted across the sky. I needed to remember it, to keep the image deep inside the vaults in my memory bank. This was the top of Everest. The dream of a lifetime. I looked around. There had to be something for me to latch on to. A perfect image I could remember that would objectify why I'd come, for now and forever. But nothing came into focus. It was hard to believe, after so many years, but the summit of Everest was just snow and ice. A mountain summit, pretty much like any other mountain summit. I was contemplating this when Pasang looked over at me and said:

"We spend two months getting to the mountain, carrying things up the mountain, climbing the mountain. We work like dogs, then spend so little time on top and now we go back down. What's the meaning?"

I shook my head. How do you define ambition? People do strange things — stand on their heads, play computer games, write a hundred thousand prayers to Buddha. You find your talent, and see how far it will take you. You do what makes you feel the most alive.

Then we put our packs back on, and after taking one last look, headed down the ridge. I thought about what lay ahead. Descending the Hillary Step, then the steep, rocky decline beneath the south summit. We'd have to plunge-step through the steep snow in that gully, then work our way, carefully, down the snowy faces to Camp 4. A faster trip than the way up, now that we were cooperating with the force of gravity. But no less dangerous. I knew I had to watch every step. Celebrating seemed a bit premature, considering how easy it would be to die on the way down. I concentrated on the task at hand.

I got down the Hillary Step easily enough, then took my time walking down the steep, rocky section beneath the south summit. Soon we were off the ridge, plunge-stepping our way through the thick snow in the gully. The sun was high now, just about noon, and I was sweating in my down climbing suit, drenching my polypropylene with the effort to keep moving. Beneath the gully we hit the steeper faces, where the snow was crustier, blended with ice. Here we descended in a kind of sidestep motion, careful to plant our crampons firmly with each footfall.

The route flattened after a while, and soon I could see the tents of Camp 4 getting closer, bright specks against the white on the South Col. I was growing tired, feeling the weight of the climb and my sleepless night. But the sight in the distance swelled my excitement again. I focused on the tents, letting them pull me like a magnet.

We approached the camp at two-thirty. Appa and Pemba were in the tent farthest uphill, and when they heard us coming they poked their heads out of the door. The Koreans had already radioed down that they'd seen us on the summit, so they shouted congratulations. Hearing this, Steve came bounding out of our tent.

"Good goin'!" he cried, and picked me up in a bear hug. Steve slapped my back and swung me around, pack and all, before gently placing me on my feet again. Seeing how excited he was charged me up again. It reminded me of what had happened.

"You did it!" Steve cried, clapping his hands. "I knew you would do it!"

Jim leaned out of his tent, but he wasn't wearing his boots, so he didn't want to come out. He motioned me over and then reached out to give me a hug.

"It's wonderful," he said, slapping my back. "I'm proud of you. You made us all proud."

Steve had already heated up water for lunch, so I dumped my pack, stripped off my heavy down climbing suit, and crawled into our tent to eat and drink. It was hard to believe it had been only twenty-four hours since we first got to Camp 4. Or that I'd spent the night lying there wide awake, too wired to sleep.

I ate lunch and rested for an hour, and Steve told me what had gone on since they got back to camp. Now he and Jim weren't going to try for the summit again the next morning — one radio call down the mountain had quickly shown how the climbers on the second and third teams felt about putting off their attempts for one more day.

The second team was already champing at the bit in base camp, poised and ready to climb higher, so now Jim, Steve, and I had to get out of Camp 4 as soon as possible.

"Are you strong enough to head down to Camp 2 this afternoon?" Steve asked. It would be a hell of a long push at the end of a summit day. Another 4,500 feet, down the nearly perpendicular Lhotse Face. But we probably had enough daylight, and it would certainly help to preserve the food and oxygen at Camp 4.

"Sure," I said. "Let's do it."

We left twenty minutes later.

DESCENDING through the ashen light of the afternoon, I plodded down the mountainside in a trance. Thoughts of my glorious morning abandoned me completely. There was no glory to this — letting my carabiner slip down the line, planting my crampons, feeling the pack rubbing that raw spot on my hips. This was little more than endurance. Patience, concentration, and tenacity. *Keep moving, try to keep up the pace.* I'd been climbing, almost nonstop, since midnight. Now I could feel the weight of every hour. The endless day burned in my thighs and tore at my calves, it ached in my knees. The lights behind my eyes grew dim, then flickered. I followed the others, not thinking about the summit, not thinking about anything. It took all my energy to keep moving.

We passed Camp 3 in the late afternoon, and rolled onward. Down the Lhotse Face, following the fixed line into the shadows. Dusk settled above us, the sky fading slowly toward night, the temperature sinking, the wind nibbling with baby teeth. Finally past the bergschrund, that gaping crevasse at the top of the Western Cwm, we walked out onto the flatter glacial terrain. Here we stopped for a moment to pull off our crampons. Too tired to wrestle my climbing boots from their protective, high-altitude neoprene overboots, I walked on slick neoprene soles. Which didn't provide much in the way of traction, a fact that became evident when I swayed back on my heels. The hard glacial crust had turned icy, and so my skewed center of gravity sent both of my feet flying out from beneath me. I was suddenly airborne, and then — wham! — I was flat on my butt.

"Dammit."

I sat in the snow for a moment, then climbed back on my feet and started down again. I walked more carefully now, keeping my weight on top of my boots. But a ridge of ice, hidden in the lengthening shadows, robbed me of my balance again. Wham! I was still sitting in the snow when Appa came up behind me.

"You're so tired," he said, holding out his hand to help me up. "I will take your pack."

And I was so tired I let him do it, too. After eighteen straight hours of climbing, the trance deepened. Even without the weight of my pack I could feel my body sinking past exhaustion. We were pushing it so hard, trying to hit Camp 2 before dark, and I had to find the energy to get there. *How do you keep going when you've got nothing left?* I thought of that night on Mount Washington, my first mountain back in 1978, with Curt and Chris and Ev. *Just keep going. Doing does it.*

And then we were there. The line of tents at Camp 2 came into view just as the shadows were stealing the last of the daylight. As we walked into camp, a few of the others came out of their tents to greet us. Peggy, Geoff, and Jean Ellis from our team, a half dozen of our Sherpas, Gary Ball and Lydia Bradey from the New Zealand team. But it was getting dark, and cold, so the hugs and backslaps didn't go on for long. The climbers heading up in the morning needed to get some sleep. I was exhausted and starving, thinking only of dinner and my sleeping bag. But then Jim came over and draped his long arm over my shoulder.

"One more thing," he said. "Time for the radio call. I'll bet some folks down below want to say hi to you."

Jim, Steve, and I crawled into their tent, and gathered around the walkie-talkie. Jim called down to base camp and made contact with Bob Singer. I could hear music in the background and shouting. It sounded like someone was having a pretty good party, even through the airwave fuzz.

"Is she there?" Bob was shouting over the noise.

Jim smiled. "Right here." He handed the radio to me.

"Hi, Bob," I said.

"Stacy!" Cheering now from the background, the clunk of glass bottles being slapped together. Then a few voices, through the noise and radio murk.

"Congratulations!"

"Thanks, guys." I was laughing now. A trickle of adrenaline shot through my dulled nervous system.

"We're celebrating for you!"

"I can tell!"

There was another wave of noise from below, and I could feel it lifting me up again. Now it wasn't just me up there, it wasn't just my success. It was Bob, too, and Larry and Charlie and everyone who put their hearts and backs into our expedition. There was more shouting, and they passed the walkie-talkie around to let everyone say hello. After a few minutes they gave the radio to Sherry Stripling. She'd already talked to Jim on the walkie-talkie that afternoon, but before she sent her dispatch back to the *Seattle Times* she wanted a few direct quotes from me.

So you did it, she said. *And now you're the first American woman to climb Everest. . . .*

She was right. But I didn't want to think about that, not yet, anyway. Not when my teammates were all around me, not when the others were still working so hard. It wasn't fair to revel in a personal achievement when I knew it had as much to do with Bob Singer and Larry MacBean as it did with me. "Well, it was a personal goal," I said, suddenly exhausted again. "I'm just glad I could do it."

Sherry paused for a moment, scribbling her notes.

"But wasn't that why they chose you to go on with the last oxygen bottle?"

With the static and the noise, I wasn't sure I heard that right. "Say that again?"

"Jim told me," Sherry said, "that he and Steve gave up their oxygen so you could go on to the summit and be the first American woman on top of Everest."

I looked up at Jim, but couldn't catch his eye. When I met Steve's gaze, he was shaking his head, smiling his crooked smile. I punched down the "talk" button.

"That's not true at all," I said. I described the lottery, the way Jim asked Pasang to choose a number, and how we'd all guessed to find the closest match. "And I won," I said. "No one gave up anything on purpose."

Sherry finished her questions, and then Bob got back on the radio at base camp. They needed me to stay at Camp 2 for a few days to coordinate the next wave of summiters, he said. But, Bob added, they would send something up to help me celebrate. "Whatever you want!"

I thought for a moment. A beer, I decided. And potato chips. "You got it," Bob said.

I got up to head over to my own tent, and Steve followed me out.

It was dark now, except for the dim lights filtering through the tents. From the outside I could see the ghostly shadows of the other climbers cast against the translucent gray walls. The shadows of people hunching over their stoves, sitting up to eat, lying back and reading. The sounds of camp life sifted out into the wind, too, the gentle roar of the stoves, the clank of the tin spoons on the tin pots. The soft murmur of conversation. After we got out of earshot from Jim's tent, I leaned up to whisper to Steve.

"What did she say about you guys *letting* me go?"

Steve shrugged. "Jim's idea," he said. "He thought the lottery sounded amateurish, so he said we should change it. That's what he fed to Sherry."

"But it's bullshit."

"Of course it is," Steve said with a laugh. "But isn't it just like the movies?"

So that was Jim's game. If not the summit, he'd settle for a glorious, golden shot of him passing off the oxygen bottle, standing on the ridge as the wind blew and the snow rushed around him — *No, you go on . . . bring it home for all of us!* Jim Frush, propelling me to destiny.

A nice little bit of double-reverse sexism to welcome me back to the world: An American Woman Finally Did It (Thanks to the Generosity of an American Man, of Course).

Screw that.

Alone in my tent, I fired up the stove to melt some water for dinner. I was really out of gas now, almost too tired to eat. I forced myself, though, shoveling in a plate of freeze-dried chicken and rice. I washed it down with a few cups of lukewarm water, then turned off the headlamp and lay back in my sleeping bag. I could feel myself fading, my toes warm, my fingers limp, my arms too tired to move. I shut my eyes, and my brain started to fade to black. But first I ran through my nightly mountainside checklist. Breathing okay, head still clear. Tired, but fed and watered. I curled up in my sleeping bag and I was asleep.

11

CHASING THE
GODDESS

I drifted awake the next morning, surfacing through a jumble of dreams and impulses. Then the familiar tightening in my chest. *Time to wake up, get the stove going, get out and start climbing.*

Then I remembered. Not today. Not tomorrow, either. I lay back again and let it roll over me. I didn't have to defy gravity anymore. It was all downhill now. I reached out and moved back the flap of my tent. The sky outside was a wash of gray and pink. But I wasn't home yet. There were still other people who wanted to head for the summit. Outside, I could hear the voices of Peggy and Jean preparing to head up toward Camp 3.

I pulled on my socks and pants, a pile jacket. I was starving, but breakfast would have to wait. I pulled on my boots, and without pausing to lace them I crawled outside and stood up on the snow. Jean and Peggy were standing a few tents away, talking quietly. When I approached, they looked up. Designated the fourth and final summit team, Jean and Peggy had stayed up at Camp 2 while the second team — Diana, Don, and Dave — and the third team — Johnny and Geoff — were sent back to base camp to rest. But then things got confusing. Geoff decided to stay at Camp 2, saying he felt strong enough to stay put and saw no use in retreating. And when Steve, Jim, and I came down a day early from Camp 4, the expedition confronted another logistical conundrum. Once again, the weather was perfect and our next designated summit team was at base camp. Instead of squandering the wide-open weather window this time, Jim and Don decided to seize the moment and send up the trio of climbers still at Camp 2: Peggy, Jean, and Geoff. And thus the fourth team became the second.

"How's it going?"

"Okay." Jean nodded. He slung his pack onto his shoulders, tightened the waist strap. I could feel their tension. It's always nerve-racking to go higher on the mountain, even when you know what you'll find up there. Peggy and Jean, on the other hand, were still strangers to high altitude. The thought of their heading up toward the summit by themselves made *me* nervous. Geoff, the one experienced climber on their summit team, decided to stay at Camp 2 for an extra day, then climb all the way from Camp 2 to meet Peggy and Jean at the South Col the next morning. So Peggy and Jean would spend the next day and a half above 23,000 feet, with no one except the Sherpas for emotional support.

Back in Seattle it had been so clear that support climbers were staying low on the mountain. But Peggy pushed herself as high as almost everyone else, so when Jim and Don started plotting summit teams both of the leaders figured she had earned a shot. And Jean wanted to go, too. He was tentative above 21,000 feet, but his marathon-honed perseverance kept him from even considering going less than all the way. He had even brought along a hand-painted banner spelling out a marriage proposal to his girlfriend. Once he got to the summit, Jean figured he could unfurl the banner, then pose for a photo while standing next to it.

I wished them good luck and watched them go. Then I went back into my tent to get the stove going for breakfast.

The rest of the day passed slowly. I ate and napped, then got up and sat in the sun, shooting the breeze with Geoff. As happy as he was to catapult up through the summit team ranks, Geoff was less pleased to be taking his shot with the expedition's two least experienced climbers. He'd catch up to them at Camp 4 tomorrow, but if Jean and Peggy weren't fast enough, Geoff made it clear he wouldn't think twice about blowing right by them.

"I don't want to go all the way up there just to baby-sit those guys," he said.

It sounded mean, but he had a point. Geoff didn't sign up to be anyone's guide. And once Peggy and Jean agreed to take a summit slot, they also took on a certain responsibility. *They knew what they were doing.* We all knew how powerful the mountain was. I hoped, if things went wrong, they would have the guts to quit.

Geoff left before dawn the next morning. Stirring in my sleeping bag, I heard him outside my tent, zipping up his climbing suit, adjusting the straps on his pack, and poked my head out into the dark to wish him well.

"Have fun up there."

He looked over at me and smiled through his dark beard. "Always," he said. "It's always fun up there." Geoff switched on his headlamp and started up the glacier, and I heard him rattling off into the blackness. Ahead, the thin beam of light danced with his choppy strides.

Up above us in Camp 3, Peggy and Jean were careening through a bad night. Their climb up the Lhotse Face had proceeded smoothly enough the day before, but when they got to Camp 3 they found the tents buried in snow. After spending hours shoveling, they settled into their sleeping bags. A hot afternoon of work was the least of their problems — at 23,700 feet the sudden leap in altitude clamped down hard on their bodies. Squeezed by the barren air and the weak atmospheric pressure, Jean and Peggy spent the evening pinned into their sleeping bags, heads pounding and stomachs lurching. When the sun finally broke through the night, both Jean and Peggy had to make a decision.

Later that morning I could see Jean coming down the cwm, walking slowly across the flat glacier. When I could hear him coming, his boots crunching against the snow, I came out of my tent and stood to greet him.

"I had to turn around," he said. His voice was flat.

I nodded. "Peggy and the Sherpas kept going?"

"Yeah."

There was silence for a moment. "I was scared," Jean said. "Goddammit. I felt like shit up there, and I got scared. I had to turn around."

It was over for him — the hope, the vision. I knew the feeling of loss. I put my arms up around his shoulders and hugged him. Jean seemed limp against me.

"It's okay," I said. "You did exactly the right thing." Jean didn't say anything, and I stepped back, still holding his shoulders with my hands. "It takes more strength to turn around than to keep going."

Jean nodded, still silent, then turned away, picking up his pack and dragging it back toward his tent.

PEGGY knew she would keep going. When Jean decided to head back for Camp 2 that morning, she wished him well, summoned their two Sherpas, and started up across the Lhotse Face to Camp 4. Adjusting a bit more easily to the altitude now, Peggy managed to push her way to the tents on the South Col by early afternoon. The three of them settled in, and were soon joined by Geoff and another Sherpa, both of whom had vaulted up the mountain from Camp 2. They crawled immediately into their sleeping bags, put on oxygen masks, and set their alarms for nine P.M.

Strong winds kept them pinned down for a few hours, but then the gusts broke down into a stiff breeze, and by two A.M. Peggy, Geoff, and the Sherpas were ready to leave. After that awful night at Camp 3 Peggy was fortunate to have the presence of mind even to lace up her boots, but she was strong.

The five climbers set out together, walking up the shallow slope of the Col toward the south face of Everest. They climbed together for a while, but as the route turned steep and the climbing more difficult, Peggy slowed down. She moved carefully, choosing her steps, making sure to plant her crampons in the crusty slope. The three Sherpas stayed with Peggy, so Geoff gained distance on them all, moving easily through the darkness. Dawn came, and as the sky lightened Peggy could see clouds gathering in the distance. She threw off her pack and collapsed in a heap. She sat there with her eyes closed, gasping for breath. When she looked up, finally, she saw Geoff. He had been resting on the south summit, having a snack and mulling the thirty-five-foot cliff on the near side of the Hillary Step. He could tell Peggy was shaky — when she finally looked at him, she shook her head. He gestured to the Hillary Step. "That's it, right there. Then it's a walk."

Geoff stood up, gesturing to the Sherpas. "You guys want to come along?" They looked at each other, and then to Peggy. She waved them on. And so they left her sitting there, still stretched out in the snow.

Geoff and the Sherpas clambered up the Hillary Step, then headed up the ridge toward the summit. They hit the top just past ten A.M., hung around for a while to take some photos and enjoy the view, then started back down again to look for Peggy. When they found her, she was on the ridge, just past the Hillary Step. On her feet, and moving slowly, but still climbing. Now she was less than half an hour from the top. Geoff and the Sherpas cheered her on, but Geoff realized she presented a problem. If she were any other climber — an *experienced* climber — it would be okay to keep descending, to head back to camp and assume she would be strong enough to get back on her own steam. But no matter what Jim or Don or anyone claimed for her, the fact was inescapable: Peggy did not have high-altitude experience.

Geoff looked at the Sherpas. "I'm heading down," he said. "You can come along or wait for Peggy." The Sherpas looked at each other, looked at themselves. Finally, one spoke up. It was Dawa Tsering, one of the two younger Sherpas who had climbed with Peggy all the way from Camp 2.

"I wait Peggy," he said. Geoff nodded. *Good man!*

When Geoff got down to Camp 2, he told us what had happened. Don radioed the good news down to base camp that night. *Guess who made the summit!* I was delighted — Peggy made it! I was happy for Geoff, too, but Peggy's ascent astounded me. Here was a woman who had climbed all of two medium-sized mountains in her life, both of them in the North Cascades. Now she'd pushed herself all the way to the top of Everest, and without even another team member to lean on. It was, we all had to agree, a stunning achievement. It would seem even more stunning when we learned what really happened up there.

After Geoff left her, Peggy's climb had become difficult. It was her glasses that started it, on the way up the ridge. The same thing that happened to me — heat escaping from the top of her oxygen mask, the steam rising right into her sunglasses, fogging the lenses. She couldn't see anything. Peggy tried wiping them off, but then lost her patience. Knowing she was already late, Peggy snatched the steamed-up shades from her nose and stuffed them in her pocket. It was, she figured, easier to squint. That was a decision she would soon come to regret.

She made the summit — stood there on top, waving her ice ax above her in the air, seeing the whole world beneath her. "Yay!" she cried. A beautiful moment, but no more than that. After squinting at the view for a minute, her eyes still uncovered in the light, Peggy turned around to follow her own footsteps down the ridge.

By the time Peggy found Dawa waiting for her just above the Hillary Step, she had been climbing bare-eyed for almost an hour. The glare beat against her eyes, but now she had little time to worry about finding a way to defog her glasses. It was close to noon, and they had to make tracks to the South Col. Peggy saw the thin rope dangling down the cliff, then hitched herself to the line and started down the wall.

She made it about a third of the way down before she felt the stake beginning to slip. Falling off the face, her feet slipping — Peggy was in midair for a moment, free-falling through space. Then she seemed to freeze in midair, as the next picket caught her, shivered with the shock of her weight, then held. The protection stopped her descent, but the momentum from Peggy's fall sent her swinging crazily on the end of the rope. She swung back and forth, helpless, one moment heading toward Nepal, the next moment swinging at Tibet. Then she regained her balance and lowered herself the rest of the way down.

Limping slightly, her knee strained by a midair collision with the ice face, Peggy took a moment to rest, waiting for Dawa to catch up. She caught her breath. An ugly scrape, but it was over, and she was okay. Actually, she was going blind.

Ever since she'd pulled off her glasses, the unfiltered sunlight — the piercing, high-altitude ultraviolet rays beaming down, reflecting up off the white snow — had been burning her eyes, quickly stealing her eyesight. When Peggy and Dawa hit the rocky, icy slope just beneath the south summit, she moved carefully, once again taking the time to consider each step. This would be a bad place to fall. The ridge fell away on both sides, and even the crest of the ridge, beneath the rocky part, was steep. Once you fell and lost control, you would be dead long before your body stopped tumbling. So Peggy moved carefully, trying hard to see it all, squinting against the sunlight, the white glare. Her eyes were swelling now, the corneas themselves shutting down to avoid the burning light. Her eyes were still open, but detail faded to black. It was all shadows and light, and nothing more.

Then she tripped. She hit the ice and rolled, then started tumbling, falling down the ridge. Dawa was above her, his mouth open, gaping at the dreadful sight of Peggy rolling and tumbling, the weight of her pack now adding to her momentum as she slid down the slope. She had to stop herself. Could she? *I'm another statistic,* Peggy thought. *Summiters who die on the way down.*

But somewhere, in all that frantic pawing, Peggy managed to grasp her ice ax and dig in the pick. Clenched in her iron fist, the ice ax held firm, digging into the snow, slowing her down. She scraped slower, losing speed, a rooster tail of snow flying behind her. Then she stopped after another ten feet. Peggy sat still for a moment, then looked back up to where she'd started. It was fifty feet above her, up where Dawa was standing. Peggy waved at him, then stood up.

Soon her eyes were swollen almost completely shut. Dawa walked just ahead of her, giving Peggy — now nearly blind — a solid form to follow down to the South Col. Exhausted and starving, the two climbers finally found Camp 4 at about five-thirty.

PEGGY was grateful to be alive, but Geoff wasn't on her thank-you list. "He didn't even wait for me," Peggy complained when she made it down to Camp 2 a day later. "He just *left* me up there. He didn't even check to make sure we got to Camp Four."

The facts behind Peggy's summit climb blew through the expedition like a bitter wind. *She almost died up there.* Our expedition was framed on a foundation of work and skill and discipline. We took only measured risks, and were always responsible for our own safety. Steve, briefly at base camp, didn't hide his anger. Peggy had endangered everyone, he argued that night. "And success in the face of stupidity," he snapped, "is still stupidity."

Up at Camp 2 I couldn't decide which was more breathtaking: Peggy's tenacity or her luck. True enough, she climbed to the summit. That fact, in some ways, towered above everything else. But getting up a mountain hardly counts unless you can get down, too. And if it weren't for Dawa, Peggy might not have come down alive. Even so, Don and Jim insisted that Peggy's success spoke for itself. No one guided her up, they said. And even if she fell twice on her way down, she was strong enough to stop herself, and then get back onto her feet. I agreed with that, but I could also understand Steve.

Peggy was lucky in the end — she escaped with minor injuries. Even her eyes healed after a few days. But luck runs in short supply on Mount Everest. And for our expedition, and for all the other climbers scuttling up her flanks in the fall of 1988, the Mother Goddess of the Earth's good luck had just run dry.

THE weather turned dark the day Peggy got back to Camp 2. Dave, Don, Johnny, and Diana passed her on their way up to Camp 3 that morning, unaware of what had taken place during her summit day, and the sight of their groggy, half-snowblind expedition mate seemed less than a good omen. Worse yet was the thick band of gun-metal clouds closing off the sky, riding the northern wind like a line of tanks. The conditions grew more violent the morning after that, and with no end to the storm in sight they decided to retreat: back to Camp 2 for the next night, then all the way back to base camp until the skies grew calm.

With the action on the mountain at a standstill, Peggy and I also hustled back to base camp. Now the expedition was officially on hold. Once Diana, Dave, Johnny, and Don came off the mountain, everyone — except for Steve, now minding the tents at Camp 2 — sat in base camp, waiting for the storm to run its course. The clouds broke up after a few days, but when the summit finally came back into view the sight wasn't encouraging. Gale-force winds were sweeping a huge plume of snow from the summit, evidence that the jet stream had already started sinking toward the top of the mountain. And unless it flew upward again — a sudden reversal back to summer conditions — our expedition was over.

We were heading into mid-October now, dangerously close to the point where the winds would blow the weather window shut for the rest of the year. We waited for an entire week, the winds on the mountain roaring without pause. Up at Camp 2 Steve spent his days working to shore up the tents. Base camp was untouched by the gales. We sat in the warm autumn sun, wearing T-shirts and shorts, but even where it was calm the deep roar of the wind was a constant backdrop, like a jet airplane hovering in the sky.

As the days passed, tension built. Earlier we had all been joined by a single ambition, a goal each of us knew we could meet only if we had the help of the others. But once some of the team members started reaching that goal, agendas and allegiances started to shift.

The team divided into two groups: climbers who had finished, and climbers who still wanted to summit. Of the five who had finished, only Geoff, Peggy, and I had reached the summit. Charlie had given up early, shifting to a supporting role in base camp. Jean, on the other hand, still wore his disappointment like a mourning cloak. He kept his eyes focused downward and rarely spoke to anyone at meals. In the end Jean even moved his tent away from the others.

My perspective was changing, too. While I was still climbing, I found it hard to think about anything but the mountain. I blocked out everything else — David, my family, what I might want to do with my life when I got home. But once I stood on top of the mountain, then came down and walked out of the ice fall for the last time, I could feel myself turning homeward. I could taste the Oregon air, I could see my house. And David! I could think about David, about the relationship that was now so important to me. There was a whole life out there and I was finally ready for it to begin.

But Steve, Johnny, Diana, Dave, Don, and Jim possessed a very different perspective. The dream of the summit. Officially we were all still committed to getting as many climbers to the top as possible. But how do you define *possible?* Winter was coming, soon the blizzards would be upon us. We had to set a schedule for our departure. Jim brought up the subject in the dining tent one day at lunch.

He began by presenting the verities of autumn in Nepal. If we waited too long, the jet-stream winds could stop us from salvaging our gear at the high camps. And one big storm could dump enough snow onto the moraine to make it impossible for yaks and porters to help us. If that happened, we'd have to leave behind thousands of dollars' worth of equipment. "We're taking a big risk," he concluded. "If we don't start thinking about leaving, we might not get out."

I saw Diana's face go stormy, the glint of desperation in her eyes. She'd worked so hard on this expedition, she'd spent so long dreaming about it, she'd invested so much of herself in what would happen when she got here. And it didn't pay off.

I'd felt her frustration. At base camp, Peggy, Diana, and I slept in the same dome tent, just as we had before we started climbing. But the warm, chatty friendship we'd had before was markedly cooler. Diana had never said a word about the summit to me after I came down, and she never mentioned Peggy's successful climb to Peggy either.

I knew Diana was burning to make the summit herself. At this point she couldn't even think about our success until she'd done it herself. So I avoided the topic. I didn't talk about the other climbers who still wanted to go up. I didn't mention that I was starting the long process of organizing and packing the gear for our trek back to civilization. When Jim brought up the subject during lunch that day, Diana looked up at him and glowered.

"I don't want to be rushed," she said. "Just because other people have made it doesn't mean *we* shouldn't get *our* fair shot."

I peered at my plate, waiting for the others to sort it out. I had my opinion, but a successful team member couldn't even appear to influence other team members to give up their own hopes. Jim didn't make it to the summit, but at least he'd already had a chance. Finally Don weighed in, his voice firm. "No matter what happens," he said, "we've got to have a definite end date. Otherwise we'll never get out of here."

Our permit kept us legal through November 3, but even if the winds lifted for a few days they certainly wouldn't stay away for an entire week, let alone two or three. Don suggested setting the deadline for October 20. That gave the climbers almost two weeks to make it to the summit, and gave the rest of us a date to plan our departure. He gazed around the table. "Any objections? Sound fair?" Diana nodded. Jim said fine, everyone else seemed satisfied.

When the winds above us ebbed enough to leave base camp on October 10, Johnny climbed up to meet Steve at Camp 2. The two of them would make up the next summit team, ascending the Lhotse Face for the South Col whenever the weather allowed them to risk the trip. Then Diana, Don, and Dave would follow, making the group's final attempt on the summit. It made for a tight schedule, particularly at the tail end of the fall climbing season. But with a little luck, we figured we might be able to pull it off.

THE Mother Goddess had been kind to us. After two years with no one summiting Chomolungma from any direction since the spring of 1986, twenty-three climbers stood on her crown during the course of one week.

But even in her most gentle moods the mountain could have moments of intense violence. In this most fruitful climbing month in Everest history, the mountain had already claimed two lives.

Early in September a sudden avalanche had roared into the Spanish Camp 3, destroying several tents and sweeping one of the group's Sherpas, Narayan Shrestha, to his death. And a day or two later a group of the survivors from that very avalanche continued up the mountain, only to find the frozen body of French soloist Michel Parmentier, who had started up from the Tibet side, near the bottom of the Hornbein Couloir. Parmentier's death was a puzzle. He was lying facedown in the snow just a few feet from his tent. Climbing alone from the north, Parmentier was rushing to the summit in an attempt to beat Marc Batard's solo ascent from the south. But with little gear and no oxygen, evidently Parmentier fell victim to a combination of exhaustion and altitude sickness. Wandering outside his tent one night, delirious, perhaps, thinking he was going to descend, Parmentier managed only a few steps before collapsing in the snow.

The deaths were sad, even sobering. But climbers climb, and others would attempt the summit. High winds or not, the five French climbers, camera crew, and their three Sherpas decided to leave Camp 2 on the morning of October 11. The Spanish climbers agreed to go along with two of their own Sherpas, and so the group set off together, dashing straight for Camp 4 against the blasting wind.

Two mornings later Steve, Johnny, and two Sherpas left Camp 2 for their crack at the summit. The heavy winds had died overnight, and now just a light breeze grazed their faces as they walked up the cwm. They crossed over the bergschrund, then started up the steep bottom of the Lhotse Face. The wind picked up a bit in the higher elevation. A definite breeze, but really not much more than that. And everyone seemed to be taking advantage of the break in the weather. It was already a busy day on the mountain. A couple thousand feet above them, just setting out from Camp 3, Steve could see the Spanish climbers heading for the South Col, small colored specks against the sheer white face. Steve kept climbing, moving quickly up the line, looking up occasionally to track the Spanish team's progress. If everything went well, he and Johnny would be that high tomorrow. In eighteen hours they could be starting out for the summit. Steve glanced up again, looking for the colored specks, and something else caught his eye.

It was moving. Another speck, only this one was coming down the face. Rocketing down, actually, out of control. Spinning on the windblown snow, bouncing off ridges, flying, then landing hard and cartwheeling for a few dozen yards.

Steve turned and gestured to Johnny. He had already seen it, so Steve turned and they watched it together. They knew it was a body, and they watched openmouthed, saw it falling like a comet past them, down past the bergschrund and then onto the flat surface of the cwm, where it somersaulted, cartwheeled, then rolled to a stop.

When he leaned over the body, Steve knew the Sherpa had been dead for at least twelve hours. He was frozen solid. Someone, it appeared, must have thrown him down on purpose. Steve looked up at the Lhotse Face above. He couldn't see the Spanish climbers anymore, they'd disappeared up on the col. Next to him the Sherpas were crossing and uncrossing their arms, their faces gloomy and clouded. No one, they knew, would ever throw a white climber's body down the Lhotse Face.

Stunned, unsure what to do, Steve and Johnny moved the body from where it had fallen, over to a more sheltered place on the glacier. Here they were met by another French climber, this one moving up from Camp 2, who told them the French team had lost two Sherpas trying to broadcast from the summit. Finding the bodies, the French leader had decided to hurl them down the Lhotse Face. Steve and Johnny, he said, were free to go back up to Camp 3.

But by now it was already past noon, far too late to get up to Camp 3 at a decent hour, so Steve, Johnny, and the Sherpas retreated for another night at Camp 2. When the next morning dawned, they were back on the mountain, bound for Camp 3. Once again the south side of Everest crawled with humans. Down below, Don, Diana, and Dave were climbing through the ice fall, heading for Camp 2 and their last shot at the summit. And the Spaniards were up above the South Col, plodding toward the summit with Lydia Bradey, the New Zealand soloist, following in their footsteps. It was a fine morning for climbing — the skies were clear, the winds light. But above Camp 4 the situation was fast changing.

The Spanish climbers' troubles had started the day before, when Sergei Martinez came down with a sinus infection. The cold, dry air had irritated the condition, but Martinez felt good enough to keep going, so the group continued up to the col and then, early on the morning of October 14, toward the summit. The Spaniards climbed through the morning, making steady progress until they reached the south summit. Then Martinez, already ill with his inflamed sinus, grew too weak to continue. He sat down to wait while his teammates made the final push to the summit. The other three Spanish climbers and their two Sherpas scampered to the top with little problem, took a few photos of themselves, then turned around to collect their sick friend. Finding Martinez in dramatically worse shape — by now he was barely conscious, almost blind, and apparently sinking into cerebral edema — the climbers made a stretcher out of some climbing rope and started pulling Martinez down the mountain. His survival, they knew, depended on a rapid descent and speedy medical care.

Meanwhile, Johnny and Steve were climbing above Camp 3, heading to the South Col. Once again they were back on track. The weather was perfect, the summit twenty-four hours away.

Then the Spanish team came into view, small dots on the ridge above them. Once he saw them, creeping down the Lhotse Face, Steve could tell something was wrong. When Steve and Johnny finally found them up near the top of the Lhotse Face, Martinez's hands and feet were frostbitten and he had full-blown cerebral edema. Seeing how close to death Martinez actually was, they turned around immediately and helped pull the Spanish climber down to Camp 2. Two nights later, when they got to the bottom of the ice fall the Spaniards rushed Martinez down the path to where the French helicopter stood, ready to fly him down to the hospital in Kathmandu.

When I saw Steve coming across the moraine in his yellow windsuit, I got up to welcome him back to camp. Steve had been at Camp 2 or higher for practically every day of the last two weeks. Since then he'd been on three summit attempts, weathered a week-long windstorm, and pulled two all-nighters tending to Martinez. And Steve had done all of this well above the 19,000-foot mark, up where the altitude python was wringing the life out of him, drop by drop. He was smiling when he got into camp, but by now even his grin looked like a grimace. He must have dropped at least fifteen pounds since I'd last seen him. Steve's cheeks were sunken beneath his beard, his eyes were hollow and dim. When I hugged him, I could feel the bones in his shoulders, like sticks poking against his windsuit. In an instant I realized how lucky I'd been. There was hell up there, and I didn't have to look beyond Steve's dim eyes to see it.

LIFE continued at base camp. The final summit team — Diana, Dave, and Don — were on the mountain, and I started preparing for our departure, gathering equipment and packing up the things we didn't need anymore. On the radio we tracked the progress of our summit team and the only other group still climbing — four Czechs attempting a lightweight sprint up the Southwest Face.

The Czech climb was particularly exciting, the Southwest Face being more than 10,000 feet of vertical rock and ice. No one had ever attempted an Alpine ascent on that face, but that was just right for Dusan Becik, Josef Just, Peter Bojik, and Jaroslav Jasko. The four Czech climbers were all slim and wiry, like a band of trapeze artists. Between them they could claim more than twenty routes on 8,000-meter peaks, many of them first ascents and most of them climbed in the barest Alpine style.

The Czechs left Camp 2 early on October 15, the same day the Spanish were descending from the South Col with the ailing Martinez. Dusan, Josef, Peter, and Jaroslav made good progress on their first day, climbing quickly through some difficult terrain. But on the second day of their attempt, all were feeling the altitude, and Peter had for some reason stopped drinking water. They were too high to turn back — it would have been just as dangerous to try to descend. Waking up on their third day facing the mountain without food, they kept moving up. By the end of the day they had made their way to the top of the Southwest Face, within striking distance of the summit. But by the next morning both Dusan's and Jaroslav's eyes were failing, their vision reduced to dim shadows. Dehydrated and starved, Peter was too weak to move. Even so, Josef decided to keep going. He climbed to the summit alone. Returning to the tent that afternoon, Josef gathered up his three sickly compatriots and started for the South Col.

But as the day wore on, the jet-stream blast had started sinking again, and by mid-afternoon the top third of the mountain deteriorated to siegelike conditions. Calling down that afternoon, the Czechs were desperate. Johnny called up to the South Col, hoping to alert Dave, Don, and Diana, who had set out for Camp 4 on their summit attempt. But as darkness fell and the winds ripped from across the Lhotse Face, Johnny's calls to Camp 4 yielded only radio static. Johnny knew they were up there — he'd followed their climb up the Lhotse Face through his binoculars and watched them climb onto the col just before sunset. But he could also see how brutal the winds were. There was no way the tents could have survived those gusts. If they were lucky, Don, Dave, and Diana would be spending the night huddling in collapsed tents. So even if the Czechs did manage to locate them, they certainly wouldn't find much help.

October 18 was a hellish night on the South Col. The wind had ripped down all but one of our tents, and left only one collapsed tent still somewhat habitable. Reaching the col too tired and too late to turn back, Don and Diana zipped into the standing tent, while Dave squeezed himself into the other. The wind was unrelenting through the night, and none of the climbers shut their eyes for more than a few moments. By morning they knew they had to get off the mountain. Johnny was relieved to hear Don's voice rasping down on the radio that morning. All the Americans were okay — tired, scared, wind-battered and cold, but still in one piece.

But Peter, Josef, Jaroslav, and Dusan had vanished. The 150-mile-an-hour winds had blown them off the face of the mountain — a terrible tragedy.

Diana, Dave, and Don limped down to Camp 2 that morning — Dave slowed by fingers frostbitten during their windblown night on the South Col — then back to base camp the next morning. Now the climb was over for everyone.

I shifted the packing into higher gear. The work was a group effort, and almost everyone who wasn't still climbing pitched in. Packing, sorting, and cleaning three months' worth of mountain-climbing gear was an enormous task. But the morning after Geoff came down from Camp 2, he stood up after breakfast and announced he was leaving camp for a few days.

"I'm going to party," he said, and then he hiked off to the nearest village with a couple of Sherpas in tow. A few days later Jim announced he was leaving camp for Kathmandu. A second summit attempt hadn't worked out for him, and when the French team asked Jim if anyone in our group wanted to fill an extra space on their helicopter, our leader volunteered himself.

"My toes got frostbit up above the col," Jim said. "Walking all the way down to civilization would be terrible for them."

So he decided to ride the chopper back. Immediately.

I'd never even heard of a leader leaving an expedition before it was finished. Not a healthy leader, anyway, and according to Steve, Jim's toes had barely been nibbled by the cold. "Frost*nip* is more like it," Steve snorted.

It certainly hadn't stopped Jim from starting a second summit attempt, although he didn't get above Camp 2. At dinner on the night he left, the rest of us sat shaking our heads with wonder.

"I can't believe he's abandoning us," Peggy said.

Cast in the light of this one episode, everything Jim had done seemed suspect. We all knew there had been a few mistakes down the line; now they added up to a troubling pattern.

Hiring Karma, for instance. While the other sirdars in base camp were busy coordinating their expeditions to the summit, ours was spending his days drinking so much rakshi we had to threaten to fire him in order to keep him sober. And what about those top-secret cornea exams? And deciding to put himself on the first summit team! A major blunder, in terms of morale, even if Don thought he deserved it. And the way he lied about the truth of our summit lottery: *Steve and I decided to let her go ahead.* Why did he have to say that? To me it seemed like gratuitous ego enhancement, as if leading a successful expedition weren't enough.

The rest of the group drew closer in our mutual anger at our absent leader. I suppose it would be miraculous for a group of such highly motivated and opinionated people to work together in difficult conditions for three months without setting off some sparks. Sherry Stripling, writing about us after she got back to Seattle, remarked that she really noticed the tension at base camp the day she walked away for the last time and couldn't stop smiling. Suddenly she remembered what *relaxed* felt like.

We still managed to stick together. By the time Diana, Dave, and Don returned from Camp 2 on October 19, the entire camp had been cleaned, sorted, packed, and made ready to go. All our last three climbers had to do was pack their own gear and lace up their boots. We walked out of camp for the last time the next morning.

I didn't look back, but I could feel the mountain receding behind me. I was glad to leave, happy to be ending that chapter in life, excited to be opening a new one. I was going home. David would be there, and I was excited to see him. But it was scary, too. And what about my career? I knew I would start my own building business. But

I also knew there were other opportunities now the First American Woman title was raising its head again. I'd tried to ignore it on the mountain, but now I had to think about it. Did anyone back home care about what I'd just done?

So I walked and I wondered. Everest was over. The mountain that had defined my life, the one goal I could never get out of my mind, and now I was finally past it. But even on top of the biggest hill on earth I knew there were other mountains to climb in my life. I was ready.

12

ANYTHING IS
POSSIBLE

AFTER three months of living on a glacier and eating food from envelopes and tin cups, the ballroom of the Yak and Yeti Hotel in Kathmandu seemed like heaven. We'd planned to have an end-of-the-road blowout, and so Bob and Larry reserved the room, while Jim hooked in a legion of guests from the American embassy, the Nepalese ministries, Sherpa friends, local climbing industry honchos, media, and, of course, everyone from the expedition. And what a scene beneath the chandeliers: tuxedoed waiters circulated with silver trays of hors d'oeuvres, while their colleagues took orders and distributed drinks around the room. We posed for a formal photograph of the climbers, and once that was finished Jim toasted friends and supporters and the expedition members: "... and here's to Stacy, the First American Woman ..." The scene took on a surreal edge. The glimmering chandeliers and the tuxedoes and the trays of crackers with the shrimps arranged on top just so, and people flocking up to shake my hand. A melée of Nepalese ministers and beaming American embassy folks, all working their way in for a few words of congratulation. "*You must be so proud . . . to be the first of your countrywomen is a great achievement!*"

When I had a moment, I looked around the ballroom. This was probably the last time we'd all be in the same room. It felt so good to see everyone, and to feel like a family. Now that we were away from the mountain, away from the tension and stress of life at high altitude, we could put aside our differences and savor what we'd achieved. I noticed Diana, wearing a beautiful silk dress. Steve was still skinny, but looking healthier, still eating as much as he could get his hands on. I felt someone tap me on the shoulder, and when I turned around it took me a moment to recognize Pasang, really turned out in pressed jeans and a nice shirt. He grinned at me, taking a second look at the dress I was wearing. Until this moment we'd only known each other in grungy mountain clothes. "Wow, Stacy," he said, shaking his head. "You look really nice!" I gave him a hug.

Diana was gracious at the party, but I knew how it felt to invest so much of yourself in something and then come back feeling empty. It was difficult for me to think about her during the climb — I had to focus on the mountain — but now that it was all behind us, I wanted to resolve what had happened to our relationship. She kept her distance, though, and when we did find ourselves standing together late that night, after the party had ended, she shook her head and backed away. "I don't think we can be friends anymore," she said. I was shocked that her disappointment in not summiting was so great, but even then I could see she was more sad than angry. Fortunately, time heals some wounds. I've seen Diana since then — at Johnny's wedding in 1992 — and it was easier for us.

ONLY three of us walked on the summit, but once we left the mountain behind we each attached our own personal significance to the climb. Mountain climbing in general is usually practiced on obscure peaks by obscure people, but the First American Woman to stand on the top of the world? That's something you could see in a spotlight. My ascent, the companion to Jim Whittaker's First American crown, was something the mainstream media could and did embrace.

Jim Frush arranged the first press conference in our hotel's garden the afternoon before the party. A handful of wire-service reporters came and directed most of their questions to Peggy and me. So many men had climbed Everest, but the women — that story still had some snap left in it. When the stories were wired over to the United States with the Kathmandu dateline, the American reporters started calling. And most of them wanted to talk to me.

First a writer from *Outside,* then a reporter from the *Portland Oregonian,* my hometown newspaper. *How's it feel to be the First American Woman? What's this about a lottery beneath the summit? How'd you decide which woman got to go first?* It was fun to talk about something I'd done that meant so much to me. I was proud of myself and proud of the expedition, this small group of climbers who worked together and managed to pull off a lofty achievement. After so much time by ourselves, it was amazing to see how interested reporters were, how they pressed for every detail. Even so, it always came back to the First American Woman title. *Do you feel like a role model?* And that was harder to talk about. All year I'd just wanted to think about the mountain, not get obsessed with the First American Woman title or what earning it might mean. I wanted to climb Everest for the same reason I climbed any mountain — because it was something I dreamed about, and then worked hard to make come true. I had seen the mountain as a personal goal, but now I had to look at it through other people's eyes.

And there were a lot of eyes swinging in my direction. "You know, I just talked to Dan," Jim said, grinning at me at the Kathmandu airport. We were about to board the flight for home, and he'd just sent word to Dan McConnell, our spokesman in Seattle. "He's got a six-inch pile of interview requests on his desk, and they've all got your name on 'em."

AFTER our plane landed in Seattle, and after we all cleared customs, we gathered at the door to the international lounge. "Everybody ready?" Jim looked us over, poised to throw it open. I felt my heart quicken, a sheen of sweat gathering on my palms. I knew David would be out there. David and my mother and father and maybe a few sisters and my brother. And what about the media? Maybe there'd be cameras, reporters. I had no idea. "You guys ready?" Jim pushed the door, and as it opened a flood of light beamed down into our faces. I took a step out into the crowd — I could feel a crowd — but I couldn't see anything. Then my eyes adjusted and I saw my mother moving toward me, clapping her hands and smiling, tears in her eyes. I ran into her arms, then hugged Sidney and Wendy and my father, my grandparents — and there was David. I ran into *his* arms, laughing and crying. He grabbed me and spun me around. "Welcome back! Congratulations!"

I kissed David, hugged him again, then looked up. I could see about a dozen lenses, all of them staring at our reunion. A flash singed my corneas, then another. It was hard to focus on anything, in the rush of emotions and the crowd of loved ones and strangers. Then Dan McConnell herded all of us into the airport subway and the press conference room on the other side. When we got there, Jim led off with a summary of what we'd done on the mountain — the dates we reached and set up each camp, the dates Geoff, Peggy, and I had summited, the names of the Sherpas who had accompanied us, and the day we left base camp and returned to Kathmandu. When he was through, the reporters fired their own questions. There were a few general queries for Jim, then someone shouted in my direction:

What's the significance of being the first American woman on the summit of Everest?

I felt the lights focusing on me, the lenses swiveling in my direction. My pulse leaped in my wrist. "It was a personal goal," I said. "As far as significance, that's for the public to decide."

When the press conference was over I took David's hand and walked out with my family, out to where they'd parked in the garage. While we were waiting for the elevator David put his arm around my shoulder and whispered in my ear. "You're a star now."

"No way," I said.

"Try answering your own phone," David said. "David Letterman's producer called last week. I think they want you to be on the show!"

We had lunch with my family that afternoon, then they drove back to Oregon and David and I found a hotel in downtown Seattle and went out to dinner. I was still on Kathmandu time, so I went to bed early, and was still sound asleep when the telephone rang in our hotel room at seven the next morning. David looked up, his eyes cloudy with sleep. "Who knows we're here?"

It was Letterman's segment producer. Somehow she'd managed to track down David and me. "Welcome home," she said. "Can you fly out this morning and do the show tomorrow?" I thought for a moment. If I was going to leave on a moment's notice, they were going to have to do something for me.

"I'll go," I said. "But can you fly my boyfriend out, too?"

"No problem."

When I got back to our house in Portland, it seemed like the phone would never stop ringing. Friends calling to welcome me home, newspaper reporters, TV news reporters. The mayor of Woodburn, my old hometown, proclaimed Stacy Allison Day, and invited me down for a small parade and to cut the ribbon on a street named in my honor (actually an alley, but I was proud). *Outside* published their story about our climb — naming Peggy and me as two of their Outsiders of the year. Peggy and I were written about in *Time,* and *Life* did a small piece about me as the First American Woman, as did *Self, Climbing,* a handful of airline magazines, and, yes, even the *National Enquirer. Esquire* proclaimed me one of the Women They Loved.

It was scary at first, peering into all those open lenses, talking into a hushed thicket of microphones. After engaging in a months-long, mostly silent, struggle with a mountain, now this electronic whirlwind expected me to describe what happened, and then interpret its significance in the moment of a soundbite. But I decided to enjoy it. If the wave's going to hit, you might as well ride it. And there were wonderful possibilities here, maybe even opportunities. Climbing stories seemed to intrigue people on a level that went beyond the average sports story. The more I recognized climbing Everest was a metaphor — a parable about everyday goals — the more I wondered if I could find a way to make the real-life parallels in my story seem even more vivid.

I called Sharon Wood (the first Canadian woman to climb Everest). How, I asked, does a mountain climber go about writing speeches for the corporate world? "Figure out what you're going to say," she explained. "And then say it." That sounded simple enough. Thanks to the burst of articles that had appeared when I got home, I got a few calls from some local builders' associations, a local medical group, a dental group, then worked my way up to a regional building association. At one meeting I met another speaker named Richard Flint. Richard is a sort of evangelical corporate self-help whiz, and he travels all over the country giving inspirational speeches about motivating employees and maximizing sales. After we shared a podium at a builders' conference in Washington, Richard came over to say he'd liked my speech, but pointed out that I could probably incorporate my inspirational messages more effectively into my climbing stories. We consulted, and together outlined a few lectures drawing parallels to the challenges faced by everyday people in everyday situations. After that I approached businesses with specific ideas — speeches not only about the real mountains I climbed, but also the ones that come along with setting business goals, solving interpersonal problems, unlocking individual potential. I began to feel more comfortable on the podium, and my presentations became smoother. Word spread, and soon I started getting calls from corporations and groups from around the nation. By 1990 I was making two or three speeches a month, in different parts of the United States.

That year I also started thinking about K2. It's such a graceful mountain, its ridges so sharp and steep, vaulting toward the sky like crystal spires. K2 is the second-tallest mountain in the world — measuring 28,250 feet, some 800 feet shorter than Mount Everest.

A head shorter, but a notch or two harder. All the routes on K2 are extremely difficult — thousands of feet of steep, technical, high-altitude climbing. And the erratic Pakistani mountain weather doesn't make the task any easier. Days of clear, calm skies merely serve as punctuation for the weeks of iron-clawed winds and brutal snowstorms.

Everest's summit may be higher, but in some ways K2's peak is the more desired accomplishment. Fewer climbers have scraped the top of the world's second-tallest mountain than the tallest. And those who do reach the summit do so at a greater cost: of all the world's 8,000-meter peaks K2 has the highest failure rate. Through 1985, twenty-six expeditions attempted the mountain; only nine sent climbers to the summit.

I wondered: *can I do it?* Can I venture to the far end of my ability one more time — and then go a little farther? Scott Fischer summited K2 in 1992 and he told me it was the most difficult mountain ever. It is a hard mountain. But I'd never climbed in Pakistan, and K2 is wild and beautiful. The thought of climbing into that beauty, the thought of making that power my own, if only for a moment, was irresistible.

But how was I going to get there? I didn't know anyone who was planning to lead an expedition. After a few months, I decided to take action. If I was really serious about climbing the mountain, I thought, I could get my own permit and lead my own expedition.

A whole new challenge. Another layer of responsibility, of pressure and expectations. Every successful climber has to approach a mountain with a dream, but when you lead an expedition you have to dream big enough for an entire group of people. More than that, you have to have the tenacity to turn that dream into reality. As an expedition leader, I'd have to find a route and then figure out how to approach it. I'd have to choose the team, give them a sense of mission, and motivate them. As on all expeditions, every climber would take responsibility for him or herself. But responsibility for the team — the group's success, the lives of the climbers — would rest most heavily on my shoulders. Could I carry it? I wouldn't know until I took that first step.

So I took a deep breath, and started climbing. I applied for a permit and got one for the summer of 1993. Then I started making telephone calls, pulling together a group of climbers. It's a new challenge, but not an unfamiliar one. In the last few years at home I've become used to climbing on the front end of the rope.

My life since Everest has required me to be a leader. I've created a career, working at becoming a better speaker, and then coordinating the engagements. When I wasn't doing that, I worked as a builder, buying and renovating houses and then selling them for a profit. A different group of pursuits, to be sure, but I approached them in the same way: I set goals and worked to reach them. I tried to learn from my failures, and continually motivated myself to succeed.

I'll use the same strategy to lead the K2 expedition. I'll work hard for the summit, but I'll make sure we all remember that the climb won't begin and end at the mountaintop. As on every other climb, there will be lessons in failure, and victories in every footfall. Even so, we'll be determined to succeed: I wouldn't bother going all the way to Pakistan if I didn't want to climb to the top of the mountain.

And we'll be safe. I wouldn't go if I didn't think I'd come back in one piece. David wants me back in one piece, too. Even when we were planning our wedding in 1992, he supported the idea of the expedition. David knows why the mountain is important to me. He knows that the deepest part of me is, and will always be, a climber.

Climbing has inspired me, shaped my life, and changed it. Climbing has given me confidence and strength. It has taught me how to be resourceful, how to challenge myself and trust myself enough to take risks. To look beyond the ordinary and to transcend myself. Climbing stays with me when I'm building a house, making a speech, or talking with David. No matter where I go, I always feel like a climber.

Everest stays with me, too. The summit was ephemeral — it was gone in an instant. Now I have to think hard to remember what it felt like up there. But the climb itself is in the marrow of my bones. It's in the friends I made while I was there. It's in what I learned about myself when I failed on my first attempt, and what I proved to myself when I dusted myself off and went back to try again. The summit was a dream, but when I was climbing, I was as wide awake, as alert, as open to experience, as I've ever been in my life. Everest is behind me now, but I can still see the shadow of the mountain in everything I do. It's a reminder, a challenge, from the highest spot on the world. *Look beyond the ordinary. There's always something more.* As long as I remember that, I know anything is possible.